T0319932

# Evolutionary Economic Thought

NEW HORIZONS IN INSTITUTIONAL AND EVOLUTIONARY ECONOMICS

**Series Editor**: Geoffrey M. Hodgson
Research Professor, University of Hertfordshire Business School, UK

Economics today is at a crossroads. New ideas and approaches are challenging the largely static and equilibrium-oriented models that used to dominate mainstream economics. The study of economic institutions – long neglected in the economics textbooks – has returned to the forefront of theoretical and empirical investigation.

This challenging and interdisciplinary series publishes leading works at the forefront of institutional and evolutionary theory and focuses on cutting-edge analyses of modern socio-economic systems. The aim is to understand both the institutional structures of modern economies and the processes of economic evolution and development. Contributions will be from all forms of evolutionary and institutional economics, as well as from Post-Keynesian, Austrian and other schools. The overriding aim is to understand the processes of institutional transformation and economic change.

Titles in the series include:

Institutions and the Role of the State
*Edited by Leonardo Burlamaqui, Ana Celia Castro and Ha-Joon Chang*

Marx, Veblen and Contemporary Institutional Political Economy
Principles and Unstable Dynamics of Capitalism
*Phillip Anthony O'Hara*

The New Evolutionary Microeconomics
Complexity, Competence and Adaptive Behaviour
*Jason D. Potts*

National Competitiveness and Economic Growth
The Changing Determinants of Economic Performance in the World Economy
*Timo J. Hämäläinen*

Conventions and Structures in Economic Organization
Markets, Networks and Hierarchies
*Edited by Olivier Favereau and Emmanuel Lazega*

Globalization and Institutions
Redefining the Rules of the Economic Game
*Edited by Marie-Laure Djelic and Sigrid Quack*

The Evolutionary Analysis of Economic Policy
*Edited by Pavel Pelikan and Gerhard Wegner*

The Evolution of Scientific Knowledge
*Edited by Hans Siggaard Jensen, Lykke Margot Richter and Morten Thanning Vendelø*

Evolutionary Economic Thought
European Contributions and Concepts
*Edited by Jürgen G. Backhaus*

# Evolutionary Economic Thought

## European Contributions and Concepts

*Edited by*

Jürgen G. Backhaus

*Krupp Chair in Public Finance and Fiscal Sociology,*
*Erfurt University, Germany*

NEW HORIZONS IN INSTITUTIONAL AND EVOLUTIONARY
ECONOMICS

**Edward Elgar**
Cheltenham, UK • Northampton, MA, USA

Published by
Edward Elgar Publishing Limited
Glensanda House
Montpellier Parade
Cheltenham
Glos GL50 1UA
UK

Edward Elgar Publishing, Inc.
136 West Street
Suite 202
Northampton
Massachusetts 01060
USA

A catalogue record for this book
is available from the British Library

**Library of Congress Cataloguing in Publication Data**

Evolutionary economic thought: European contributions and concepts/edited by
    Jürgen G. Backhaus.
        p. cm. – (New Horizons in institutional and evolutionary economics)
    Includes bibliographical references and index.
    1. Evolutionary economics. 2. Evolutionary economics-Europe. I. Backhaus,
Jürgen G., 1950- II. Series.

HB97.3.E959 2003
330.1—dc21                                                                2003049045

ISBN 1 84064 678 0

Typeset by Cambrian Typesetters, Frimley, Surrey
Printed and bound in Great Britain by MPG Books Ltd, Bodmin, Cornwall

# Contents

# Figures

# Tables

# Contributors

**Richard Aréna** is Professor of Economics at the University of Nice-Sophia Antipolis, where he teaches and publishes articles in the history of economic thought, industrial organization, theory of the firm, business cycle theory, monetary economics and the economics of knowledge. A founder of the European Society of History of Economic Thought, he is Director of the French research network History of Economic Thought and Economic Methodology (CNRS). In addition to his books, covering subjects ranging from Neo-Ricardian economics to the circulation of money, he has edited special issues of *Economica* magazine.

**Jürgen G. Backhaus**, PhD and JSD University of Konstanz, holds the Krupp Chair in Public Finance and Fiscal Sociology at the University of Erfurt. Before that, he was the Professor of Public Finance at Maastricht University. Since 1994, he has been editing (with Frank H. Stephen) the *European Journal of Law and Economics*. In 1999 he published the *Elgar Companion to Law and Economics*.

**Ursula M. Backhaus** received her education at the University of Constance (Diplom-Volkswirt, 1979) and Auburn University (Master of Science in Economics, 1983). As a forecasting analyst for a leading manufacturer of agricultural implements she specialized in empirical applied econometrics and agricultural economics. In 1987, she became a Fellow in Health Economics at the School of Health Sciences at Maastricht University. Since 1992, she has been a research associate at the IssF Foundation. Most recently, she translated Schumpeter's Seventh Chapter, 'The Whole Picture of the Economy'. This chapter had been omitted from the 1934 translation of Schumpeter's *Theory of Economic Development*. The original appeared in Leipzig, Duncker & Humblot, 1912, pp. 463–548. Forthcoming in Vol. 1 of the new series *The European Heritage in Economics and the Social Sciences*, Kluwer, Boston.

**Dr. Simon Duindam**, PhD University of Maastricht, is currently working at the Open University of the Netherlands as an Associate Professor in Economics. In his daily work he is busy with the innovation of education in economies by means of multimedia, the internet and innovative didactic techniques, in disciplines like public finance, personal finance, institutional economics and monetary economics. In 2000 he published the book *Military Conscription, An Economic Analysis of the Labour Component in the Armed Forces.*

**Staffan Hultén** is an Associate Professor in Business Economics at Stockholm School of Economics, and is since 1996 a recurrent Visiting Professor at Ecole Centrale Paris. In 2000 he was visiting Professor of Strategy and Management at INSEAD. He has carried out numerous industry studies based on an evolutionary research methodology. Last year he published together with Professor Robin Cowan, MERIT, an edited book entitled *Electric Vehicles. Socio-economic Prospects and Technological Challenges,* (Aldershot: Ashgate).

**Hans Maks**, PhD University of Groningen, holds a Chair in Economics at Maastricht University. Before that, he was Associate Professor of Micro-economics at the University of Gronigen and Professor of Microeconomics at Maastricht University. His fields of interest are: microeconomics, welfare economics, competition and regulation and history of economic doctrine. He is Supervisor of the NWO-program 'Competition and Regulation' (NWO, National Foundation of Scientific Research), Member of the Appeal Committee Competition Act (Mededingingswet), Chair of the session 'Competition and Regulation' of the Flemish Scientific Economic Conference 2002 and guest editor of a special issue on Competition and Regulation of *Maandschrift Economie* published in June 2001. He co-organized a Walras-Pareto Conference at Maastricht University in June 2001.

**Dietmar Meyer**, PhD Hungarian Academy of Sciences (1984), is with the Department of Macroeconomics of the Budapest University of Economic Sciences. He held chairs of General Economics at the Highschool for Applied Sciences, and of Economics at the Budapest College of Management and Macroeconomics at BUES. His fields of research are theory of economic growth and business cycles, mathematical economics, evolutionary approaches to economic theory, and history of economic thought.

**Stéphane Ngo Mai** is Associate Professor of Economics at the University of Nice Sophia Antipolis. He teaches macroeconomics, economics of innovation and economics of the firm. His main fields of interest are evolutionary dynamics, self-organization approaches and economics of knowledge. He has recently published in those fields in *Revue Internationale de Systémique, Revue d'Economie Industrielle*, and in edited books.

**Helge Peukert**, Dr.phil. and Dr.rer.pol. University of Frankfurt, is Privatdozent at the University of Frankfurt, and Lecturer at the Krupp Chair in Public Finance and Fiscal Sociology at the University of Erfurt.

**Erik S. Reinert** received his undergraduate degree from the University of St. Gallen, Switzerland, and holds an MBA from Harvard University and a PhD in economics from Cornell University. He works as the Head of Research of Norsk Investorforum, Oslo, Norway, a private sector think-thank, and has been working with the Centre for Development and the Environment of the University of Oslo since 1995.

**Bernard Verstegen**, who received his PhD from the University of Groningen in the Netherlands, is currently working at the Open University of the Netherlands as an Associate Professor in Economics and Accounting. He has done research in the areas of consumer theory, methodology, institutional economics, and management accounting and published in these areas in international journals.

# 1. Evolutionary economic thought: European contributions and concepts

## Jürgen G. Backhaus

'Evolution is a process in which a *system* under consideration *transforms itself over time*' (Witt, 1994, p. 83[1]).

This definition is sharp and workable from the point of view of analysing economic systems and their ability to transform themselves over time without outside interference. Hence, the definition is extremely well geared to questions of transformation economics, in other words the study of countries undergoing deep change. An analysis following this direction will pinpoint areas and issues where outside intervention is needed, and by implication will show ways of allowing such economic systems to transform themselves. True enough, one important application of evolutionary economics today is the study of economic systems transition. However, evolutionary economics has a much broader history and it refers as a label to very different approaches, of which some are broadly compatible with Witt's definition, others much less so.

The concept of evolution has its roots in Greek philosophy. Although Aristotle applied the notion of biological development to ontogeny, the development of the individual from fertilized egg cell to adult, he failed to apply it to phylogeny, the sequence to adult forms in time. The same position was still taken by Hegel. But the Pre-Socratic Ionian philosophers were led to the concept of evolution by the distinction which they made between the shifting temporal flux of phenomena and the eternal changeless reality beneath. Towards the end of the eighteenth century, the notion of evolution was in vogue and with Malthus' *Essay on Population* (1798) it became combined with his contention that periodical checks on the numbers of human groups are biologically necessary. Hence, the notion of evolution became combined with the other notion of the survival of the fittest, although the process of evolution as such should not be confused with the method by which it takes place. In the nineteenth century, historically working economists practised what today may be called evolutionary economics, and in the case of Schmoller, the influence of the experimental laboratory method practised by his grandfather clearly had an impact on his own approach to his work in the social sciences, primarily economics, although history consists of non-repeatable occurrences which are thus outside the realm of scientific investigation but not outside that of scientific imagination and speculation. The method of large numbers of similar case studies practised by Schmoller was supposed to overcome the inherent difficulties imposed by the lack of laboratory experiments in the social sciences. The new development in experimental economics still has to be considered far too limited in its applications to provide the necessary basis for social policy oriented economic research.[2]

Shmuel Eisenstadt in his entry on social evolution there states two conditions for evolutionary social science, clearly including economics. To wit:

> An evolutionary perspective, from the point of view of human societies, makes sense only so far as at least some of the processes of change that are inherent in any social system create the potentialities for the institutionalisation of more differentiated social and symbolic systems. From the point of view of human society or culture as a whole, such a perspective makes sense only in so far as there exist some mechanisms for the transmission of various institutional and adaptive techniques and for creating some common, inter-societal, adaptive and integrative capabilities and frameworks (Eisenstadt (1968), *Social Evolution*, IESS5, pp. 228–34).

These two elements, institutions of evolutionary change and particular processes (such as competition) which generate such change are therefore the focus of our attention. To give an example, in the context of the economics of transition, we are interested in the basic institutions of the market economy[3] as well as the processes that bring about change which Schumpeter had identified as entrepreneurship, with the additional understanding that such entrepreneurs can be both individuals or social organizations such as specific enterprises.

This broad perspective serves to argue for the need to take stock of European contributions to evolutionary economics with a view to broadening the perspective of current discourse and seeking to redress the balance of past and present approaches. Obviously, in one volume we can only hope to focus on a subset of such different perspectives, and this is also the reason why the focus is on European contributions, as they tend to be overshadowed by American ones.

For one thing, any economy is embedded in culture. Cultures are different, but with care, in each culture a *key* to development can be found.

Secondly, the works we cover ask very different questions from what is currently on the agenda:

- Schmoller is interested in a comparative programme of development which uses *all* available instruments a modern government in change of a developing economy has at its disposal. He didn't think of World Bank and IMF advice, 1917–1936 marks a big difference in this respect
- Yet, how about inherent impediments to development, due, for instance, to the class structure of the society in question?

- Which brings us right to the main thinker in this anti-evolutionary way of thought – Karl Marx – who has to be considered as an inspiration for many evolutionary ideas.
- The great integrator and interpreter of the most diverse ideas hence has to be called upon: Werner Sombart. Once the grand picture has been painted, let's turn to
- the early history of path dependency, which was turned into a law-like relationship by
- Adolph Wagner. However, Wagner stood somewhat uncomfortably between the Austrian 'theory based' advocacy of particular (in his case self perceived) social policy and
- the radical empiricism of Gustav Schmoller, which is the concluding topic of this volume.
- Yet do not forget the thoughtful underpinning of the entire edifice emphasized by the early Schmoller.[4]

Evolutionary thought tends to be identified with models that allow for evolution from a given set of resources to a higher order of an economy such as from a migrant herding economy to a settled economy with agriculture, and hence to crafts, industrialization and the welfare state.

While such stage theories of economies are not beside the point, this volume wants to go *beyond* and at the same time behind *Rostow*. There is a set of European contributions to the question of how economies develop which should not be overlooked. Where is the difference from the received wisdom?

It is the purpose of this volume to encourage research on ideas that are not commonly available. In a recent comment on the Nobel Award it could be read: 'what is the idea?' – the award was given for a technique – in contrast, we want to emphasize ideas which are ideally suited to be tested by this laureated technique.

## NOTES

1. Witt, Ulrich (1994), 'What evolutionary economics is all about', in, Ulrich Witt (ed) *Evolutionary Economics*, Edward Elgar, Cheltenham.
2. In the *Encyclopaedia of the Social Sciences*, the entry on evolution by Joseph Needham, while explicitly referring to Malthus, makes no further reference to evolutionary economics. In contrast, the post World War II *International Encyclopaedia of the Social Sciences* has no fewer than six separate entries on evolution, to wit: 1) the concept of evolution; 2) primate evolution; 3) human evolution; 4) cultural evolution; 5) social evolution; 6) evolution and behaviour.
3. Backhaus, J., 'Basic institutions of the market economy', working paper no. 11/1999, University of Maastricht.
4. Schmoller, G. (1917), *Grundriß der allgemeinen Volkswirtschaftslehre*, Leipzig, Duncker & Humblot, I, p. 112.

# 2. Growth or development: the concept of the historically writing economist

## Jürgen G. Backhaus

### INTRODUCTION[1]

In his review of economic development 'From the beginning to Rostow' Robert Dorfman[2] gives a sketch of his view of the history of economic thought on the subject of development. In this history of thought, he notes a big gap between the contributions of Mill and Marshall.

> For about a hundred years after the end of the classical period, the problems of economic growth seem to have lost their urgency. At any rate, other problems such as justifying and redressing the income distribution or explaining and moderating the business cycle displaced economic growth at the top of the economists' agendas. As evidence, when you read the sections on economic growth and progress in Marshall's *Principles of Economics*, you are struck by how closely they echo the corresponding sections in Mill's *Principles*, written 40 years before[3] (p. 573).

This gap needs some explanation. The purpose of this chapter is to bridge the gap and to provide the missing link. The first part gives some reconstruction of Robert Dorfman's lineage of the history of development economics up until Rostow.[4]

The second offers an amendment to Robert Dorfman's family tree of development economics in emphasizing the work of the historical school, notably of Gustav Schmoller (1838–1917). It is emphasized that Schmoller's is a complex evolutionary theory emphasizing institutional prerequisites for economic development, going far beyond a theory of stages. This is illustrated in the third part with respect to the institution of money.

### A GAP IN DEVELOPMENT THEORY

From the point of view of the history of economic thought, the one hundred year gap between Mill's *Principles* (of 1848) and the post World War Two development literature aimed at developing the newly emerging post colonial Third World[5] is somewhat mystifying, because precisely in the middle of these two dates, Schmoller's *Blueprint* appears in 1900 and 1904 respectively.[6] In this massive work, Schmoller indeed offered an institution-based blueprint for economic development and growth primarily of industrializing and agriculture based economies of the European mainland type which differed substantially from Mill and Marshall in its evolutionary perspective. Dorfman's article is surprising in yet another way. What started out as a review of Rostow's *Theories of Economic Growth* from David Hume to the present (1990) ultimately became a review article containing two distinct parts. Part one is Dorfman's alternative *History of Economic Thought* in a nutshell and part two (sections 4–8) is the review. In our context, we are only concerned with Dorfman's alternative history of economic thought. In order to establish the context, in this section I shall offer a short summary, relying heavily on original quotations; since only in this way can the context of the peculiar gap theory be authentically established.

Dorfman begins his historical sketch by emphasizing that economic development, from the very start, was and remained the leading concern of economists, following the example of Adam Smith. He notes strongly that the inquiry into the nature and the causes of the wealth of nations was essentially about economic development. He continues that phase of the focus of economists' attention to the middle of the nineteenth century, but then claims that economists became concerned with short-run problems until shortly after the Second World War.

> For about a century after Mill's *Principles*, however, the centre of economists' attention shifted to business cycles, the distribution of income, the growth of trusts and monopolies, and other short-run problems. Immediately after World War II, a second shift of focus occurred. The colonies of the Europe-based empires were transformed into about a hundred new nations, a 'third world', as they came to be called. The poverty and instability of those new countries promoted economic development once more in a place near the top of economists' agendas. (p. 573)

Since Dorfman let economics begin with Adam Smith, he is circumspect enough to note that Adam Smith took his cues largely from the physiocrats in criticizing Mercantilist doctrine. Hence, he emphasizes the importance of the physiocrats' contribution. Their lack of success he attributes not to the (lacking) validity of their doctrines but rather to interest group interaction.

> The Contrôleur Générales des Finances, A.R.J. Turgot, was greatly influenced by the physiocrats and tried to implement some of their recommendations, but crop failures frustrated his efforts and the nobility was so strongly opposed that he was dismissed from the cabinet. Thus ended the first effort at development planning. (p. 574)

From the point of view of economic theorizing and development in main-land Europe, this account is remarkable in that the first chairs in political economy were actually founded in 1723, 99 years before such a chair was established at Oxford. By that time, economics was already a flourishing discipline and part of the curriculum for civil servants in most Central European countries, and the economics profession was very active. As a consequence of the disastrous war variously called the Thirty Years War and the Eighty Years War and ended through the Treaties of Münster and Osnabrück in 1648, the population in the German countries had been reduced from 17 to 8 million people. A massive effort at reconstruction had become necessary and the Treaties had established a large number of fairly independent states competing with each other within the constitutional context of the reconstituted Holy Roman Empire. Hence, individual rulers depended on economic development for their political survival and, since colonization was not an alternative, internal colonization (that is development) became the central focus of economic policy throughout. The respective doctrine developed and taught at the universities, Cameralism, in direct opposition to Mercantalism emphasizes development over taxation, stable currency over devaluation, religious and professional freedom over oppression and regulation and so on. This clearly market based, development oriented political economy which put the state into the centre of economic activity should be seen as the proper starting point of economic doctrines concerned with economic growth and development. Interestingly enough, the emphasis of the Cameralists was clearly on institution building and economic development and evolution over economic planning, for which the necessary policy instruments were clearly not yet available.

The next important stop in Dorfman's journey through the history of economic thought on development issues, after an extensive discussion of Adam Smith, is the interchange between Ricardo and Malthus. Again, political considerations guide his interpretation. Witness the following account of their rent theory.

> According to Malthus and Ricardo, rents are determined by the margin of cultivation, the least fertile land, and the least productive units of the natural resource that are used. The rents for supramarginal units for resources are the rents for marginal units plus differential rents, which capture for the landowner the excess profits that would otherwise be earned by capital employed on the supramarginal unit rather than at the margin. Thus, much of the fruit of economic growth is plucked by the landowners, that is, in early nineteenth century Britain, by the landed gentry. (p. 576, footnote omitted)

This analysis clearly rests on some institutional assumptions which determine on the one hand the demand for foodstuffs, on the other hand the cost of transportation, on the one hand the mobility of labour and on the other hand government policies with respect to imports, but also land ownership. These institutional presuppositions are not made explicit in the account.

From the point of view of a specific agenda other than economic development, the account of Mill's position on female emancipation is also coloured. Witness this:

> Mill's program depended heavily on education. The ignorant and illiterate certainly cannot appreciate the advantages of family planning; universal education is a prerequisite of population control. Along with education of men and women equally, Mill advocated a general improvement in the social status of women. He was an early proponent of women's liberation, and pointed out that liberated women would contribute significantly to limiting family sizes. (p. 577)

From the point of view of the economic development of a country, the issue of female emancipation turns on the need to maintain an able and healthy labour force, so as to sustain a continuous growth process. A mainstay of Cameralist doctrine emphasized the importance of household formation and a sufficient capital basis; hence, the Cameralists advocated the institution of savings associations for the formation of the dowry; the availability of farm-land for trained farmers who had not inherited such; the availability of craft openings for those qualified, and so on. There is, thus, a clear connection between education on the one hand and economic development on the other; there is in addition an important role for female emancipation in the development process, as women could be expected to have a pivotal role in households which we have to picture as being both productive and consumptive units. Issues of health care, sanitation, food variety and such like play an important role in addition to other household production skills such as sewing, gardening, poultry management and management skills as such. The issue of the number of children turns primarily on the economic functions in these households. If children play an important role in household production, even increasingly skilled production, and in transgenerational capital formation, the number of children may be small or large depending on the specific circumstances of the household, but not depending on the level of education of women. Dorfman in his account stays true to Mill, who, at this juncture, indeed leaves the realm of economic analysis for political considerations.

With respect to technology, Dorfman arrives at the following conclusion:

> From the modern, that is, twentieth century, point of view, only Marx seems to have paid adequate attention to the idea that technological development might be an important secondary, or even primary, impetus to economic growth. (p. 578)

This is said despite the importance of the role technology consistently plays in the Cameralist literature starting with Wolff in 1754, Justi, Becher, and all the others; continued in Roscher's work, being central in Schmoller's and being one of the three pillars of explanation (next to the spirit and the form of capitalist development) in Sombart.

Apparently, apart from Marx, who cannot be considered part of the classical school, in competition with the classical school Dorfman considers two alternative theories of economic development, those of Alexander Hamilton and Friedrich List on the one hand, and of John Rae on the other. List's role is emphasized in the context of German unification under Bismarck (p. 579), although List had campaigned for a wider integration of the entire German Federation, including not only Austria, of course, but also the lowlands and ultimately even England. He took his own life in 1846, and Bismarck accomplished German unification (without Austria) in 1871. List's ideas are much more significant for European integration than they are historically, for explaining the German unification of 1871. John Rae is primarily identified as a precursor of the Austrian capital theory. To conclude his review of theories of economic development, Dorfman offers an account of Schumpeter's work, based both on his *Theory of Economic Development* and his *Theory of Capitalism, Socialism and Democracy*. Finally, there is a short account of the work of Ramsey and von Neumann, which is interesting to quote: 'von Neumann's model, like Ramsey's, invoked such drastic simplifications that no economist would expect to lead to interesting and significant findings' (p. 581).

Hence, it should be worth our while to look for an institutionally rich theoretical framework, and to this we now turn.

## THE BLUEPRINT: A CLASSIC IN DEVELOPMENT THEORY

This section offers an overview of one of the magisterial works in development economics, this sub-discipline being conceived as being the centre of political economy. This work has to be classified as being one of the cornerstones of the discipline as such. Only the fact that it has not been translated into English can explain the mysterious treatment of the history of development economics by Robert Dorfman, that we have just been introduced to. The work itself, the *Blueprint*,[8] is only the tip of the iceberg of an enormous amount of research that has been conducted by students and colleagues who came to be convinced by the validity of the research programme not only due to its obvious political success, but also due to its scholarly merits. The research programme had been supported by the publication of a journal, the creation of an independent organization of researchers devoted to social policy issues with no links to the state, when obviously the focus of the research was state policy, no funding from any interested source being accepted (although available) and rigorous adherence to the received standards of scholarship being upheld. This occurred in a climate that was not necessarily hospitable to such a movement.

The programme was one that attracted mostly scholars from Prussian universities, but not only from there. There were many co-travellers of Russian, Polish, Czech, Slowak, Bavarian, Austrian, Swiss, Italian, Hungarian, Romanian, Bulgarian, Greek and even Turkish origin. Those in the Western hemisphere should not be overlooked either. We are looking at a voluntarily organized research initiative even without a legal form, started at the private house of the instigator, Gustav Schmoller, and intended to change the way economic policy would be conducted in the Germany in which he worked.

The most important aspect here was the issue of change. Schmoller wanted change, but he wanted a change not in a disruptive but rather in an evolutionary way. In order to achieve this result, he wanted to base every particular proposal for change woven into a careful analysis of the starting point of the change, typically a study, indepth, into the conditions of the problem that needed yet to be redressed, and on this basis he wanted to see competing advice on the problem thus identified. Typically, the first stage would be conducted through doctoral dissertations under his colleagues' guidance. Witness that this 'proto-graduate school' was a private initiative. On this factual basis with notions of what the problems were that could be redressed by identifiable entities, such as legislatures or agencies, the next stage would be to invite a group of senior professors to discuss the possibilities of launching such a research programme so as to make it the major focus of the association's meeting. Those invited to take these decisions had a hard choice to face. If they declined, they would be out of the proto-decision making process. It was well-known that Schmoller's activities, often disliked by various government agencies, ministers and sometimes even the chancellor, would often result in policy initiatives through one of the various powerful parties in the imperial diet. In his later writings, Schmoller became fully aware of the implications of his activities, and he grew to develop a fully fledged public-choice and rent-seeking analysis under this imprint.[9]

In taking account of restrictions on political initiatives, Schmoller was not bound by any belief into a particular constitutional set-up. He adopted monarchy, based on Roscher's analysis, as the most viable form for Germany at the time. It was, of course, a constitutional monarchy under a federal constitution, hence totally bereft of immediate policy weight. The weight of the emperor in political terms came only from his success as the King of Prussia.

If we want to put Schmoller's *Blueprint* into the proper light so that it can be understood by scholars trained in the Anglo-Saxon tradition, we need to accept that the two volumes deemed incomprehensible by Salin[10] exercized a strong influence on many future scholars but also economic practitioners. It was often the case that a family might decide on a son's course of study, as they had to finance it. Frequently, students would cheat on their parents and take up a different subject. Economics as a subject turned out to be unbelievably popular in Berlin at the time when Schmoller worked there, next to such illuminaries as Adolph Wagner, although he was by all accounts a poor lecturer. The heat of the action seems to have been in the large figure 'one hundred people' doctoral seminar where grilling discussions took place. Schmoller himself says that his style of lecturing is often misunderstood and that this is the reason that he took the time to rewrite the *Blueprint*. The King of Prussia (Emperor William II) was convinced by this argument and granted him a retirement salary so as for him to be relieved of his teaching duties, enabling him to finish the *Blueprint* in its second edition. It is to this *Blueprint* that we shall now turn.

The model of the more encompassing theory of economic growth and development can be readily gleaned from the structure of the *Blueprint*. The book starts appropriately enough with a short definition of what economics is. Paragraph three of this short introductory chapter defines economies as social organs and organs of the political economy. Economics in this case are households, firms, co-operatives, churches, farms or whatever other group of persons economically working together and taking part in the economy. Political economy is a notion in the state sciences such as state, nation, people and the like involving the institutions in which economic activity can take place. As well as defining the notions, the introduction to the *Blueprint* has two further parts. Part Two looks at the psychical, ethical and legal foundations of economy and society. In turn, these foundations consist of nine aspects. First the purposes and the means of the social association involving the association due to different agent agendas, the association in peace, the association in war and the association in common settlement. Second, the psycho-physical means of communication, notably oral and written language. Third, social consciousness and collective forces; fourth, individual sentiments and needs; fifth, human instincts; sixth, the human commercial instinct and economic virtues; seventh, ethics; eighth, ethical institutions and ninth, the general interdependence between economics and ethics.

The third part of the introduction is a history of economic thought dealing in its first paragraph with economic thought in antiquity and the Christian tradition, secondly with the renaissance of science and the natural law in the seventeenth century, thirdly with the main economic systems of the eighteenth and nineteenth centuries dealing with Mercantilism, classical economics and socialist thought, fourthly the method of economics and fifthly the development of economics to becoming a science in the nineteenth century emphasizing, in particular, its empirical focus.

The remainder of the *Blueprint* consists of four books. Book One deals with land, people and technology. Book Two deals with the social constitution of the economy, its evolution, its organs, and its current state. Book Three with the social process of allocation and income distribution, and Book Four with the evolution of economic activity as a whole.

Book One has four chapters. Chapter One deals with the dependence of the political economy on its natural endowment. Chapter Two deals with races, nations and the people. Section 60 specifically looks at the various causes of the formation of races and people, notably the climate, the way of life, education and race composition.[11] Chapter Three is devoted to economic demography, and Chapter Four to the development of technology from an economic point of view.

Book Two, devoted to the economic constitution, is almost five times as long as Book One and has eight chapters. Chapter One deals with the household economy, Chapter Two with the settlement arrangements of social groups, notably the city and the village, and Chapter Three with the economies of the state, the municipalities, and other public bodies. Chapter Four deals with the division of labour in society and economy. Chapter Five deals with property and its distribution. Chapter Six is devoted to the formation of social classes. Chapters Seven and Eight are both devoted to the enterprise. Chapter Seven deals with the evolution of forms of commerce and production focussing on older and simpler forms, whereas Chapter Eight deals with the newer more complex and composed forms.

Books Three and Four are actually bound in Volume Two. Book Three on the social process of allocation and distribution has nine chapters. Chapter One deals with economic competition. Chapter Three is devoted to measures, weights, coins and money and banking. We shall return to this chapter in the third section of this chapter. Chapter Four is devoted to value and price theory. Chapter Five deals with wealth, capital, credit, capital rent and interest. Chapter Six is on banking. Chapter Seven is devoted to wages and the labour contract. Chapter Eight is the core chapter dealing with the new social institutions (the entire Bismarckian system of social security) in both its public parts and the complementary private and commercial systems of insurance. Chapter Nine deals with the income and its distribution.

Book Four on the evolution of economic life as a whole has four chapters. Chapter One is on cycles and crises. Chapter Two is on the class struggle, class dominance and its reduction through state, law and reform. Chapter Three deals with international trade, and speaks of trade relations, trade wars, and commercial policy. Finally, Chapter Four is devoted to the economic and general evolution of mankind and its single peoples, through rise, peak and decline.

As we can see, the evolutionary aspect permeates the entire work. This is strongly evident as we look at Schmoller's *Theory of Money*.

## AN EXAMPLE: THE THEORY OF MONEY IN A DEVELOPMENT THEORY

This section is devoted to Schmoller's *Theory of Money* as it is contained in his *Blueprint*.

Schmoller's theory of money can be found primarily in his *Blueprint*,[12] but also in his many detailed studies in economic history.[13] If we only concentrate on the *Blueprint*, we have to consult primarily Volume II. Volume I offers a discussion of the role of money in mercantilism which differs substantially from Adam Smith's presentation (pp. 85–6 and a succinct statement on methodology on pp. 119–120). The main body of this literature however can be found in Volume II. Here, at a minimum, it is necessary to consult pages 24–6, pages 57–105, and pages 169–83. In what follows, I should give a brief representation of Schmoller's approach, supported by extensive quotes from the (untranslated) *Blueprint*.

### A Point of Method

Schmoller's contributions to a theory of money occur in the context of explaining the emergence of institutions that allow for market exchange. Obviously, market exchange on a grand scale is only possible with a very liquid medium of exchange and account, and – as we shall see shortly – also store of value. However, Schmoller does not wish to insert his theory of money into a rash genetic general design; he is particularly concerned with linking the institution of money to other institutions, notably those of the law and customs. Hence, what disappears in the institutional assumptions in modern monetary theory is actually the focus of Schmoller's approach. 'The approach of the younger historical school', he explains,

> is different from that of a generalized genetic approach [he refers to the older histor-ical school] in that the younger scholars wish to depart from the polyhistoric gath-ering of facts to specialized focused research of specific epochs, people and economic situations. This requires primarily monographic research in economic history and a linking of every modern specialized research with its historic roots; this approach emphasizes research into the development of every single economic institution before a general analysis of entire economies of the world economy can be attempted. This new approach is similar to those rigorous methods now employed in legal historical analysis, and it is being supplemented through schol-arly travel and interviews in order to supplement book knowledge as well as philo-sophical and psychological research. (*Blueprint*, p. 120)[14]

### A Point on Mercantilism

Schmoller is, of course, famous for his study of the economic policies of Prussia during the 18th century.[15] Hence, it is not surprising that in the long introductory chapter to the *Blueprint* which is entitled: 'Introduction: Notion. Psychological and customary basis, literature and method [of political economy][16] there is a section on mercantilism (pp. 85–6).[17] In this survey, he emphasizes the real world context in which mercantilist writings developed. This is, by the way, typical Schmoller as a historian of economic thought. In doing so, he first makes the point that the territorial states that developed during the 17th and 18th centuries had to emulate those economic policies that had already been developed in the cities during the late 14th, 15th and 16th centuries. The territorial states which were, partly as a consequence of the Thirty Years War (1618–1648) and then further on as a consequence of the Napoleonic wars during the late 18th and early 19th centuries, forged by 'blood and iron' and continued to be in an extremely precarious position, constantly on the outlook not to be ravaged by a mightier power in the case of smaller states, constantly switching between trade and war in jockeying for resources in the case of the larger powers. Hence, he suggests, it is understandable that some smaller powers entertained the notion not to participate in international trade at all.

The basic underlying idea of mercantilism was that the state had the duty to develop the deep division of labour which can only be accomplished through the introduction of money. Hence, the state had to create those institutions in which market exchange could take place; yet there was an ulterior purpose, economic policy always being in the interest of the newly developing territorial states. The civil service which had to build and maintain the economic institutions of market exchange and the standing armies which had to protect that very production (of agriculture and manufacture) and trade (in the case of colonial trade a navy had to be maintained as well) required substantial revenues through taxation, and this, in turn, required the extensive use and frequent circulation of money. Hence, monetary policy was the prerequisite of developmental policy on the one hand and public finance on the other. Not so much the vain quest for gold and silver, as Smith seemed to have suggested, but the needs of these public bodies (civil service, army and navy) dictated mercantilist policy. 'Even Colbert (1619–1683)', Schmoller writes, 'has devoted much more attention to the international administrative unity of France than to its external consolidation.'[18] Since the traditional institutions such as staple rights, road duties, internal tariffs and so on were still in existence, economic policy had to emphasize a deeper and deeper penetration of monetary exchange, and the circulation of money became the focus of policy. 'Not money as the sole object of wealth is the centre of analysis, but the circulation of money, since money is seen as the swingwheel of economic exchange.'[19] This is a radically different interpretation of the basic essence of mercantilist doctrine from what the mainstream of textbook authors in the history of economic thought offers. The emphasis is on the one hand on the institutions that allow markets to emerge, a point extremely important today for transitional economies, and on the other on the circulation (as opposed to the institution) of money, which presupposes all those aspects that make money acceptable as a unit of exchange, a unit of account, and a store of value.

## Transaction Costs and the Emergence of Markets

This is a story of how commodity markets turned into markets for money and credit, and how credit appeared as an institution for minimizing transaction costs, facilitating exchange over large and at that time physically unbridgeable distances. It is the story of the emergence of the bills of exchange, an institution the uses of which somehow had to navigate around the usury doctrines taught and applied by the Catholic Church. In a nutshell[20] the story goes like this. In order to penetrate the local economies with market exchange, regular markets had to be granted that also allowed access by foreign traders. Originally, this was a matter of exception, in order to protect local business. Prudent city leaders noticed that it was important to reign in the local interests favouring protection (and high prices) in order to develop the economic strength of the city. Market privileges, that, of course, had to be granted by the emperor – since a market needs the rule of law – became more numerous, and some cities reverted to attracting more and more traders on more and more numerous occasions. What originally had been annual markets became biannual markets and ultimately veritable fairs, and these fairs in some cities turned into places where international credit transactions could be handled under the rule of the (local) law. Instead of putting the foreign traders under the law of guests, increasingly prudent city fathers noticed that more traders could be attracted if the legal conditions under which they were allowed to trade were more favourable. Hence, a competition started to create favourable rules for international exchange, notably the international exchange also of monetary instruments, since there was still a large variety of different, often debased, local currencies.

Fortunately, bills of exchange that carried a discount rate did not violate Church-based usury laws. As is well known, Church law (canonical law) has an internal and an external application, since the worldly power (the emperor) is considered to be the sword of the Church and hence has to enforce the worldly aspects of Church doctrine. However, the discount rate carried by bills of exchange was considered not an interest rate, but rather a premium due to the fact that they were entered in one currency to be paid out in another instead. Hence, the discount rate was supposed to have a time element only due to the necessity of transferring one currency into another, which necessarily allowed for travel that is time consuming. This hurdle having been surmounted, new international forms of credit transactions could take place, the nuclear form of our international money markets. The numbers here are interesting and worth reporting; at a quarterly fair in Piacenza at the beginning of the 17th century, there was a turnover of 16 million ducats. An Antwerp around 1550, Ehrenberg talks about a turnover of 40 million ducats in bills of exchange. (*Blueprint* II, 26) In appreciating these numbers, please note that the point of these discussions is to see the context in which international financial markets could emerge. Schmoller throughout uses a transactions cost approach, emphasizing the institutions that were necessary to make this happen. This is notably the market police, the market law with its very fine rules, the market court with its appeals structure. There was even a system in place to deal with questionable bills of exchange. These are, of course, the requisite institutions for facilitating international financial exchange. Schmoller's history-based theory is then an institutionally rich theory of international financial markets, based on a large number of studies of real markets.

## Technology, the Development of the Division of Labour and Public Institutions

An important aspect of Schmoller's monetary theory is his insistence on interconnecting technology, the development of markets and hence the division of labour and the concomitant development of supporting public institutions. One should immediately emphasize that this development is not necessarily a one-way road. Repeatedly, and an example will be given shortly, Schmoller points out that next to progress there is always a potential for retrogression, that it takes well-advised and well-intentioned governments to ensure benign political, economic and technological progress. Only in this sense was Schmoller a cultural optimist, that he worked on identifying potentials for progress, well aware that such progress would require strong efforts not only on the part of outstanding and leading individuals but also on the part of entire social groups, testing their cohesion and long-term viability. The discussion Schmoller placed in Book 3 of the *Blueprint* is devoted to the social process of circulation of goods and distribution of income. There, part one discusses traffic, the emergence of markets and commerce, which we have just looked at, Part 2 economic competition and Part 3 measures, weights, coins and monetary affairs. Chapter 4 looks at value and prices. The remaining chapters are respectively on wealth, capital, credit and rent (5), banking (6), the labour contract (7), the new social institutions, in other words the welfare state (8) and finally income and its distribution. The reason for the peculiar positioning of this aspect of his monetary theory (next to measures and weights) lies in Schmoller's insistence that for these earlier periods technology matters a great deal and to an extent technological restrictions hamper economic development.

In his typical circumspect style, Schmoller sets out the research programme in its complexity:

> We can readily see the parallel development of on the one hand the fuller perfection of the notion of an economic value and on the other hand the deeper division of labour and the more extensive traffic. This parallel development occurs in stages. In a sense, the epochs of money and minting became at the same time epochs of economic development more generally. This is a complicated process in which technical properties of metals and the needs of trade, the customs of markets and merchants interact with state institutions in an iterative process, with groping attempts and missteps of all kinds, setbacks certainly not lacking, with egotistical interest of individuals again and again challenging state institutions of commerce and correcting them, yet those state institutions always recurring in an improved form and finally dominating, since only these state institutions can guarantee, in a sustained way, the successful completion of the task to provide a generally accepted medium of payment and exchange.[21]

The medium of payment and exchange obviously refers to the two basic functions of money, providing a unit of exchange and a unit of account. Before looking at the state institutions that could accomplish this function, Schmoller first emphasizes the economically relevant properties of those precious metals that can serve the purpose of preserving, accurately representing and transporting value.

> The function of preserving the value is performed by the secondary demand for those metals, these being the raw materials for the more refined tools, jewelry and the more refined implements. Secondly, this value must be contained in a rather small physical entity. As compared to wheat, Roscher had pointed out that gold is 447 772-fold more readily transportable, the figure for silver is 15 544. In addition to this ease of transportation the importance of the durability is also stressed. The metal is not depreciated by either exposure to air or water, the stamps remain legible, the metal even survives fire. (p. 69)

The devastating debasements of the currency from the high Middle Ages on are a well known fact. It is interesting how Schmoller, using the interplay of economic, technical and political factors, finds an explanation. First of all, from the year 800 on the stability of the currency initiated by the Carolingians is astonishing. The penny (denarius) in the year 800 stood at 1.7 grams silver, in 950 at 1.5, in 1150 at 1.4. Only in the 14th century did it come down to 0.5 grams (p. 71). Hence, with the same theory, one has to explain both, the relative long period of relative (and not absolute) stability and the sudden decline in the 14th century, but differently so in different locations. The explanation turns on the costs of minting.[22] The cost of minting stood at about four to six per cent. Hence, it was the practice, once a year, on the major market day to mint new coins and recall the old ones. Typically, 13 old pennies had to be turned in for 12 new ones, the objective being that the new coins would all contain the same amount of silver. The difference (1/13) was called the mint treasure. Given the high cost of minting, the pure profit from minting, despite this mint treasure of 1/13, was not extraordinarily high and provided sufficient incentive for the local sovereign as a feudal representative of the king who had received a minting privilege to provide the market with sufficient and equal currency.

This was a sustainable regime as long as the volume of market transactions was small. When markets became more frequent and the volume of transactions increased, larger and larger amounts of pennies had to be minted, and more frequently so. In Brandenburg, for instance, in the 14th century it became a custom to require 16 old pennies for 12 new ones, pushing the mint treasure to 25 per cent. Conversely, this amounted to a 25 per cent tax on liquidity, a result those merchants who held large amounts of liquid currency were unwilling to accept. Hence, this unaccepted cost of monetary transactions, in the form of the liquidity tax, forced the monetary innovation, the large gold guilder or florint (1252) or Venetial dukat (1284) became this substitute large coin representing 240 pennies, and remained fairly stable over many centuries. In the northern part of the Holy Roman Empire starting in the Tyrrol and then going to Joachimsthal, the thaler (or American dollar later) would be the silver substitute. Interestingly, the pennies were minted well below par, but they remained accepted due to their transaction value and as they remained tied to the larger stable coins. An economic theory must explain a historical event occurring or not occurring, as well as its timing. The introduction of the large (golden) coin coincides with the degree of economic development. Those cities that are farthest advanced economically introduced the coin first. 'In the 14th and 15th century, the gold guilder is practically a common European currency.'[23]

With more and more extensive and intensive commerce, the demand for liquidity obviously increased. That also increased the need for issuing small currency. Given, however, the technological constraint of high costs of minting in particular for small currency, the issue necessarily arose as to who would bear these high costs. Conceivably, three possibilities are available. The first possibility consists in reducing the value of the currency with each new process of minting. Hence, we have the liquidity tax previously mentioned. Secondly, one could, as did England (p. 656) allow free minting, which meant that whoever would mint (according to standard, obviously) would have to bear the cost of minting. The third possibility pioneered in Florence and Venice, later in Upper Germany consisted in defining two types of coins, those (large) coins that would be minted at par, and those that would still contain the par value but only owe their vinculation to the large coins. This, again, was a measure that required a public initiative, since the value of the small change was only linked to the inherent metal value by an act of law. In this innovation lies the kernel of the later state theory of money propagated by Knapp. The technological breakthrough of being able to mint fairly precisely occurred shortly before the French Revolution, but this date coincided with great political upheavals including the introduction of paper money with which Schmoller dealt in a separate chapter.

An interesting insight in Mercantilist thought, so deeply misunderstood by Smith, is also provided with a technological reason. The larger the political constituency and hence commercial area, the larger was the amount of metal necessary for the regular minting dates, a logistical problem of a supreme order. But, as we had seen before, the provision of an equal and reliable currency was necessary for markets to function at the respective dates. It was this necessity that explains the emphasis of mercantilist writers, who wrote for the rulers of very large areas, to emphasize the need always to have sufficient amounts of specie under control. The smaller Cameralist countries could profit from the competition among currencies even at times when they would not themselves be able to reap the benefits of seigniorage from minting. Having detailed this historical development with its transactions costs aspects, the technological constraints and the political institutions, Schmoller then proceeds swiftly to defining the functions of money in essentially the same way as we know monetary theory today.

> Money is not only in fact but also in concept on the one hand endowed with a natural essence and on the other hand with a legal form. It is a medium of exchange in sale and purchase, but it also represents economic values and is used as a medium of account, as an instrument to fix in a precise way economic processes. It allows for quantification of economic events. It took a gradual historical process for these different economic functions of money to evolve. Only modern states provide money that can fulfil all these functions. (Blueprint II, p. 79)

A fascinating example of how far the transactions costs approach to a historical theory of money can be pushed is provided in Schmoller's theory of bimetalism. The inherent volatility of quotations due to the different prices of gold and silver respectively, as long as they were within reasonable bounds, was easily absorbed in market transactions. The currency minted in the metal expected to be appreciating in value was used as the credit money, in other words the currency in which credits had to be repaid. The system broke down when, due to new technologies (of mining) enormous changes occurred; different changes in technology affected mining of gold and silver differently at different times, but ultimately silver engaged in a free fall with respect to its value. Now, the original volatility by far exceeded the transaction costs and credit relations, and bimetalism as a system collapsed.

It is interesting to reflect on why credit relations were in this way organized as insurance contracts. In fact, the creditor assumes the risk of the debtor's default, while the debtor assumes the risk of changes in the value of the currency, which are beyond either agent's control. The entire risk of the moral hazard is thus shifted to the creditor, while the market risk lies supremely with the debtor. Clearly, usury laws could thus be readily circumvented. Yet insuring contract performance must still have been a formidable challenge.

## On Hyperinflation

The most astonishing aspect of Schmoller's monetary theory occurs when he discusses the effects of the change in the value of money on economic activity starting from small changes over history due to technological or legal imperfections or the slow process of modern banking institutions to develop but leading all the way to the economic and social effects of hyperinflations. This discussion can be found in the second volume of the *Blueprint* on pages 685 to 765 in Chapter 4 of Book 3 (in the second volume) entitled 'Value and Prices'. It is impossible to summarize the densely written 80 pages of theory and history in just a few paragraphs. However, the reader may be helped by a characterization of the approach taken which may serve as a reading guide. Throughout, value and prices are seen in the context of the monetary expression in which values can be formulated. As we have seen, the monetary items available cannot themselves be taken for granted, transaction costs are high, as are the costs of maintaining monetary value due to purely technical imperfections, but to the extent that these imperfections can be overcome and money becomes more pervasive it has a different effect on the valuation of things. Monetary valuations as compared to others based in religion, ethics, customs and the like take the lead and become more and more the norm.

Obviously, changes in the value of money affect different parts of the economy differently depending on the extent to which it has been penetrated by money. This is true in the simple sense of backward areas in the history or geography being less affected by monetary fluctuations than highly integrated activities which experience changes in monetary values by the day, or even by the minute. The better one is equipped to hedge against these risks of changes in monetary values, the more one is also able to profit from these same changes. Some parts of the economy will necessarily depend on regular payments, sometimes on an annual basis as with leases in agriculture, sometimes on a quarterly basis as was still the custom with the salaries of Prussian civil servicemen. Taxes will often be due on an annual basis, salaries of employees on a monthly basis, workers' recompensations on a daily basis and the like. Some fees may require a lengthy process of review, hence they cannot readily fluctuate in recognition of changes in the value of the currency.

Unleash on such a structured system a process of hyperinflation, detailed in the final part of that chapter. Gradually, paper money will not only drive out other means of payment, it will suffocate all lines of monetary transactions that are more cumbersome. Those who can appropriately judge the inflationary process and can hedge against its risks will be less affected and may even profit from it. Others may be defenceless against its repercussions. Some suppliers of government will be paid on the spot with freshly provided new currency, others at the regular intervals with a currency by then already devalued. Parts of the economy that are more exposed to foreign trade will be affected differently from those that are more cushioned internally. Those who rely on fees for their services will find their position challenged, the fees meaningless and a general erosion of the practices in their professional trade being widespread and hard to contain, then professional practice being corrupted and this corruption affecting different people very differently. A general erosion of civilization will rapidly take place and will be hard to reverse (he has a chapter on reversal). The extent of social injustice will be generally perceived as large, but it will motivate the differently affected pockets of the population differently, some despairing, some going along, the common good suffering in both cases.

This discussion is extensively supported by all kinds of quantitative material of both historical and contemporary cross-sectional type. However, the ultimate conclusion of the in-depth economic analysis is worth noting, as it shows how Schmoller is trying to summarize his economic argument in a general form. He says:

> It has to be hoped that civilized governments will revert ever less frequently and to an ever smaller extent to his policy which is not only disastrous to the financial infrastructure but more importantly to the economy as a whole

## CONCLUSION

In conclusion, we have to note that Dorfman's thesis of a one hundred year gap in economic theorizing on development is clearly untenable. Just a little over fifty years after Mill's *Principles*, Schmoller published his *Blueprint* which is an extremely ambitious social and economic theory of development and wealth creation, taking an evolutionary point of view and emphasizing the state and its economic functions in creating institutions in which markets can evolve.

## NOTES

1.  This essay is dedicated to the late Zoltan Kenessey (1929–1998), formerly director of the International Statistical Institute of the United Nations in Voorburg, Netherlands. When the

June 1991 issue of the *Journal of Economic Literature* reached our desks, we had just spent a week discussing the work of Werner Sombart. (See Jürgen Backhaus (ed.), *Werner Sombert Social Scientist*, I, II, III (Marburg: Metropolis, 1996).)

Earlier conferences had been devoted to the work of Gustav Schmoller and the scholarly landscape in which it had occurred (see Jürgen Backhaus (ed.), 'Essays on Gustav Schmoller', *History of Economic Ideas*, I.3; 1993, II.1, 1994; and Jürgen Backhaus (ed.), 'The Economics of Science Policy'; An Analysis of the Althoff System', *Journal of Economics Studies*, 20.3–4, 1993). In a letter with a copy of the Dorfman review article as an enclosure, Dr. Kenessey asked me to write an essay explaining the contribution of the historical school, since even eminent people such as Robert Dorfman apparently are ignorant of it. Unfortunately, due to his untimely death last year, I have not been able to benefit from his critical input.

2.  Robert Dorfman, Review Article; 'Economic Development from the Beginning to Rostow', *Journal of Economic Literature* 29, June 1991, pp. 573–91.

3.  'The main difference is that Marshall's optimism is more moderate than Mill's as one would expect, moderation being one of Marshall's most constant characteristics.' Dorfman, 1991, (pp. 579–80).

4.  This refers to Walt Whitman Rostow, *Theories of Economic Growth from David Hume to the Present*. New York: Oxford University Press, 1990.

5.  Dorfman counts Marshall (1890) out, because of the strong resemblance to Mill asserted.

6.  Gustav Schmoller, *Grundriß der allgemeinen Volkswirtschaftslehre (Blueprint)*. Munich and Leipzig: Duncker & Humblot, I, 1900; II, 1904; second and substantially revised edition 1919.

7.  'The Kanitz Act Proposal'. In: Jürgen Backhaus (ed.) (1999), 'Freedom, trade and the nation state', *Journal of Economic Studies*, **26**(4/5), 438–48.

8.  Edgar Salin called the *Blueprint* 'einen unbezwingbaren Berg'; he obviously never succeeded in reading it.

9.  Currently, this aspect is the most central and volatile aspect of US policy, pervading every aspect of life, not just underlying the main issue in economic policy.

10. Gustav Schmoller, *Grundriß der allgemeinen Volkswirtschaftslehre I, II*. Munich and Leipzig: Duncker & Humblot, 1923, second edition. It is important to consult the second edition, since this is the final statement made by Schmoller as a conclusion of his entire life's work.

11. Schmoller himself cites the following of his own contributions next to those notably by Bücher, Brentano, Inama Sterneck and Schönberg: 'Geschichte der deutschen Kleingewerbe im 19. Jahrhundert', 1870; 'Straßburger Tucher- und Weberzunft', 1879; 'Wirtschaftliche Politik Preußens im 18. Jahrhundert', J.f. G.V. 1884–87; 'Die Tatsachen der Arbeitsteilung', das. 1889; 'Das Wesen der Arbeitsteilung und der sozialen Klassenbildung', das. 1889; 'Die geschichtliche Entwicklung der Unternehumung', das. 1890–93; 'Zur Sozial- und Gewerbepolitik der Gegenwart', 1890; 'Einige Grundfragen der Sozialpolitik und Volkswirtschaftslehre', 1898; 'Umrisse und Untersuchungen zur Verfassungs-, Verwaltungs- und Wirtschaftsgeschichte', 1898; *Acta Borussica*, from 1892 up to 14 Bde.; *Staats- und Sozialwissenschaftliche Forschungen*, from 1878, 126 Hefte, to Heft 101 in sequence.'

12. The German text reads: 'Der Unterschied der Jüngeren historischen Schule von ihm ist der, daß sie weniger rasch generalisieren will, daß sie ein viel stärkeres Bedürfnis empfindet, von der polyhistorischen Datensammlung zur Spezialuntersuchung der einzelnen Epochen, Völker und Wirtschaftszustände überzugehen. Sie verlangt zunächst wirtschaftsgeschichtliche Monographien, Verknüpfung jeder modernen Spezialuntersuchung mit ihren historischen Wurzeln; sie will lieber zunächst den Werdegang der einzelnen Wirtschaftsinstitutionen als den der ganzen Volkwirtschaft und der universellen Weltwirtschaft erklären. Sie knüpft an die strenge Methode rechtsgeschichtlicher Forschung an, sucht aber ebenso durch Reisen und eigenes Befragen das Bücherwissen zu ergänzen, die philosophische und psychologische Forschung heranzuziehen.'

13. Gustav Schmoller, *Wirtschaftliche Politik Preußens im 18. Jahrhundert, 1884–1887*; this study has been (mis)translated as a study in Mercantilism, when in fact he deals with a Cameralist approach to economic policy.

14. In the German original: 'Einleitung. Begriff. psychologische und sittliche Grundlage. Literatur und Methode'.
15. By the way, this history of thought of political economy which covers essentially the first 120 pages of the first volume of the *Blueprint* would be a worthy project for translation into English; it is still brilliant in its concise statements.
16. 'Selbst Colbert (1619–1683) hat unendlich mehr für die innere Verwaltungseinheit Frankreichs als für dessen Abschluß nach außen getan.' (*Blueprint* I, p. 85)
17. 'Nicht sowohl das Geld als einziger Gegenstand des Reichtums steht so im Mittelpunkt der Betrachtung, als die Zirkulation desselben, das Geld als Schwungrad des Verkehrs.' (*Blueprint* I, p. 86)
18. Please note that this nutshell is literally based on hundreds of detailed investigations, enumerated on page 120 of the *Blueprint*, Volume I.
19. 'Wir können so sogleich verfolgen, wie die ganze Ausbildung des wirtschaftlichen Wertbewußtseins sowie der höheren Arbeitsteilung und des großen Verkehrs diesen Stadien der Geldentwicklung parallel ging. Die Epochen des Geld- und Münzwesens wurden in gewissem Sinne zugleich die Epochen der volkswirtschaftlichen Entwicklung überhaupt. Es ist ein komplizierter Prozeß, wobei die technischen Eigenschaften der Metalle und die Verkehrsbedürfnisse, die Sitte des Marktes und der Kaufmannschaft einerseits, die staatlichen Veranstaltungen andererseits immer wieder zusammen-wirken und ineinander greifen, wobei tastende Versuche und Fehlgriffe aller Art, ja Rückschritte nicht fehlen, das egoistische Interesse des Einzelnen immer wieder die staatlichen und Handelseinrichtungen über den Haufen wirft order korrigiert, und diese doch immer wieder siegreich in verbesserter Form sich behaupten, weil nur sie dauernd der großen und schwierigen Aufgabe, ein allgemeines Tausch- und Zahlmittel zu liefern, gerecht werden.
20. Part of the cost is also the inaccuracy of the minting process which always leads to the heavier coins being retained and the lighter ones remaining in circulation.
21. 'Der Goldgulden ist im 14. bis 15. Jahrhundert fast eine Europäische Münze'. *Blueprint* II, p. 654.
22. 'Das Geld hat tatsächlich oder begrifflich ein natürliches Substrat und eine koventionell rechtlich geordnete Form. Es ist nicht bloß Tauschmittel bei Kauf und Verkauf, sondern zugleich Zahlmittel für Steuern, Besoldunge, Ausstattungen, Ablösungen, Schenkungen. Das Geld wird zum Repräsentationsmittel aller wirtschaftlichen Werte und zum Mittel der Rechnunb, Fixierung, numerischen Präzisierung aller wirtschaftlichen Vorgänge. Diese verschiedenen Funktionen des Geldes haben sich historisch nach und nach entwickelt. Im modernen geldwirtschaftlichen Staate sind sie alle voll und ganz vorhanden.'
23. 'Es ist zu hoffen, dass gesittete Regierungen immer seltener und in immer geringerem Maß zu dissem für Volkwirtschaft und Finanzen gleich verhängnisvollem Mittel greifen werfen. (*Blueprint* II, p. 765).

# REFERENCES

Backhaus, Jürgen (ed.) (1993), 'The economics of science policy: an analysis of the Althoff System', *Journal of Economics Studies*, 20, 3–4.
Backhaus, Jürgen (ed.) (1994), 'Essays on Gustav Schmoller', in *History of Economic Ideas*, vol. I issue 3, Pisa: Gruppo Ed. In Internazzionale.
Backhaus, Jürgen (ed.) (1996), *Werner Sombart Social Scientist*, vols. I, II, III. Marburg: Metropolis.
Dorfman, Robert (1991), 'Economic development from the beginning to Rostow', *Journal of Economic Literature*, **29**, June, 573–91.
Rostow, Walt Whitman (1990), *Theories of Economic Growth from David Hume to the Present*, New York: Oxford University Press.

Schmoller, Gustav (1884–7), *Wirtschaftliche Politik Preußens im 18. Jahrhundert*, Leipzig: Duncker & Humblot.

Schmoller, Gustav (1900), *Grundriß der allgemeinen Volkswirtschaftslehre (Blueprint)*, vol. I, Munich, Duncker & Humblot: vol. II (1904), Munich: Duncker & Humblot, second and substantially revised edition published in 1919, Munich: Duncker & Humblot.

Schmoller, Gustav (1870), *Geschichte der deutschen kleingewerbe im 19. Jahrhundert*, reprinted 1975 Hildesheim, NY: Olms.

Schmoller, Gustav (1879), *Straßburger Tucher- und Weberzunft*, Straßburg: Trübner.

Schmoller, Gustav (1889), *Die Tatsachen der Arbeitsteilung*, reprint.

Schmoller, Gustav (1889), *Das Wasen der Arbeitsteilung und der sozialen Klassenbildung*, reprint.

Schmoller, Gustav (1890–93), *Die geschichtliche Entwicklung der Unternehmung*, Leipzig: Duncker & Humblot.

Schmoller, Gustav (1890), *Zur Sozial- und Gewerbepolitik der Gegenwart*, Leipzig: Duncker & Humblot.

Schmoller, Gustav (1898), *Einige Grundfragen der Sozialpolitik und Volkswirtschaftslehre*, Leipzig: Duncker & Humblot.

Schmoller, Gustav (1898), *Umrisse und Untersuchungen zur Verfassungs-, Verwaltungs- und Wirtschaftsgeschichte*, Leipzig: Duncker & Humblot.

Schmoller, Gustav (ed.) (1892–), *Acta Borussica*, 14 volumes; comprises a total of 126 volumes since 1878, Berlin: Parey.

# 3. Some evolutionary features in John Hobson's economic analysis

## Stéphane Ngo Mai and Richard Aréna

### INTRODUCTION

The assessment, throughout the last century, of John Hobson's contribution to economic analysis has been a rather controversial issue. For some commentators Hobson's economic analysis is nothing more than muddled thinking. This position was quite widespread in England during the heyday of Marshallian supremacy and indeed blocked Hobson's academic appointment.[1] His analytical 'heresies', such as the underconsumption/oversaving thesis or the marginal productivity critique, led many economists to regard him much as trade unionists regard a blackleg, or at best as a mere crank.[2] These negative judgments have probably overinfluenced further academic commentators. Without any kind of demonstration, J. Schumpeter, for instance, is very abrupt:

> ... the possibility that owing to his inadequate training, many of his propositions, especially his criticisms, might be provably wrong and due to nothing more but failure to understand, never entered his head, however often it was pointed out to him.[3]

This creed sharply contrasts with the tribute that J.M. Keynes paid to Hobson. Indeed seven pages of Chapter 23 of the *General Theory* are dedicated to a comment on Hobson and Mummery, early work the *Physiology of Industry*. Then J.M. Keynes, himself, contributed to the belief that Hobson was one of his few forerunners and modern commentators have tried to reassess this influence.[4] In the same line of thinking, the economic analysis of Hobson has sometimes been presented as an ancestor of Harrod and Domar growth models. Indeed, Harrod wrote a preface of a re-edition of *The Science of Wealth*[5] and Domar did explicitly refer to Hobson rather than Keynes as a predecessor.[6] Similar considerations were noticed by J. Robinson: 'Mr. Harrod's analysis provides the missing link between Keynes and Hobson.'[7]

Other commentators have developed the idea that Hobson's contributions to economics did fill the analytical gap between the classical and the Keynesian approaches.[8]

From a quite different standpoint, Hobson is sometimes presented as 'A British Institutionalist.'[9] J. Schumpeter, for instance, stressed accurately the point:

> Hobson's insistence upon what he considered to be irrational behaviour of consumers and upon the institutional factors that, rather than 'rational choice', determine this behaviour really implies a research program of the historico-sociological sort. This is important to realize because it supplies one of the links between Hobson and American institutionalism.[10]

Indeed, Hobson did personally know and corresponded with Thorstein Veblen, they cited each other, and Hobson even wrote a book, an article and an obituary on Veblen.[11] However recent reassessments of this connection tend to demonstrate that the analytical link is rather tenuous[12] though broad influences can be detected.

In the face of such an apparent imbroglio one could contend that Hobson's economics is nothing more than a collection of disparate superficial analysis and this would explain the diversity of opinions. This chapter supports the opposite idea: far from being a collection of disparate superficial analysis Hobson's economic analysis conveys a general vision of the scope and nature of economics which is certainly idiosyncratic, but also self-consistent.

This chapter is neither an attempt to assess Hobson's status as an institutionalist nor as a Keynesian economist or otherwise, it is rather an attempt to enter into Hobson's economic theory in order to evaluate his methodology and his analysis. We indeed contend that a genuine economic theory is clearly detectable in Hobson's analysis and that it can be evaluated quite separately from Hobson's ideological position.

As R. Harrod reminds us in the preface to the fourth edition of *The Science of Wealth*,[13] 'J. Hobson is best known for two theories, one, his theory of the unproductive surplus, and the second, his explanation of the causes of industrial depression. There is a link between those two theories.'[14] Now it is precisely this link that we shall here study in order to stress the importance of the role of institutions in Hobson's economic analysis. This chapter includes three parts. The first one is dedicated to an exposition of the quite distinctive evolutionary conception of Hobson's economic analysis. The second considers his study of depressions and business cycles within his industrial dynamics analysis. The third emphasizes the importance of institutions in the Hobsonian explanation of depression through the specific roles they play both in his normative and positive theories of distribution.

## HOBSON'S EVOLUTIONARY CONCEPTION OF ECONOMIC ANALYSIS

> In an age when human problems of a distinctively economic character, relating to wages, hours of labour, housing, employment, taxation, insurance and kindred subjects, are pressing for separate consideration and solution, it is particularly important to enforce the need of a general survey of our economic system from the standpoint of human values.[15]

It is important to note, at the very outset, that Hobson's economic analysis is quite distinctive. The apparent multidisciplinary nature of his work combined with his so-called humanistic foundation have turned many readers off. Yet, we think that it is possible to isolate a pure economic analysis in Hobson's contributions. For the Hobsonian assumption according to which *one has to assume that a human valuation of economic processes is possible and desirable* is certainly not a logical precondition for understanding his economic theory. Now, while a humanistic conception of the functions of economics – expressed in the Ruskinian phrase 'there is no wealth but life'[16] – necessarily implies, according to Hobson, a sort of *methodological organicism,* this latter, in turn, does not necessarily lead us out of economic frontiers.

> To a Greek or a Roman, the idea that the city existed merely for the production of good citizens, and without an end or self of its own, would never have seemed plausible. . . . Society must then be conceived, not as a set of social relations but as a collective organism , . . . . Finally a social interpretation of industry is not possible except by treating society as an organic structure.[17]

Nevertheless, these teleological and methodological positions do not imply, in our author's view, the enlargement of the ordinary definition of the boundaries of economic studies. For, referring to the *industrial system*[18] for instance, it seems possible to disconnect the teleological analysis from the methodological one; studying *first* the system from an 'objective' and 'narrow economic point of view' and interpreting it *then* from a subjective standpoint. In other words, in Hobson's analysis, methodological organicism is a necessary but not sufficient technique to cope with the human valuation issue. Though our author would probably have refused to accept an economic analysis that divorced the economy from the society, an important feature of his theory remains: his economic analysis can be evaluated quite independently from his humanistic study.

The theoretical foundations of Hobson's approach to economics may then be evaluated on the ground of the positive or normative economic results to which it leads rather than on the ground of teleological issues.

The 'organic structure' of Hobson implies that the economy is not a collection of separate individuals whom contractual exchange relations are supposed to connect. Rather, as J. Maloney[19] pointed out, in Hobson the economy appears to be an 'evolving organism':[20]

> Thus the growth of harmonious and conflicting desires of consumers weaves the closest and most intricate network of relations between all the various productive processes of the industrial world. The closer we examine any section of the industrial system, the more numerous and complex the relations between the businesses, the trades, the groups of trade contained in it (. . .) we come unconsciously to shift the metaphors we use, and to regard industry less as a stream or a machine and more as a live organism . . .[21]

This evolutionary conception of economics implies in Hobson's view that agents do not exist a priori and economic relations or institutions are not described as the mere results of individual interaction. Agents and 'the industrial system' are defined simultaneously. There is no logical necessity to begin with isolated individuals.

> In accordance with our method of procedure, we first assume the existence of a fully equipped industrial system and consider the costs of its upkeep . . .[22]

This kind of 'methodological organicism' is postulated in Hobson's work in order to construct *an image of the actual concrete system of industry* which happens to be a preliminary to deal with most economic issues. Note, as J. Rossman[23] observed, that Hobson's generic economic study is more concerned with the provisioning of a society than with pure allocative issues. In this respect the 'industrial organism' is thus seen as the core of economic analysis, for it is the location where the *creation of wealth* takes place.

Since the industrial system is fundamentally described as an 'evolutionary process' and not as a stationary one,[24] one must pay attention to *the history of structural change* and to *the basic incentives to change*.

> In the structural changes of modern industry and in the social changes which accompany them an ever-growing importance attaches to the discovery, selection, training and economical application of these finer sorts of psychical forces which are the chief direct instruments of progress in the arts of industry.[25]

On one hand, Hobson did not hesitate to resort to the history of economic facts to perform positive economic analysis. His *Evolution of Modern Capitalism* is, according to Schumpeter, a very good work on the history of capitalism. This allows him to call upon 'economic facts' to produce economic analysis. And even more, he did not hesitate to discard orthodox, quite normative, concepts such as marginal productivity or Say's law, in the very name of 'industrial facts'.[26]

On the other hand, his insistence upon incentives to change led him to discard the orthodox rationality of economic agents. For Hobson, agents are endowed with different bounded economic rationalities; *imitation, routine, creation* are the basic ingredients of agent behaviours. Those behaviours play different but complementary roles in the progress of industry.[27] Let us quote a long but significant passage:

> All social progress, indeed all social changes . . . come about in the following way. Some unusually powerful, original, or enterprising person, assisted often by good fortune, makes what is called a discovery, some true and useful way of doing things or thinking about things, or even of saying things. This new truth, new phrase, new dodge, is capable of being recognized as interesting or useful, not only by its discoverer, but by the many who had not the wit or the courage or the luck to discover it for themselves. By suggestion, infection, contagion, or conscious imitation, or by any combinaison of those forces and habits that constitute the social nature of man, the novelty becomes adopted and applied by an ever-growing number of persons, over a widening area, until it becomes an accepted practice or convention of the whole society.[28]

Although agents belong to a 'connective tissue', just as organs are characterized according to their place within the organism, it is clear in Hobson that the figure of the entrepreneur deserves special attention. The peculiar and important role of the 'ability' of the entrepreneur clearly appears in economic dynamics.

> . . . in ordinary steady industry . . . the kind of and degree of skill and other powers of the entrepreneurs are not scarce. Little foresight or strategy is required: even the method of organization is stereotyped. . . . The real power of the *entrepreneur* lies in areas of progressive industry. Ability is creative, labour is imitative. Such is the radical nature of the distinction that is drawn.[29]

It is worthwhile to note that creative and imitative behaviours in Hobson's analysis are – as in modern evolutionary theory, the basic microelements that explain macrochanges. This mechanism is for instance used by Hobson to deal with the evolution of standards of consumption.

> It may be well here to revert to the distinction which we found convenient to employ in our analysis of the human value of different forms of work, viz the distinction between creation and imitation. Here it will take shape in an enquiry as to the ways in which new wants are discovered and pass into conventional use.[30]

A diffusion process based upon imitation clearly stands here as a micro–macro linkage.

The 'innovation' which stands at the origin of such processes may introduce, in Hobson's view, hazard into the picture. The role of 'accident' or 'small historical events' is well acknowledged by Hobson.

The first men, who chewed the sugar-cane or tried the fume of the *herba nicotina*, must be deemed to have done so 'by accident'.[31]

More generally, our author does not seem to describe a purely deterministic world. Hazard plays a significant role in his evolutionary view. 'On the side of consumption as of production a progressive society that has not abandoned itself to excessive rationalism will recognize the desirability of keeping a scope for "bonne chance" and "hazard" '.[32]

Now once a discovery has been made, depending 'on its merit, it may become a collective habit. '. . . this personal habit becomes the customary habit of the group, moulded by a tradition continuously supported by a repetition of the feeling which attended the first chance experience'.[26]

In Hobson's opinion those processes may be variously estimated from the 'organic' standpoint, they are 'natural' and 'reasonable' and thus lead to a safe evolution of standards of consumption. But their sensitivity to initial conditions and path is such that a manipulation is always possible.

> A falsification of the standard, involving the admission of wasteful or positively noxious consumables may arise, either in the initial stage of invention, or in the process of imitative adoption.[26]

## HOBSON'S CONCEPTION OF INDUSTRIAL DYNAMICS: DEPRESSIONS AND BUSINESS CYCLES

We shall now describe shortly the main Hobsonian economic mechanisms of industrial depression and business cycle from both a macro and industrial point of view.

One of the foundations of the Hobsonian view of the economic development of modern capitalism is the possible existence of a 'right' ratio between the volume of saving and the amount of spending:

> . . . there exists at the present moment a right proportion between saving and spending in the income of the industrial community yielding the maximum rate of consumption over such a period of time as is open by reasonable foresight to capitalist investment. Industrial progress, or the economical working of the industrial system, consists largely in the ascertainment of this proportion and the adjustment of industry to it: any disregard or disturbance of this proportion involves industrial wastes.[33]

Strong tendencies related to the very working of the capitalist system prevent the practical durability of such a 'right proportion'. Among those tendencies, the famous Hobsonian underconsumption theory plays a major role. In fact as modern commentators have stressed there exist at least two distinct mechanisms in Hobson's underconsumption analysis.[34] One, by far the most analysed by Hobson, refers to an oversaving–overinvestment hypothesis. The other, a 'footnote explanation', refers to hoarding but seems to have been a bit neglected by Hobson.[35]

The first explanation is delineated in Hobson and Mummery's 1889 book.

> Now saving, while it increases the existing aggregate of capital, simultaneously reduces the quantity of utilities and conveniences consumed; any undue exercise of this habit must therefore, cause an accumulation of capital in excess of that which is required for use, and this excess will exist in the form of general over-production.[36]

It is quite clear here that overproduction arises because capital is accumulating so fast that demand for goods cannot keep up with supply.

Two main macroeconomic conditions to hold such a view are of course that (i) intermediate consumption is derived from final consumption, (ii) saving is equivalent to investment. Now the main explanation for the divergence from the 'right proportion' between saving and consumption has to be detected in Hobson's distribution theory.

We shall here briefly sketch out the essential of Hobson's distribution theory in order to complete our general picture, leaving a more detailed description of this important piece for the next section.

Because of the asymmetry of agents in the labour market, wage earners can hardly obtain more than a minimum (subsistence) wage while profit earners, that is entrepreneurs, can gain extra funds. This 'extra fund' notion has to be understood in regard to the cost element which founds the normative theory of Hobson's distribution analysis. The cost of each productive services includes two aspects. The first is a maintenance payment that allows the service to sustain its productive power from a technical point of view. The second is a more sociological element which includes a payment that sustains the will or motivation to provide the ongoing effort of work[37] (more on this in the third section).

Now in regard to this normative point of view, the effective remuneration of services depends also upon social standards, customs, bargaining power and relative scarcity. That is why the entrepreneurs'

> ... strong strategic position in the industrial system makes it tolerably certain that a large share of their income represents, not a necessary cost, a natural stimulus to the production and display of such ability, but a scarcity rent or unearned income which they take because their superior bargaining power enables them to exact it.[38]

It is now easy to understand that, as soon as wealthy agents are quickly satisfied with their current level of consumption and then save extra funds, a phenomenon of oversaving, overinvestment and underconsumption can occur. This results in an industrial depression characterized by a depressed trade where 'more has been produced than can be sold at the lowest profitable prices, and markets are congested with stock, but less is being produced than could be produced with existing means of production.'[39] This is clearly a departure from Say's law on the ground that 'the fallacy involved in the supposition that over-supply is impossible consists in assuming that the power to consume and the desire to consume necessarily co-exist in the same persons.'[40]

The only solution to avoid such an industrial depression is to respect the 'right' proportion between saving and spending. It requires regularity. Thus 'in a condition of steady consumption the continuous existence of capital, and of the same number of forms of capital, is maintained by a force which owes its impetus to a constant demand for commodities'. Moreover, 'the profits which form the money incomes of all capitalists concerned in production, the wages of all the labourers concerned, and the rent of all the natural agents required, are in a regular condition of commerce, paid out of the prices paid by consumers, that is, out of retail prices'. [41]

This situation according to which demand is constant corresponds to what Hobson and Mummery called 'the normal rate of demand for commodities', but demand is generally growing. In this case, it is obviously more difficult to obtain the 'right' proportion. It is indeed necessary to increase saving in proportion with demand:

> if saving is being effected, not merely during one day or one week, but regularly and habitually, the constantly increasing total of capital thus brought about will require a regular and habitual increase in the rate of consumption to prevent oversupply in the earlier stages of production.[42]

Hobson's industrial dynamics theory then refers clearly to a quite unstable process of growth. One can note that to the explanation in terms of a wrong distribution of incomes, Hobson adds a pure technological change explanation. In a way, in Hobson, as M. Rutherford[43] put it, 'technological change "exacerbated" the failure of consumption to keep pace with productive power'.

Hobson's work on industrial depression leads to a business cycle theory. Indeed, in our author's view, deflation is not sufficient to solve the problem of oversupply. Both price and quantity adjustments are involved in Hobson's analysis of trade depression. This economic mechanism involves a sharp distinction between makers and traders and then between wholesale and retail prices. In the *Physiology of Industry*, for instance, Hobson and Mummery stress the fact that during a boom, when demand is high, the makers can charge high prices while traders can make only normal profits; for competition happens to be weak in the case of the former while hard for the latter.

Wholesale prices are high relative to retail prices. In an oversaving, overinvestment and overproduction context, the situation is reversed: retail (fix) prices are high relative to wholesale (flex) price, traders' profits are high relative to makers' profits.

Now in such a scheme, as R. Backhouse[44] made clear, '*when during a boom, profits in making are very high, capital moves into making goods and output rises. In the depression, on the other hand, when profits are high in trading, especially in retailing, capital moves into retailing, but this does not result in any increase in output. . . . The labour attracted into retailing is thus less productive than it was in manufacturing, with the result that output is reduced.*'

To sum up the arguments on oversaving, overproduction phenomena lead first to a deflation characterized by a sharp decrease in prices and the costs of makers' activities. This is not sufficient to solve the underconsumption crisis since '*the general fall of money income which has necessarily followed from a fall of prices, uncompensated by a corresponding expansion of sales ["rigid" retail prices], induces a shrinkage of consumption*'.[45] In a second step, productive services are attracted towards traders' activities with the immediate consequence of a falling output. In a third step, once production is below (final) consumption, output and prices begin to increase.

> Before the turn in the commercial tide, current production even falls below the level of current consumption, thus allowing for the gradual passage into consumption of the glut of goods which had congested the machine. After the congestion which had kept prices low is removed, prices begin to rise, demand is more active at each point of industry, and we see the usual symptoms of reviving trade.[46]

## THE ROLE OF INSTITUTIONS IN HOBSON'S DISTRIBUTION ANALYSIS

Institutions are concomitant with economic analysis in Hobson. For, as we have seen above, the combination of an organicist methodology with a dynamic approach led our author to envisage organizations as a direct unit level of analysis and to answer questions such as the emergence and evolution of conventions, standards or collective habits. His insistence upon history, sociology as well as psychology can be understood as a methodological answer to his research programme and well adapted to deal with institutions. Apart from these methodological issues it is interesting to point out in more detail where institutions play a specific and important role in Hobson's industrial dynamics.

In this perspective, we shall concentrate our attention upon the Hobsonian analysis of distribution which happens to be at the very core of the explanation of economic depression. Indeed Hobson's business cycle theory is founded on his underconsumption/oversaving analysis, which itself lies upon a specific analysis of the distribution of an 'unproductive surplus'.

> My proposition is that the existence of a 'surplus' income, not earned by its recipients and not applying any normal stimulus to industry, has the effect of disturbing the economical adjustment between spending and saving, and of bringing about those periodical congestions and stoppages of industry with which we are familiar.[47]

This 'unproductive surplus' conjecture comes from a division of the product into 'costs of subsistence', 'costs of growth' or 'productive surplus' and an 'improductive surplus' which Hobson operates before dealing with distributional issues.[48] The idea is that modern industry continually tends to increase the product above costs of subsistence. The growing surplus should then be distributed in order to secure the maximum of *stimuli of growth*. Unfortunately there exist no strong natural economic laws that ensure such a peculiar distribution.

> But the fact that this surplus, which should be absorbed in stimuli to progress, may instead, be forcibly diverted as excessive and 'unearned' payment by the owners of some one or other factor of production, breaks this natural harmony and furnishes a ground for class or trade conflict.[49]

The important point to stress here is that an Hobsonian *normative* distribution theory is necessary to fully understand his unproductive surplus conjecture. This normative theory is more or less explicit in Hobson's analysis and is based *upon conventional, organic and human* factors. In any case the prescriptions of such a theory are neither natural nor necessary for the industrial system to survive.

The conventional or institutional feature within Hobson's normative distribution can be seen for instance in the 'family wage' to which he refers: the true maintenance wage is composed of the added wages of the wage earners in an ordinary family'.[50] This reference to a family wage allows understanding of the existence of less than personal maintenance wages.

> Where it is customary, for women and children, as well as men, to work for wages, their wages usually fall considerably below the level sufficient for their full personal maintenance, the trade in which they are engaged being to this extent parasitic upon the trade of the chief wage earner.[51]

This may also explain the coexistence in the same place of different industries, for instance a low-wage female-dominated industry such as textiles, with a high-wage male-dominated industry such as metal. Moreover this coexistence exercises a depressing influence upon the wages of the male metal workers, who will not offer the same amount of resistance to reductions of wages.

Conventional standards of living, legal and customary considerations as well as time and place determine in every class the proportion of each individual wage to the aggregate family wage and this proportion will play an important role in the price an entrepreneur will have to pay in setting up a business.

The organic feature of Hobson's normative distribution theory is straightforward:

> These laws of the maintenance and growth of the industrial system are recognized to be analogous in their nature and operation to those relating to a biological organism which provides itself with food to repair its waste of tissue and of energy, and to provide for its growth. In neither case is the method of maintenance and growth purely physical: the psychical factor enters into both.[52]

From this social standpoint Hobson describes his normative theory through the 'necessary/unnecessary payment' notion. The idea is that the excessive wages, interest and rent which distribute the unproductive surplus correspond to unnecessary payments in the sense that, if any change in economic circumstances caused them to be withheld, this withholding would not cause the owners to refuse the use of the corresponding factors of production. In other words a hypothetical abolition of such 'unnecessary payments' would in no way damage the maintenance or growth of the industrial system. It is precisely this characteristic which leads Hobson to propose a taxation of such 'excessive payments':

> They are also unnecessary in the sense that, after they have been paid, they can be taken in taxation without any disturbance of the industrial use of the factor of which they rank as surplus payment.[53]

It now appears clearly that 'a socially sound and just distribution of the surplus would be one which absorbed it entirely in what may be called the "costs of growth" '.[54] The unproductive surplus ceases to be a surplus and becomes a cost as soon as it is directed into higher wages of efficiency for workers and into further income for the enrichment of the common life.

This latter aspect leads us to the human feature of Hobson's normative distribution theory. Here again this latter is not so much defined by its beneficent effects on the industrial system as by the negative consequences that its non-application calls forth. Then for Hobson:

> The surplus element in private income thus represents the human loss from defects in the current distribution of wealth, not only the loss from wasteful and injurious consumption but from wasteful and injurious production, an exaggeration of human costs and a diminution of human utilities.[55]

Not only does the payment of unproductive surplus happen to be wasteful in the sense that it takes large sections of the income that would have been needed to raise the economic and human efficiency, or to improve the quality of the public services, but it is also injurious.

Hobson outlines the chief injuries that such excessive payment causes. Here are some examples: (i) for much, if not most, of this surplus, 'being devoted to luxury, waste, extravagance and "illth", furnishes by its expenditure not human utility but human cost', a diminution of the sum of human welfare compared to what should or could be; (ii) it encourages by imitation wasteful methods of expenditure and tends 'by suggestion to sap the wholesome respect for work in the standards of the rest of the community'; (iii) it calls into being and sustains 'a leisured or unemployed class whose existence represents a loss of productive energy'; (iv) it imposes upon the workers a great cost in the shape of irregularity of employment and a considerable burden of costly saving by way of insurance against this irregularity, for the surplus is largely spent upon 'capricious and ever-shifting consumption'.

It is worthwhile to note that free competition does not stand for Hobson as a means to impose his normative theory of distribution. If he recognizes that freedom and fluidity of factors of production associated with free competition will drive costs to their maintenance component and then that consumers will reap the surplus through low prices, he also recognizes that such a situation would lead to a stationary economy. In Hobson, free competition does not work as a mechanism that would distinguish costs of subsistence *and costs of growth* on one side and unproductive surplus on the other side. With free competition only costs of subsistence are covered.

> If the industrial system is to grow in size and improve in quality, this actual industrial surplus must be utilized to stimulate and feed this progress. . . . Now under the conditions of absolutely free competition, with payments of all factors at a minimum, no provision exists for securing this or, indeed, any apportionment of the surplus.[56]

Because free competition eradicates all incentives to change in price variables, Hobson denies its relevance to founding, as such, a thinkable normative theory of distribution. Nonetheless this does not mean that with regard to other issues Hobson still maintains this position. Quite frequently he extols the virtues of competition. And as we will argue below he even seems favourable to competition as regard of distribution if some institutions such as the State complete the picture.

In the face of this more or less explicit normative theory of distribution, Hobson proposes a quite explicit positive analysis which studies the mechanisms of appropriation of the unproductive surplus. To begin with he notes that:

> The hypothetical abundance, mobility and freedom of competition, which should prevail among all owners of capital, ability and labour, keeping down all their remuneration to a common minimum, are everywhere falsified by industrial facts.[57]

The actual determination of wages, interest and rent are, on average, more determined by 'customs, personnal considerations, public opinion, and legal enactments' than by competitive conditions. Furthermore, in every process of every industry, some factors are relatively scarce, either by nature or *by human contrivance*, and can then extort a piece of 'surplus'. This is for Hobson a generic consideration that applies to the determination of wages, interest, rent as well as profit. Because a standard wage, for instance, is built up 'partly on competition, partly on custom, partly on economic force', it may entails some 'forced gains' or 'excessive payments' which are generally obtained by a direct or indirect control of the market – trade unions for instance.

As we already mentioned the Hobsonian entrepreneur has a peculiar role in his economic analysis on account of the determinant part they play in directing the working of the industrial system and in introducing changes. Yet Hobson contends that it cannot be regarded as a sufficient reason for refusing to apply his main principle of distribution, that is the distinction between necessary and superfluous payments.

Here again our author opposes a positive analysis to a normative theory. While this latter is based upon the existence of a profit 'as the price of progress' (for being the first to innovate) which is eliminated by the emergence of competition through competition, the positive analysis rests upon 'the hypothesis that competition normally works as freely and as keenly among entrepreneurs as among labourers is notoriously false'.

Moreover, 'in actual business, . . . the entire residue of the product, or its value, after defraying the expenses of buying the other factors falls to the entrepreneur as his profit'.[58] In other words, profits are larger, as on one hand the entrepreneur can buy productive services cheap and on the other hand he can sell the product dear. Their ability to do this rests fundamentally upon the checks they set on competition.

> After land, or capital, or labour of some sort has taken its pull out of the surplus product by exacting some surplus in the price it compels the entrepreneur to pay, the rest of the surplus tends to remain for long periods of time with the entrepreneurs as an excessive profit.[59]

Thus it appears that this profit is not derived from any personal ability. Furthermore, its amount is not necessarily attached to any incentives. More precisely, 'there is no reason to suppose that a Rothschild will give out more skill in the act of finance, if circumstances enable him to earn £1000 a day instead of £100, or that a Rockefeller requires 10 000 000$ a year to stimulate his organizing genius to function'.[60] It is then quite clear that for Hobson and from a positive standpoint 'the price of ability is not closely fixed by competition, even in indirect ways, but is determined by a combination of customary, personal and competitive considerations.'[61]

Finally, it is worthwhile to note that Hobson's proposition to reconcile a normative theory of distribution – based on competition, that leaves no place for incentives to change – with a positive analysis – which shows that a large quantity of 'surplus' is everywhere diverted into unproductive channels – refers to a quite important institution: *the State*.

> It suffices to recognize that a strong and progressive State is essential to the stability and progress of industry, and must, therefore, rank as a co-operative agent in the production of the income which the private owners of land, capital, labour and ability seek to secure for themselves as costs and surplus.[62]

Indeed in Hobson's analysis competition does not suffice to secure a 'progressive industry' since it tends to direct the surplus to consumers and then eradicates incentives to innovate. While it is difficult to discriminate between costs of growth and unproductive surplus, the State can secure a share of the surplus by taxation and then transform unproductive surplus into productive surplus. The institution of a State appears then in Hobson's analysis as a necessary answer to the divorce between his normative and positive theories of distribution:

> Only when the capacity of the State to utilize for maintenance and growth a share of the 'surplus' is recognized shall we be in a position to rectify the defect in the apportionment of the product which our method of exposition has involved.[63]

## NOTES

1. cf. e.g. Kadish (1994) p.141–49.
2. cf. e.g. Cole (1940) p. 354.
3. J. Schumpeter (1954) p. 832.
4. cf. e.g. Backhouse (1994), King (1994).
5. Hobson (1911 [1950]), preface.
6. Domar (1947) p. 52.
7. Robinson (1949) p. 79, quoted by King (1994) p. 105.
8. cf. e.g. Arena and Ngo Mai (1996).
9. cf. Seligman (1962) quoted by Rossman (1991) p. 199.
10. J. Schumpeter (1954) p. 823, note 24.
11. Hobson (1936, 1926).
12. cf. e.g. Rutherford (1994).
13. Hobson (1911 [1950]).
14. Italics added.
15. Hobson (1914) p. 1.
16. Quoted by Hobson in *Work and Wealth*, p. 9.
17. J. Hobson (1914) pp. 14, 15.
18. Hobson (1909 [1969]), Chap. XIX.

19.  J. Maloney (1985), p. 143.
20.  See also Hodgson (1993).
21.  Hobson (1909 (1969)] p. 31.
22.  Hobson (1909 [1969]) p. 69.
23.  Rossman (1991) p. 199.
24.  The notion of 'static industry' is sometimes used by Hobson as a useful analytical device.
25.  Hobson (1909 [1969]) p. 315.
26.  See for instance Hobson on marginal productivity (1909 [1969] Chap. V, appendix or on SAY's law [1894] p. 288.
27.  Hobson ([1914], pp. 40, 50) refers to the French sociologist Tarde on this point.
28.  Hobson (1914), p. 40.
29.  Hobson (1909 [1969]) p 126.
30.  Hobson (1914) p. 130.
31.  Hobson (1914) p. 131.
32.  Hobson (1914) p. 127.
33.  Hobson (1909 [1969]) p. 55.
34.  cf. e.g. Backhouse (1994), King (1994).
35.  cf. e.g. King (1994).
36.  Hobson and Mummery (1889 [1956]) preface.
37.  cf. e.g. J. Rossman (1991).
38.  Hobson (1910) p. 134.
39.  Hobson (1894) p. 274.
40.  Hobson (1894) p. 289.
41.  Hobson and Mummery (1889 [1956]) p. 71.
42.  Hobson and Mummery (1889 [1956]) pp. 50–1.
43.  Rutherford (1994) p. 191.
44.  Backhouse (1994) p. 87.
45.  Hobson (1894) pp. 286, 287.
46.  Hobson (1894) p. 288.
47.  Hobson (1909 [1969]) p. 294.
48.  This provides a link between the Classics and Hobson which is however rather scarcely mentioned. It gives an essential key for the understanding of Hobson's theoretical background. cf. Arena and Ngo Mai (1996).
49.  Hobson [1909] pp. 79, 80
50.  Hobson (1909 [1969]) p. 84.
51.  Hobson (1909 [1969]) p. 85.
52.  Hobson (1909 [1969]) p. 76.
53.  Hobson (1909 [1969]) p. 111.
54.  Hobson (1914) p. 177.
55.  Hobson (1914) p. 188.
56.  Hobson (1909 [1969]) p. 136.
57.  Hobson (1914) p. 181.
58.  Hobson (1909 [1969]) p. 131.
59.  Hobson (1909 [1969]) p. 134.
60.  Hobson (1909 [1969]) p. 133.
61.  Hobson (1909 [1969]) p. 164.
62.  Hobson (1909 [1969]) p. 81.
63.  Hobson (1909 [1969]) p. 82.

# REFERENCES

Arena, R. and Ngo Mai, S. (1996), 'Post-classical and pre-Keynesian features in John Hobson's contribution to economics', *Annual European Conference on the History of Economics*, Research Centre on the Portuguese Economy working paper, February, Lisbon.

Backhouse, R. (1994), 'Mummery and Hobson's *The Physiology of Industry*', in J. Pheby (ed.) *J.A. Hobson After Fifty Years – Freethinker of the Social Sciences*, New York: St. Martin Press.

Cole, G. (1940), 'Obituary: J.A. Hobson', *The Economic Journal*, June–Sept.

Domer, E.D. (1947), *Essays on the Theory of Economic Growth*, New York: Oxford University Press.

Hobson, J. (1894), *The Evolution of Modern Capitalism – A Study of Machine production*, London: Unwin Brothers.

Hobson, J. (1909), *The Industrial System – An Inquiry into Earned and Unearned Income*, reprinted (1969) New York: Augustus M. Kelley Publishers.

Hobson, J. (1911), *The Science of Wealth*, preface by R. Harrod reprinted (1950) Oxford: Oxford University Press.

Hobson, J. (1914), *Work and Wealth: a Human Valuation*, New York: The Macmillan Company.

Hobson, J. (1923), *The Economics of Unemployment,* London: Macmillan.

Hobson, J. (1926), *Free Thought in the Social Science*, London: Allen & Unwin.

Hobson, J. (1936), *Veblen*, London: Chapman & Hall.

Hobson, J. and Mummery, A. (1889), *The Physiology of Industry : Being an Exposure of Certain Fallacies in Existing Theories of Economics*, reprinted (1956) New York: Kelley and Millan.

Hodgson, G. (1993), *Economics and Evolution*, Cambridge: Polity Press.

Kadish, A. (1994), 'The non-canonical context of *The Physiology of Industry*', in J. Pheby (ed.) *J.A. Hobson After Fifty Years – Freethinker of the Social Sciences*, New York: St. Martin Press.

Keynes, J.M. (1936), *The General Theory of Employment, Interest and Money*, vol. VII, reprinted (1973), in *The Collected Writings of J.M. Keynes*, London: Macmillan.

King, J. (1994), 'J.A. Hobson's macroeconomics: the last ten years 1930–1940', in J. Pheby (ed.), *J.A. Hobson After Fifty Years – Freethinker of the Social Sciences*, New York: St. Martin Press.

Maloney, J. (1985), *Marshall, Orthodoxy and the Professionalisation of Economics*, Cambridge: Cambridge University Press.

Marshall, A. (1901), Letter to Professor R. Ely, 11 July, reprinted in J. Maloney, *Marshall, Orthodoxy and the Professionalization of Economics*, Cambridge: Cambridge University Press.

Pheby, J. (ed.) (1994)**,** *J.A. Hobson After Fifty Years – Freethinker of the Social Sciences*, New York: St. Martin Press.

Rutherford, M. (1994), 'J.A. Hobson and American Institutionalism: underconsumption and technical change', in J. Pheby (ed.), *J.A. Hobson After Fifty Years – Freethinker of the Social Sciences*, New York: St. Martin Press.

Rossman, J. (1991), 'Hobson's surplus income and its distribution'**,** *Journal of Economic Issues*, XXV, 1, March.

Schumpeter, J. A. (1954), *History of Economic Analysis*, Oxford: Oxford University Press.

Strachey, J. (1935), *The Nature of Capitalist Crisis*, New York: Covoci Friede Publishers.

# 4.  Karl Marx – an evolutionary social scientist?

## Dietmar Meyer

## INTRODUCTION

At first sight the title of this paper seems to be provocative. On the one hand, it points out that it is very difficult – may be entirely impossible – to find a Marxian school or Marxian schools of economics among the mainstream approaches. On the basis of this statement, it has to be remarked that the so–called mainstream economics using the general equilibrium approach, calculus of optimisation, and so on are not able to interpret Marx's way of thinking about economic and social problems in its original sense. Because of the different theoretical – but mainly methodological – basis of these approaches, the reformulation of Marx's economic and social ideas or of Marxian theories in the language of mainstream economics is impossible without distorting their original meaning. (For example, see the discussions about Bródys or Morishima's pioneering research, Bródy 1970, Morishima 1968). This fact allows us to draw simple but very important conclusions about the often emphasised 'general' methods used by modern – mainstream – economic theories: worldwide discussions of Marx's theories at the beginning of this century as well as in the 1960s and 1970s have shown the impossibility of exactly and fully integrating the results found more than 100 years ago into modern economic theories.

Once Albert Einstein said that the greatest happiness for a scientist is to find his own former results as special cases of more developed and more general theories years later. If Marx lived in our age, he would not feel this greatest happiness mentioned by Einstein.

If some parts of Marx's theory are outside of contemporary mainstream economics, answers to a lot of questions have to be given:

- Are these outside parts essential and inherent parts of the Marxian approach or do they play second fiddle?
- What is (are) the reason(s) for being outside of modern economics? Is it the different methodology used by Marx and modern economics, respectively?

– Last, but not least: if these elements prove themselves to be essential parts of Marx's way of thinking, can we find among them – referring to the title of this paper – evolutionary approaches or ideas?

On the other hand, there is the argument that Marx's theory contains more elements of a revolutionary approach than of an evolutionary one. His scientific programme does not only lead to an understanding of the intrinsic laws of capitalist motion (in *Capital*), but contains a program for the conscious change of the existing social order as well. (see the *Communist Manifesto*).

In the frame of the present chapter it is entirely impossible to give a complex analysis either of Marx's approach to social sciences or only of his – enormous – economic writings. Instead of this attempt the chapter tries to concentrate on some characteristic and not so often mentioned and discussed aspects of his theory only. From some points of view, investigations in the history of economic thought mean a re-evaluation of earlier found and formulated results. In the present chapter the following problem has to be analysed: can elements of a theoretical economic approach developed decades after Marx's death be found in the writings of a social scientist of the 19th century? The key point of the analysis is the structure of Marx's labour theory of value and its role in the social theory as a whole. Outside of the general parallelism between Marx and Darwin in their theoretical way of thinking about problems of society and nature, it will be shown that Karl Marx – not only from a methodological point of view – involved elements and approaches in his theory which have been introduced in this detailed form into biology in the 20th century after the discovery of the DNA-structure.

Re-evaluation of earlier theories obviously also entails their reinterpretation. Thus some ideas expressed in this chapter may eventually not be found in exactly this form in Marx's work. However, the author has tried to formulate his opinion in a way that does not contradict Karl Marx's original approach.

## INDIVIDUAL BACKGROUND OF MARX'S SOCIAL THEORY AND SOME GENERAL CONCLUSIONS

The event evoking Marx's studies of abstract social sciences is well known from the literature: as a young lawyer, Marx was faced with the case of larceny of wood. Poor peasants had stolen wood from a rich landowner's forest to heat their rooms. The judgement resulted in the punishment of the peasants which was generally thought to be in harmony with the legal system. Still, the peasants felt the judgement unjust because their low income made it impossible to buy wood, thus theft seemed to be the only possibility for having a warm house. Was it the legal system as a whole or was it only the individual application of legal rules by the judge which brought about injustice? Is the principle of equality before the law valid for every man in a society or does it imply that the generally formulated legal system is advantageous for some groups and disadvantageous for others? What does 'just society' mean?

The next step of Marx's thinking is very logical again: if society proves to be unjust, one has first to find the reasons for its injustice, at least. Later, possibilities to change this society into a just one should be found.[1] If social scientists or politicians detect the reason for injustice and if the change in society seems to be practicable, the achievement of the change will or should be a conscious and deliberate action.[2]

All these facts imply that the main question in Marx's approach is the evaluation of the existing social structure. What are Marx's principles for this evaluation? By means of which principle or principles can one decide whether a society has to be considered as just or unjust? This is the problem that had to be solved by Marx.

Nevertheless, at this point some facts of great importance for the understanding of Marx's scientific programme are worth mentioning. It should be emphasized that Marx's educational process started in a school with a strong humanist orientation. His interest in Greek classics and in great ancient philosophers' writings was further stimulated by his later father-in-law, Mr. Westphalen (see Gemkow 1975, pp. 15–19). Thus, the characteristics of the (ancient) classics, the ideas of humanism, democracy and harmony, determined his way of thinking from the beginning. The continuity of this effect can be seen in the often-quoted, theatrically written sentence of his schoolleaving examination,[3] and later in his doctoral dissertation – dedicated to Westphalen (!) – prepared about questions of Greek philosophy after intensive studies in philosophy, law and economics in Berlin and Bonn (Marx [1841] 1981a).

This focus formed by his education and by his own interests cannot be separated from the geographical endowment of Marx's earlier life. He was born in Trier, he studied in Bonn, in other words he spent his youth in the Rhineland, a multicultural region of Germany. In his everyday life he could experience different cultures, different languages and different behaviour of the people of this region. The colourful reservoir of different languages and different ways of thinking – or more generally formulated – between different cultures, assumes at least two things: the tolerance and acceptance of these differences; and a leading principle, a fundamental idea – as the basis for ordering the various ways of thinking, behaviour, and so on. In a more or less natural way Marx found his own leading principle in the ancient classics. From this point of view, humanism, harmony and democracy had been generalizations of the daily experienced differences in behaviour, thinking, and so on and formed an integral part of Marx's way of thinking about languages, cultures and societies.

It can be assumed that these facts from Marx's private life can serve as a reason for the pursuit of general treatment of problems – a frequent, characteristic element in Marx's writings. In this field his 'philosophy' was that every concrete problem could be understood and solved if it was separated from all other problems. However, for a scientist a solution seems to be acceptable only if it can be applied to other problems as well. As a result, *tolerance, the acceptance of differences and the belief in having a common basis at the same time,* or using other words *the duality between the existence of variances and a special kind of stability* is an immanent part of Marx's way of thinking. This duality – let us use this expression again – is one of the main characteristics of evolutionary processes which will be explained later. Here it should only be remarked that Marx's basic, philosophic approach contains important elements that were found later in evolutionary approaches as well. At the same moment, it should be mentioned that the individual way which led Marx to theoretical social research, a way characterized by the acceptance of the individuals' autonomous activities and the rejection of 'unjust' political and economic power, can be considered as the basis for revolutionary elements in this theory.

However, the acceptance of varieties and the stability of their common basis are *only necessary, but not sufficient* for the existence of an evolutionary way of thinking. In the history of sciences many examples can be found of the assumptions of stable principles successfully explaining the investigated phenomena, but they are far from evolutionary approaches. In biology the answer to the question 'What is life, where does it come from?' was for a long time determined by the following idea: life was produced by the so–called *immortal primary matter.* In other words, species can vary but their stability as *living* species is given by this primary matter. Thermodynamics of the 18th century assumed that the *matter of heat* was responsible for different temperatures. The function of the matter of heat was the same as that of the primary matter in biology: a stable assumption for the interpretation of different temperatures. In some sense Adam Smith's well-known 'invisible hand' can be considered as a similar stable principle. Comparing all these examples, one has to see that they are characteristics of the era of the so-called *classicism* (!) of the 18th and 19th centuries.

With regard to the ideas mentioned above, a new conclusion could be drawn: on the one hand, it is necessary to have a more or less basic principle, that is, a fundamental idea for any scientific explanation of a great variety of phenomena. On the other hand, the suitable condition for an evolutionary interpretation is the *interaction* between the stable principle and these varieties that is, the influence of both sides on each other.[4] In other words: transmission mechanisms have to be found.

Returning to Marx, the question, or more exactly, the questions which have to be analysed can be formulated as the following:

1.   What is the basic Marxian principle of social and economic life?
2.   What is the stable element within this principle?
3.   What is the interaction between this stable element and the great variety observed in real social and economic life?

## THE THEORY OF LABOUR VALUE IN MARX'S SOCIAL SYSTEM

As mentioned above, Marx's problem was to find a criterion for a just society, and as a second step to analyse the society of his time on the basis of this criterion.

According to Marx a just society has to be harmonious and characterized by equality: equality of every man before the law, equal exchange of commodities, and so on. This equality is closely connected to the human element of society, that is, the same rights are ensured for everybody and nobody suffers from disadvantages during the exchange of commodities. Accepting this view, Marx was faced with the following problem: the wide spectrum of economic activities and the great number of different commodities taking part in the processes of exchange had to be reduced to a common element connected with the human factor. This common element could be considered as a part of any economic activity beginning from production onwards through distribution to consumption.

The element chosen by Marx was labour.[5] Everybody[6] is capable of working. Any thing produced and exchanged involves labour: labour is used directly in production and indirectly in an earlier period of time for the production of machines and tools applied in the contemporary production process. Thus, capital – the counterpart of labour – can also be traced back to labour: capital goods are commodities of accumulated labour. Labour is embodied in goods produced in an earlier period but used in the production process of the present period. This duality between capital and labour – or in Marx's words, the contradiction between them and their yields (profit and wages) – was the basis for Marx's interpretation of the development of the capitalist society. It was the specification of Marx's principle used in his theory about the development of social-economic formations, that is, the antagonistic contradiction between the *relations of production* and the *forces of production*. The interaction of these elements was essential for Marx in order to understand social development. In the society under investigation in *Capital*, labour and especially capital were not simple factors of production as later in the neoclassical approach. For Marx, capital was a relation of production and the most important force of production was the economically active human factor, the human being (Marx 1970).

From the theory of labour value in Marx's social and economic system, it follows that a certain quantity of labour corresponds to every commodity exchanged on the market, that is, the quantity of labour necessary for the production of the commodity under investigation. However, it is independent of the fact whether it is the directly or indirectly necessary quantity of labour in contemporary production processes. This quantity of labour embodied in every commodity was called by Marx *labour value*[7] (Marx 1965). Equal exchange means the exchange of equal quantities of labour, or an exchange of equal values.

Labour is measured in time. Thus equal quantities of labour exchanged by the producers of different commodities mean the exchange of an equal number of labour hours. The *first problem* connected with this conception is the occurrence of different productivities during the production of the same goods. Let us assume that two economic actors – and only these two firms – produce the same goods. However, producer No. 1 needs – for instance – five hours, while producer No. 2 needs – for instance – ten hours for the production of one unit. Thus, there exist different *individual* values of the same kind of goods. Assume further that the quantities of these goods supplied by the producers on the market are the same. If these goods will be exchanged for other goods at the same time – for instance, both producers exchange their goods for goods produced in 15 hours by economic actor No. 3 – then the equal exchange means that every good of producer No. 1 and producer No. 2 has to be accounted by the *average labour time* necessary for the production of one unit, in the example 7.5 hours. Marx called this average labour time the *market value* of commodities (Marx 1966).[8] Thus, one unit of goods produced by economic actor No. 3 will be exchanged for two units of the other goods on the market independent of their places of production or the applied technologies. This exchange can be considered to be equal from two points of view: firstly, it was an exchange of equal quantities of labour; and secondly, the technological differences between the producers were equalized by the market. Of course, producer No. 1 will earn 150 per cent of his *own individual value* from the exchange of two units of his goods for one unit of the goods produced by his partner. He can sell two units for a value of 15 hours. In this time he is able to produce not two, but three units of his product. The contrary is true for the situation of economic actor No. 2: in the exchange he can earn only 75 per cent of his own *individual value*.

The value of 2.5 hours earned by producer No.1 is the profit based on the better technology. In the case of producer No. 2 the difference between the earned market value and the individual value is his loss. The sum of profit and loss is equal to zero – a result corresponding to the neoclassical theory, or the theory of general equilibrium.

At this point it should be mentioned that all these different kinds of Marxian labour values were determined only by technology. Its individual value was shaped by the amount of labour used for the production of goods by separated economic actors, while the market value took into account the difference in technologies. In any case, the market conditions, especially on the demand side, were left aside. More exactly, the hidden assumption was used that all commodities supplied on the market could be sold. However, what will happen if the market is in disequilibrium and if an excess supply exists?[9]

This question is discussed in Volume III of *Capital* but in a somewhat contradictory way.[10] On the one hand, Marx wrote that the continuous adjustment of demand and supply implies equilibrium in the long run. His analysis concerning the capitalist society naturally referred to the long run. Thus the short run disequilibrium of markets was not a problematic case requiring investigation (see Chapter 10 of Volume III of *Capital,* Marx 1966). On the other hand, a new interpretation of the *value* category can be found in the same chapter. Neither the individual quantity of labour used for the production of a certain commodity by separated economic actors, nor the average quantity of labour used by the firms of a sector producing the same good is the basis for the labour value of the commodity. Instead it is the *socially accepted*, the *socially recognized amount of labour* that is necessary for the production of one unit of the commodity. This new form of labour value is called the *market price* (!) of the commodity.[11] Market price will differ from market value if supply differed from demand, that is, if the market is in disequilibrium.[12]

Summarizing Marx's theory of labour value, the following conclusion can be formulated. In an economy with a more or less stable structure and a more or less stable technology used by the producers, the market value will be unchanged for a long time – or will change to a lesser degree. On the basis of the actual relation between demand and supply the (Marxian) market price will/can differ at any moment from the market value. The profit (or loss) earned by economic actors depends on two factors: on the technology used in the production process and on the actual situation on the market. Differences between technologies are given and well known to every economic actor. Thus differences of profits are based on the technological spectrum of the sectors in the economy as a whole. Of course, these differences are also stable and are independent of the market processes.

A rather different situation is created if the differences between demand and supply, or between (Marxian) market value and (Marxian) market price are taken into account. They are consequences of market forces influencing the conditions for production and for sale unexpectedly. Obviously, they have only a mild effect. However, the change of the conditions mentioned above is unquestionable. They imply the adjustment of both producers and consumers. The producer 'who supplies goods or services may thus respond to tendencies . . .' (Witt 1998, p. 7), which can be a newly discovered opportunity for action (Witt

1998, p. 11). In Marx's theory of labour value the behaviours of consumers and producers are closely related to labour transmission mechanisms – supposing the short run disequilibrium situations on markets. Therefore, one has to agree with Laibman's opinion stating that the Marxists 'do not imagine a serene process of competitive leading to a stable – stationary – price-profit configuration' (Laibman 2000, p. 328). Taking into account the continuously changing relations between demand and supply based on the also continuously changing behaviour of producers and consumers it can be said that these labour transmission mechanisms have an evolutionary character. In the sense of evolutionary theories, they are 'slight differences in the ... endowments ... giving rise to differential reproductive success for the ... carriers of those endowments' (Witt 1998, p. 6). Thus it can be emphasized that in Marx's theory of labour value at least one evolutionary element exists, or more exactly, there exists an element necessary for speaking about this theory as an evolutionary one.

Before finding other evolutionary elements in the Marxian approach, let us turn to Darwin, who is sometimes considered as the 'father of evolutionary theories' and who lived more or less in the same era as Marx.

## DARWIN AND THE EVOLUTIONARY APPROACH IN BIOLOGY

During his expedition on the *Beagle* (December 1831 – October 1836) Darwin was faced with a lot of phenomena, especially in South America, that could be interpreted only with the assumption of slow but continuous modification of the different species. At the same time it seemed to be clear to Darwin that the experienced changes could not be interpreted by the different natural endowments to which these species had been perfectly adjusted. Having returned to England, Darwin began to analyse this problem and tried to find an indirect proof that species are able to evolve (Darwin 1959, p. 99). Fifteen months after he had started his investigations, Thomas Malthus' *Essay on Population* came into Darwin's hands. The basic idea of Malthus, now called the *Malthusian Law of Population,* made it suddenly clear to Darwin that advantageous modifications of species let them survive, while disadvantageous modifications imply their death.[13] Darwin applied this principle of 'struggle for life' to solve the problem mentioned above, or as he wrote: 'This principle of preservation ... I have called "Natural Selection" ' (Darwin 1872 quoted by Barlow, 1933, p. 438). The application of Malthus' Law of Population to the processes in fauna and flora was an important step in the direction of an evolutionary theory in biology. However, with good reason Darwin can be considered as an evolutionary scientist of the 19th century.

Without discussing Darwin's principle in detail some remarks should be made. First of all, the 'survival of the fittest' is a *principle*. It is more an assumption than a theory. Its role is similar to what classic philosophy and culture was in Marx's way of thinking, or what the role of the human element was in his theory of labour value. In other words, it is the first step (paradigm) of a theory of which details will be given later. Concerning the expression 'principle', the second remark is that *principles do not reflect history*. Principles can be formulated either in an intuitive way[14] or by using a lot of historical facts and experience (as done by Darwin), but the principle itself is a logical construction, the 'abstraction of experiences' (Eigen and Winkler 1975, Chapter 5.2). In Darwin's case it means that his principle can explain the natural development of species – which species may precede and which may follow another. Still, in the same age different species on a different level of development can be found at the same geographic place as well as in different regions, which evoked Darwin's result.

Secondly, the formulation of this principle was the result of a *macroscopic* approach. Darwin tried to give an interpretation of the development of the phenotypes but he was unable (or he was not interested) to give microscopic explanations for it. Darwin's macroscopic approach led to a tautology: the survivor is that individual who has been adjusted in the most efficient way to their endowment, or 'the survivor is who survived' (Szentágothai 1981). The answer to the next question – what the microscopic conditions for survival are – was found in the 20th century after intensive research in microbiology, genetics and so on. However, the macroscopic approach was sufficient for Darwin: with its use he was able to give a phenomenological interpretation of the development of species. Here it is worth mentioning that Darwin understood his principle as being true not only for one individual. 'Survival of the fittest' meant not only the surviving of that individual with the best properties and capabilities for this but also that their descendants would inherit the same capabilities and properties (Darwin 1980, p. 76).

This macroscopic approach is important from two points of view, both of which are the basis for critics of Darwin's principle, and both are closely connected to each other.

The title of Darwin's famous book is *The Origin of Species* ... which suggests that every living individual in fauna and flora has an ancestor with similar properties and capabilities. This ancestor has again an ancestor, and so on; every living or dead individual can be traced back to ... to what? Somewhere and sometime there had to exist an individual being, the ancestor of *all* living or dead individuals in fauna and flora. But accepting Darwin's concept for this individual, the same must be true for this individual as well: it must have an ancestor with properties very similar to those of itself. Thus the question is: what is the origin of life? Does Darwin's principle imply the old assumption of the existence of the 'immortal primary matter'?

The second question is connected with the change of properties of the species' different generations. If every individual can be traced back to a 'common ancestor', then all information necessary for these changes must be included in this common forefather. Nevertheless, due to the wide spectrum of individuals, how is it possible? The older the ancestor is, the bigger the set of information belonging to itself and its descendants. However, this is a contradiction the principle of evolution which means that development is moving from simple structures to more and more complex ones. The conclusion can be drawn that the common forebear must be very simply constructed, but at the same time it has to contain all necessary information for the functioning of the principle of selection.

From the further development of biology it is well known that the problem was solved in the 20th century by research in microbiology. Detecting the role and the structure of DNA and understanding the role of genes, as controllers of the synthesis of protein molecules were important results in the field of modern biology from this aspect. From the present point of view, it is essential to see that after having ordered the individuals according to the principle of Darwin there is another 'reduction', that is, tracing back all possible information (sentences) needed for the construction of protein to only some letters. The translation of only four letters of the nucleic acid to the 20 letters of protein molecules is the process in which all possible proteins are born, and this is also that place where their wide spectrum can come into existence. The problem of copying original information and the possible errors in this process are the basis for the countless number of protein molecules and consequently, for the innumerable forms of life (for a more detailed explanation see for example Crick 1967).

Summarizing the results, one should not forget that using microscopic analysis could solve the problem of contradiction in Darwin's concept. This form of investigation completed the evolutionary theory in biology, which is again an argument for understanding evolution as an interaction between microscopic and macroscopic elements.[15] The macroscopic principle is the 'basic idea' – the stable element, or metaphorically, the Christmas tree. The microscopic processes are responsible for the great number of variations of concrete phenomena; they are the elements of change, or again metaphorically, the ornaments on the Christmas tree.

## BACK TO MARX: SIMILARITIES BETWEEN MARX'S AND DARWIN'S APPROACH

After the short trip to the field of biology, let us return to Marx. Some similarities are obvious: both Marx and Darwin formulated principles for the interpretation of the development of the (capitalist) society and of the species, respectively. Both interpretations used the philosophical category of contradiction. In Marx's system the contradiction between relations of production and the forces of production, or in the case of the capitalist society of the last century, the contradiction between capital and labour can be found, while Darwin emphasized the contradiction between individual properties, capabilities and endowment. In both approaches adjustment processes play a central role. They are endowed not only with one active side but characterized by the interaction between the two parts of the contradictions. In Marx's system – based on the adjustment of forces of production to the relation of production – labour is subordinated to capital. But during the adjustment to the given conditions of production, distribution and consumption, the relations of production will be modified, which implies a new adjustment process of the forces of production. In Darwin's concept the slow but continuous adjustment of species to their endowment yields the 'survival of the fittest', which exactly means new species and thus new contradictions, and so forth.

With these similarities in mind it is no surprise that Marx had a high opinion of Darwin's approach and his results. In a letter to his friend Engels he wrote about the *Origin of Species* that this 'book written in the rough English style contains the natural-historical foundation of our concept' (Mark and Engels 1985, p. 131, and my translation). Marx's mentioned high opinion about Darwin's work was expressed in two remarks additionally made in Volume I of *Capital* by referring to Darwin's scientific results as 'epochmaking' (Marx 1974, p. 361). The view that Marx had planned to dedicate parts of the *Capital* to Darwin was for a long time expressed in the international literature about the history of sciences (see for example Wessel 1978, pp. 172–9, Urena 1977, p. 555, and for a clearing up of this question Colb 1982).[16]

The evolutionary element in Darwin's theory was important for Marx in order to show that there exists a theory in natural sciences that explains the past, present and the future, that is the development without teleological arguments. If this could be done in biology, why should it not be true for the social sciences too? If the existing political, social and economic order doesn't express *Genesis*, it seems to be an acceptable idea that the – unjust – social order should be, or must be changed by mankind himself.[17] This is exactly the point on which Marx disagreed with Darwin, or better disagreed with his followers who re-applied the Malthusian-Darwinian 'struggle for life' to social problems, considering this as the only principle of social dynamics.

In contrast with Lamarck, who had propagated the more passive phenomenological adjustment of individuals to their environment on the basis of physiological behaviour, Darwin explained natural selection of individuals as a result of 'numerous . . . variations, aided in an important manner by the inherited effects of use and disuse of parts' of their bodies (Darwin [1859] 1980,

p. 210). In other words, Darwin emphasized the given properties of individuals as essential elements of evolution, a process in which the individuals' active behaviour will in time follow the existence of variations. A much higher degree of individual activity can be found in Marx's understanding of social development: Because individuals are able to realize their own position in the social system as a whole, and because they are conscious of the role played by any participant in the game called social life, people can develop a strategy for changing the system of social conditions. This extremely great activity, not to say the possibility of influencing social and economic life autonomously, is the point where Marx's evolutionary approach switches to a theory of revolution.

Otherwise expressed, Darwin's theory was important for Marx to understand the evolution of the human body, but he did not consider it as sufficient for understanding changes in the development of human society. By h involving revolutionary elements, the Marxian way of thinking about developmental problems of social structures not only differs from Darwin's method, but also from that of the social Darwinist's. Professor Hodgson is correct, writing that 'there is a very little in the writings of Marx or Engels on, or against social Darwinism' (Hodgson 1998, p. 300). Neither this, nor the fact that Engels after the death of Marx 'did not even express scorn for Haeckel's racist ideas' (Hodgson 1998, p. 301) implies the acceptance of social Darwinism by Marx and Engels as a general theory about social dynamics. Comparison of the philosophies of the approaches discussed, especially the important role of the human individuals' 'Bewußtseinsfaktor', often mentioned by Marx as well as by Engels, shows just the opposite.

But let's return to the parallelism (Colb 1982, p. 462) in the theoretical work of Darwin and Marx. The conceptual coincidence of the approaches of Marx and Darwin in interpreting development as a form of natural and social motion seems to be obvious. In the following paragraphs two further examples should be mentioned showing the similarity between these grandiose scientists of the 19th century.

In Volume I of *Capital* one can find the Marxian interpretation of the origin of money. The introduction of money starts with the so–called *simple exchange* of different commodities, both satisfying needs of economic actors. This simplest form of exchange is possible in a non–monetary economy, but requires that economic actor No. 1 produces and supplies goods necessary for economic actor No. 2 who produces and supplies a commodity chosen by actor No. 1. An interpretation of this change is also possible from the aspect of the theory of labour value. The commodities exchanged express their values, or in Marx's words, in the simple exchange the value of any commodity is expressed by the use–value of that commodity to which it has been changed.[18] The next form of exchange is the so-called *extended exchange* of commodities when a certain commodity can be changed into a lot of other commodities or any other commodity. The (labour) value of this commodity can be represented by the use-value of numerous goods. The exchange form of *general equivalent* means the contrary of the previous form: any commodity can be changed into a product or at most into a few, well defined goods. The value of any commodity is expressed only by a limited number of goods. In history goods endowed with this function were, for instance, noble metals, salt, skins of animals, and so on. The next step – the monetary economy's exchange of commodities – means that only one commodity – *money* – took over the role of the limited number of goods of the previous example by a social agreement (!) (Marx 1965).

This introduction concerning the 'origin of money' is logical, like Darwin's principle. In the same way as species on different levels of development can be found in a certain age in Darwin's concept, differently developed Marxian forms of exchange leading to the formation of money could be found (for examples see Aninkin 1981). In the Marxian approach the development of the 'species', that is, the development of money from a great number of more or less randomly realised simple changes corresponds to the Darwinian explanation of the origins of his species. Furthermore, the most undeveloped Darwinian species contains all the information for the phenotype of the most developed species in the same way as the Marxian simple change contains all properties of the monetary change.

The second example is connected with the main problem of Darwin's concept, that is, with the microscopic foundation of his principle. It was mentioned that Marx's approach was similar to Darwin's. He started his social studies with the question of a just society, that is, with a macroscopic problem. Capital as the engine of development, and the interpretation of the antagonistic contradictions between capital and labour made it possible to explain differences in income, wealth, and so on and to interpret the continuously growing polarization within societies in the middle of the 19th century.

However, in contrast with Darwin, Marx tried to give a microscopic foundation, using – and in some sense developing – the already existing classical theory of labour value. Doing so he had to introduce labour as the only factor of income production or of wealth. Still, at the same time he was faced with a 'Darwinian problem': labour exists in several forms and its actual form depends on the concrete form, special purpose or function, planned usage, and so on, of the produced commodity in the same way as the different Darwinian species were concrete expressions of 'Life'. To solve this problem Marx had to reduce any concrete form of labour to its common properties. Thus he created the category 'abstract labour' as that kind of labour connected with any human display of strength. With this in mind the Marxian value must be interpreted more exactly: Value – independent on its concrete form – is the quantity of *abstract* labour contained in one unit of a commodity. The abstract labour, that is, the stable element of value is similar to the genes in biology. In biology the reductions were: species    common ancestor    genes. In Marx's system they were the following: commodities    labour value    abstract labour.

Still, biologists know a lot about genes but Marxian economists knew and know almost nothing about abstract labour. Nevertheless, the structure of these theories seems to be very similar. Furthermore, the concept of the theory of labour value based on abstract labour is accepted. The value, market value or market price of every commodity can be determined and accounted for.[19] The 'only' thing one has to do is calculate the (weighted average, socially neces-sary) quantity of (abstract) labour contained in one unit of this commodity.

In Marx's understanding the labour force is the most important commodity, the only one producing more value than necessary for its consumption. For Marx this is the guarantee for extended reproduction, or for the growth of the economy and for development. Thus, the question concerned with the value of labour forces is very essential: what is the value of labour forces? Because of the consistency of the theory the answer must be that it is the (weighted aver-age, socially accepted) quantity of (abstract) labour necessary for the produc-tion of the labour force. It means the following:

- labour necessary for natural surviving, thus labour contained in the consumption of goods satisfying basic needs of the labour force
- labour necessary for medical treatment
- labour necessary for human development, thus labour connected with education, and so on

Of course, all these types of concrete labour are embodied either in machines, equipment, and so on that is, capital goods) produced in earlier peri-ods or they are connected with activities done by economic (social) actors in the present period. In other words, the value of labour forces is traced back to the value of 'normal' commodities, while the value of these commodities depends on the value of the labour force. It was considered as an inner contra-diction of the Marxian theory of labour value for a long time (see for example Böhm-Bawerk 1896). However, the original Marxian definition of the value of labour forces contains one more element than those mentioned above:

- *the historical–ethical element.*

The latter means the cultural level of development of the society, traditions, and so on, that is, elements changing slowly but expressing concrete relations of production and being modified by activities of the forces of production. From this point of view, the Marxian historical–ethical element can be considered as a feedback part of Marx's theory of labour value and of the Marxian system as a whole. The historical-ethical element is the main part of interaction between species and their endowments implying the slow, but necessary changes of the endowments for evolutionary processes.

## CONCLUSION AND MARX'S APPROACH IN RETROSPECT

In the present chapter an attempt was made to show – especially from an evolutionary point of view – some interesting elements of Marx's social and economic system. It could be seen that his approach and his analysis were in many fields similar to that of Darwin, who was one of the predecessors of the evolutionary way of thinking. At the same time some examples were presented showing that Marx's analysis was deeper than Darwin's because in contrast with the latter Marx tried to find the microscopic foundation of his basic principle, that is, a microeconomic foundation which was the frame for interactions necessary for evolutionary processes. Thus, if Darwin is usually considered as the father (or one of the forefathers) of evolutionary thinking in biology, the same has to be said about Marx in the field of social sciences.

The statement formulated at the end of the last paragraph is based on the comparison between Marx's and Darwin's philosophical approaches to problems of social and natural sciences. The period of scientific work of Marx and Darwin was the 19th century, thus the following question seems to be legitimate: does the development in economic theory observed in the last 120 years support this opinion, or is this obvious similarity between Marx's and Darwin's ideas only a – more or less randomly occurring – coincidence? What is the evaluation of Marx's approach[20] 'in the light of modern economic theory' – to use the title of an article written by Michio Morishima (Morishima 1974)?

While the first years after the publication of Volume I of *Capital* were characterized by silence, Volume III edited by Engels has evoked hard discussions about the relation between the (labour) value of Volume I and the prices of production of Volume III. Until today a lot of economists and mathematicians show great concern about this contradiction between the two volumes – about the so-called transformation problem. The original papers as well as the mathematical methods developed in the 1930s by Wald and von Neumann and later used for the modelling of Marx's theory have expressed the mainly static approach in the interpretations of Marx's labour theory of value.

Change in this process could be observed at the beginning of the 1960s when the standard work on *neo-Ricardian* economics was published (Sraffa 1960). However, Sraffa did not use the dynamic approach as well, but he was interested in a similar problem to the one addressed by Marx years before: to find the stable standard of value, that is, independent of changes of wages or of profit. Having done so, Sraffa returned to an unsolved problem of Ricardo and therefore to the common roots of the labour theory of value. Marx's standard of value was a certain quantity of (abstract) labour embodied in every commodity. From this point of view, the standard of value in Marx's system was independent of concrete commodities.[21] Sraffa found his standard of value in a couple of commodities. Both, Marx as well as Sraffa, could show that their standards of value were unique. Thus having once found these standards, they could isolate the effects of any commodity's price changes. Investigations of the price movements (Sraffa), or of their background (Marx) were possible now – as Sraffa wrote – in the airtight sphere (Sraffa 1960, Chapter 4). Further, the similarity between Marx and Sraffa can also be observed in the special role of the value of the labour force (Marx) and wages. Again both, Marx and Sraffa, have mentioned exogenous elements influencing labour forces' value or wages. In Marx's approach this was the historical-ethical element. Sraffa could imagine that wages – as a result of their historical development – might contain parts of the surplus product (Sraffa 1960, Chapter 2). Thus he assumed different amounts of wages in order to analyse their effects on the rate of profit or prices (Sraffa 1960, Chapter 3). Therefore, Sraffian wages are influenced by social conditions. This is a point in which he completely differs from the marginalist approach[22] and in which he is familiar with Marx's evolutionary elements in the sense mentioned above. The influence of Marx is obvious and indisputable. 'Sraffa would not have been able to write *Production of Commodities by Means of Commodities* if Marx had not written *Capital*' (Dostaber 1982, p. 102).[23] Some decades later Walters and Young have emphasized the same fact, when they write that 'there is some recognition within Sraffian theory of the importance of institutions and the historical evolution of critical values (e. g. wages) . . .' (Walters and Young 1999, p. 113).

Neo-Ricardian economics in the sense used by Sraffa has added institutional and sociological elements to the classical theory of labour value expressed by Ricardo who had used the pure technological conditions for the determination of the commodities' values, wages and profits. In neo-Ricardian understanding the field of economic theory will expand in relation to its interpretation of the marginalists. Economic analysis means to pay attention to historical, human, social and other factors too. From this chapter's point of view, Sraffa's return to classical economics was not a mechanical one because it took into account evolutionary elements as done almost 100 years before by Marx. Sraffian economics differ from Marx's approach in the unit and in the substance of the standard of value. On the one hand we find embodied labour (Marx), on the other physical units (Sraffa). As expressed above, Marx applied his definition of value to both kinds of commodities, to physical commodities and to the labour force. He made the exception that the historical-ethical element would influence only the latter. In this way his standard of labour not only contains the labour, labour is the only essential part of it. In spite of this model, Sraffa reduced the standard of value to commodities necessary for the production of all commodities – *except the commodity labour force.* Therefore the evolutionary element is related in Marx's theory of labour value to a special commodity, but in Sraffa's production theory it is expressed by the institutionally determined wages. Sraffian wages are in this sense a collective term reflecting all properties of the labour force expressed by Marx explicitly, that is, qualification of the labour force, cultural condition of the society under consideration and so on. With this in mind, R. Meek's opinion that the different units and the substances of Marx's and Sraffa's standard of value are 'two sides of the same coin' (Meek 1980, p. 163) has to be formulated more precisely: they are at least *formally* – from mathematical formalism's point of view – two sides of the same coin.

This formal identification of Marx's and Sraffa's approaches in particular, but also the attempt to appreciate 'the significance of P. Sraffa's theoretical work for the legacy of Karl Marx' (Brody 1977, p. 219), led to new – from theoretical aspects more or less sterile, but from methodological aspects interesting – discussions between neo-Marxists, neo-Ricardians and neoclassical economists in the 1970s and 1980s.

More or less at the same time – at the beginning of the 1980s – the so-called Radical Political Economy was established in the USA. The roots of this direction can be found in Marx's political economy. Similarly to the neo-Ricardian, supporters of the Radical Political Economy tried to apply classical approaches to the economic and social processes of the 20th century. The main field of their interests was the labour market whose structure in economic life was changing dramatically in the years since Marx had been published his writings. In the first publications of the radicals, the ideas and approaches of Sraffa are observable – as for example the analysis of joint production. But the influence of Marx is also recognisable for example in emphasizing the political and social consequences of their economic theories.

Since the second half of the 1980s Radical Political Economy has been moved away from Marxism and neo-Ricardianism towards neoclassical mainstream economics considering this as a generalization of Marx's theory. Bowles and Gintis, two determining theorists of this direction, used the principal-agent approach to develop their theory about the labour contracts as 'contested exchanges' between workers maximizing their utility and employers (Bowles and Gintis 1990). This explanation of labour market processes reminds one of the – also neoclassically based – *theory of efficient wages:* to ensure the productivity of labour, all workers not satisfying the employers' expectations are in danger of losing their jobs. On the other hand wages are being paid high enough that incumbent workers try to retain their jobs. The effect is labour market equilibrium, but – because of the relatively high wages – at less than full employment.

Unemployment as an intrinsic property of capitalism was explained by Bowles and Gintis and their understanding of neoclassical microeconomics. Thus for them and their followers as well as for the representatives of Radical Political Economy 'the axiom of rational self-interested individual action . . . provides the microeconomic basis for the study of economic power' (Spencer 2000, p. 550). Thus 'the key insights of the Marxist analysis of capitalist production can be enhanced by concepts drawn from neo-classical economics' (Spencer 2000, p. 544). Summarizing the development of Radical Political Economics since about 1985 it has to be emphasized that on the one hand this direction is trying to give the microeconomic foundation of social and macro-economic problems investigated by Marx as well as by the neo-Ricardians. In this context they accept one point of Marx's evolutionary thinking: the inter-dependence of the microscopic and of the macroscopic level. But on the other hand they are reducing the socially determined behaviour of economic actors to that of an *homo oeconomicus*. From this chapter's point of view this is equivalent to giving up essential evolutionary approaches found in earlier theories.

Beginning with the second half of the 1970s and parallel with the dynamic expansion of evolutionary ideas in economic theories, subjective factors in the form of different kinds of expectations play a more and more significant role in economics. The introduction of adaptive or rational expectation into economic models is closely connected with the greater weight attached to microeconomic approaches. After decades of macroeconomic dominance on the basis of John Maynard Keynes there was some recognition that the 'expla-nation of macroeconomic phenomena will be complete only when such expla-nations are consistent with microeconomic choice theoretic behaviour and can be phrased in the language of general equilibrium theory' (Drazen 1980, p. 293). This was the conclusion of the unsatisfactionary results of the so-called disequilibrium theory, but it was also a more general development in the field of economic theory (see for example the Radical Political Economy mentioned above).

To explain trade at non-equilibrium prices post-Keynesian economists have used and are using fixed price models and assumptions about quantity rationing or incomplete information. The modifications of this kind of theories really meant additional conditions for the behaviour of economic actors in the form of inflexible prices and wages – quite in harmony with Keynes – or in the form of uncertainty. Therefore traditional optimization techniques of the general equilibrium theory for the description of the behaviour of economic actors could be used in the future too. From this point of view it is not surprising that the challenge formulated by Drazen made it obvious: mainstream economic theory could imagine its microeconomic foundation only in the frame of the general equilibrium theory. Keynesian macroeconomics was considered to be inconsistent with traditional microeconomics.

In the last 20 years economic theory was faced with a problem already earlier discussed in connection with possible evolutionary elements of Marx's theory. Just as Marx tried to find a microscopic foundation of his basic macroscopic principle for the explanation of economic and social development, modern economic theory has been forced to do essentially the same. This had been shown above for special cases of Sraffian economics and Radical Political Economy. Now directions of (post-)classical lines and also the post-Keynesian economic theory have to be analysed from the same point of view.

Post-Keynesian theory had been established more or less at the same time as Sraffa had finished his work *Production of Commodities by Means of Commodities*. Neither this parallel development, nor the close co-operation between Sraffa and Keynes were reasons to consider Sraffian theory as a part of post-Keynesianism. In the 1960s and in the 1970s similar approaches and methods could be observed in both Sraffian and post-Keynesian economics. The joint philosophy of these directions was for example the firm conviction that in any economy dominant forces can be found moving this economy towards a so-called normal (stable or stationary) position. Another joint element was to emphasize the historical determinism of economic and social processes as well as the importance of uncertainty and institutions. Some of these factors, however, can be found in Marx's writings too. Therefore it is no wonder that some post-Keynesian economists undertake these methodological elements of Marx's approach in their interpretation (Runde and Lewis 1999).

Marx's post-Keynesian evaluation is characterized by the different starting-point of Marxism and post-Keynesianism in explaining distribution. As a social scientist influenced by classical economy and social thought Marx had considered historically and social-institutionally given wages as an independent variable. It could be seen that the historical-ethical element introducing evolutionary aspects into the Marxian model is related to the labour force, that is, it is a determining fact of wages. Thus wages are determining profits and through savings and investments the rate of accumulation too. In spite of this, post-Keynesian economics takes profits as depending on autonomously determined investments generating, via income, distribution savings.[24] First of all this means that the saving rate cannot be assumed as exogenous. Secondly, the field for possible evolutionary effects is the investment demand, and not yet the historically developed wage of the workers. If this kind of theory should be developed, subjective motivations of investors, profit expectations, or more generally formulated, the behaviour of producers have to be explained evolutionarily. From an evolutionary point of view there is no essential difference in which field evolutionary aspects occur. The main point is that both Marxian theory and post-Keynesian economic theory have based evolutionary elements of their approaches on human and institutional behaviour continuously changing over time. Last but not least this may be the reason for a possible – and for (some) post-Keynesian economists an acceptable – interpretation of Marx's ideas in evolutionary game theory (Beed and Beed 1999, p. 174).

Analysing the relationship between Marxian and post-Keynesian theory on the basis of recently published articles in the *Journal of Post Keynesian Economics*,[25] it has to be remarked that a surprising way of thinking seems to enter post-Keynesianism. Concretely formulated: finding its own place and its own theoretical positions in economic theory, post-Keynesian economists (such as Dow 2000, Dunn 2000) emphasize the difference between their direction and other – 'orthodox' – economics, however constituted (Dunn 2000, p. 346). These rather defensive ambitions to distance the field and subjects of post-Keynesian economics from other – not necessarily mainstream – economic theories are manifested in such statements as:

- 'The enemy of my enemy is my friend.' (Dunn 2000, p. 349)
- in the total rejection of Sraffian economics because of 'adopting the common language of closed system mathematics' (Dunn 2000, p. 350), and finally
- in the belief that 'the aim of economic science is explanation, not prediction' (Dunn 2000, p. 348).

This is not the place to discuss this approach to economic research and to economic theory, nor the role of mathematics in economic science. From this chapter's point of view it should be noted only that evolution is based on a – consciously or unconsiously – offensive and autonomous behaviour. Secondly, the interpretation of economics as a science that only explains processes, but does not predict possible developments is totally contradictory to the Marxian approach (see for example thesis No. 11 about Feuerbach mentioned in footnote 4).

Returning to the questions in the introduction to this chapter it has to be pointed out that the Marxian approach contains clear evolutionary elements that can be considered as methodologically surpassing those of Darwin in deepness and complexity. Of course, Marx's evolutionary ideas belong to the 19th century, with all their advantages and disadvantages. In the case of Darwin's evolutionary theory a more organic development could be observed in the 20th century. Nevertheless, modern economic theories show some very impressive similarities to Marx's approach.

If one accepts the concept of evolution used in this paper, namely that evolution is a complex interdependence between stable development and continuous disturbance of this stability, the consequences for the transition process seem also to be clear. The question is not: should the Marxian approach in the transition process be followed, or not. It is much more important to recognize the importance of messages coming from the evolutionary theory: development of complex systems is a very slow path-dependent process. Traditions, mentality, history and institutions are determinants of these dynamics as well as short- or long-term influences by education, ideology and politics. During the latter a very specific and clear interpretation of Marx should be found and should also be taken into account; not mechanically, but in the evolutionary understanding.

## NOTES

1. See Thesis No. 11 about Feuerbach: up-to-date philosophers only tried to interpret society, but it is much more important to change it.
2. The thesis of the Marxian so-called 'dictatorship of the proletariat' was later misinterpreted by politicians and ideologists of former socialist societies.
3. 'Die Geschichte nennt diejenigen als die größten Männer, die, indem sie für das Allgemeine wirkten, sich selbst veredelten; die Erfahrung preist den als Glücklichsten, der die meisten glücklich macht.' (Marx 1981b, S.594)
4. This is a kind of different understanding of evolutionary economics, which can be found for example in Boulding (1991) where evolutionary economics is interpreted as a part of large evolutionary processes, and is mainly based on insufficient information. The author's approach rather agrees with the opinion that 'the principles of natural selection and genetic adaptation appear    to be the archetype of evolutionary thought' (Witt 1998, p. 5), while, of course, he does not reduce this approach to biological problems and mainly emphasizes *the interaction* between natural selection and genetic adaptation.
5. The following few paragraphs very briefly contain the main elements of Marx's theory of labour value; as mentioned above, in the author's interpretation.
6. Labour as the basis of Marx's political economy expresses the central role of human elements in his social theories. From this point of view, the acceptance of the classical theory of labour value expounded by Smith, Ricardo and others within – using a modern scientific category – *systems* of social sciences shows the adherence to the (Greek) classics again.
7. Of course, Marx had not introduced the theory of labour value; it was a result of earlier social-economic research done mainly by Adam Smith, David Ricardo, to mention only the most important representatives.
8. In the case of more than two producers or if the quantities of commodities produced by them not being equal, the calculation of the market value corresponds to that of the weighted average. That's why the simplification will have no influence on the analysis.
9. Excess demand is not interesting for the analysis because in this situation it is possible to sell all produced goods.
10. It is well known that only Volume I of *Capital* was written by Marx (published in 1867), Volume II and Volume III were edited by Engels using Marx's manuscripts; the volumes were published after Marx's death, in 1884 and 1893 respectively. The editor of Volume IV – the so-called 'Theories Surplus Value' – was Karl Kautsky. The last three volumes of *Capital* are 'second hand editions', and it is not sure that they express Marx's original ideas and original opinion.
11. The Marxian *market price* is not a category expressing the value – taken in the widest sense

– of a commodity in money; thus it is not the 'price' of modern monetary economies. In Marx's model there is no money, and as shown above, these market prices are a certain quantity of labour, that is, really a special form of a (labour) value.

12. The role of utility in Marx's theory of labour value was discussed by Johansen (1970), Meyer (1984), Morishima (1968), Toms (1983).

13. The fact that the principle of natural selections based on an economist's idea means that the contemporarily observable attempts to find new economic paradigms using biological analogies are only a return to classical economics. They show that the 'post–classical' (neoclassical, new classical, and so on) schools contain only one aspect of original classical economics – the perfect markets, the belief in harmony, and so forth. The other characteristics of classical economics – the dynamic elements, attempts to explain economic and social development – remain outside of these approaches.

14. Einstein's principle of relativity.

15. The same could be experienced in physics. The formulation of the Second Law of Thermodynamics at the end of the 19th century was the result of a phenomenological approach to thermodynamic problems. This law expresses the fact that processes connected with heat change – or more generally with change of energy – have a certain direction; they are irreversible. The dual but microscopic side of this field of modern physics is statistical mechanics assuming a lot of particles. From their interaction the macroscopically observable thermodynamic processes are derived (Prigogine – Stengers 1986).

16. The opinion is based on a letter written by Darwin on 13 October, 1880 where he wrote that he should 'prefer the Part or Volume not be dedicated to me ( . . . ) as this implies to a certain extent my approval of the general publication, about which I know nothing' (quoted from Colb 1982, p. 466). This letter was an answer to a letter of Dr. Aveling, later for a short period partner in life of Marx's daughter Eleanor, where he proposed to honour his work and himself by dedicating a planned book about Darwin to the great scientist. After the death of Karl Marx some documents of his life and manuscripts came into the possession of his daughter Eleanor. She and Dr. Aveling died in 1898. Their documents as well as Marx's personal inheritance were passed to the Archive of the German Social Democratic Party which in the 1920s sent copies of those documents to the Marx Engels Institute in Moscow. In 1931 this institute published Darwin's letter to Dr. Aveling as a letter directed to Marx. It may be that the background of this historical offence was a pure misunderstanding, a simple blending of letters. On the other hand, it should not be forgotten that some years ago – in the years around 1925 – a great retorting of theoretical approaches to social problems could be observed in the Soviet Union. Scientific policy had been changed to dogmatic direction, and therefore Marx as well as the political economy in his sense was pushed more and more into the background and became only a political reference for any statement, activity, or whatever of the contemporary Soviet leadership. From this point of view Stalin and his followers took full advantage of 'Darwin's letter to Marx', emphasizing that Marx's theory is and will be also an 'epochmaking' building of thoughts in the field of social sciences, similar to the approach of Darwin to natural sciences – at this time generally accepted or at least discussed worldwide.

17. Compare this consequence of an evolutionary approach to social sciences to Feuerbach Thesis No 11, cited above.

18. It is worthwhile to mention that in this simple form of exchange Marx formulated the close connection between value and use–value, that is the germ of the idea about the interaction between labour (value) and utility, later the basis for distinguishing between market value and market price (see above).

19. Writing his book *The Theory of Political Economy*, Jevons was aware of the fact that measuring utility is a problem. However, he argued that some decades or centuries ago people knew about the phenomenon of electricity but they were not able to measure it. When he published his book, it became possible. Why should it be impossible to measure utility some decades or centuries later . . . e.m. (Jevons 1924).

20. For the author it would be dilettantism to write about biological problems, about attacks against Darwin, arguments of neo-Darwinists about the ideas of their famous ancestor. Therefore the following paragraphs will concentrate on Marx, on the question of how his approach had been considered in the 20th century, especially in the last decades.

21. The question whether labour value or the commodity is the basic category in Marx's theory has been investigated recently by Lysandrou (2000).
22. It is well known that this direction of economic theory was the target of Sraffa's critics expressed in the book mentioned.
23. On the other hand, Sraffa was the economist who called Keynes' attention to the writings of Karl Marx (Behrens 1985).
24. About these opposite causal relationships and about their effects on modelling see Kurz and Salvadori (1995, Ch. 3).
25. Issues No. 1 and No. 3 of vol. 22 (2000).

# REFERENCES

Aninkin, A. (1981), *Gold*, Berlin: Verlag Die Wirtschaft.

Barlow, Noea (1933), *Charles Darwin's Diary on the the Voyage of H.M.S. Beagle*, Cambridge: Cambridge University Press.

Beed, Clive and Cara Beed, (1999), 'Intellectual Progress and Academic Economics: Rational Choice and Game Theory', *Journal of Post Keynesian Economics*, **22** (1999–2000), 163–85.

Behrens, R. (1985), 'What Keynes knew about Marx', *Studi Economici*, (2) 3–14.

Bowles, S. and H. Gintis. (1990), 'Contested exchange: new microfoundations for the political economy of capitalism', *Politics and Society*, **18**, 165–222.

Böhm-Bawerk, E. v. (1896), 'Zum Abschluß des Marxschen Systems', in *Festschrift für Karl Knies*, Berlin. Haering, pp. 1–188.

Bródy, A. (1970), *Proportions, Prices, and Planning*, Budapest-Amsterdam, Akadémiai Kiadó – North-Holland.

Bródy, A. (1977), 'Marx after Steedman', *Acta Oeconomica*, **19**, 219–22.

Boulding, K. E. (1991), 'What is evolutionary economics?', *Journal of Evolutionary Economics*, (1), 9–17.

Colb, R. (1982), 'The Myth of the Darwin – Mary letter', *History of Political Economy*, XIV (4) 461–82.

Crick, F. (1967), *Of Molecules and Men*, Seattle: University of Washington Press.

Darwin, C. (1859), *On the Origin of Species by Means of Natural Selection or the Preservation of Favoured Races in the Struggle for Life*, London: John Murray. For this chapter the German edition had been used, (1980), *Die Entstehung der Arten durch natürliche Zuchtwahl*, Leipzig: Verlag Phillip Reclam.

Darwin, C. (1872), *On the Origins of Species by Means of Natural Selection or the Preservation of Favoured Races in the Struggle for Life*, sixth edition, London: John Murray.

Dostaber, G. (1982), 'Marx et Sraffa', *L'Actualité Économique*, (1–2), 95–114.

Dow, S.(2000) 'Post Keynesianism and critical realism: what is the connection?', *Journal of Post Keynesian Economics*, **22**, 15–33.

Drazen A. (1980), 'Recent developments in macroeconomic disequilibrium theory', *Econometrica*, **48**, 283–306.

Dunn, St. P. (2000), 'Whither Post Keynesianism?', *Journal of Post Keynesian Economics*, **2** , 343–64.

Eigen, M. and R. Winkler (1975), *Das Spiel. Naturgesetze steuern den Zufall*, Munich: R. Piper & Co. Verlag.

Hodgson, G. M. (1998), 'A reply to Howard Sherman,' *Review of Social Economy*, **LVI** (3) 295–306.

Hollander, S.(2000), 'Sraffa and the interpretation of Ricardo: the Marxian Dimension', *History of Political Economy*, **32**, 187–232.

Jevons, S. (1924), *The Theory of Political Economy*, Cambridge: Verlag von Gustav Fischer.

Johansen, L. (1963), 'Labour theory of value and marginal utilities', *Economics of Planning*, **3**, 89–103.

Kurz, H. D. and N. Salvadori (1995), *Theory of Production: A Long-Period Analysis*, Cambridge: Cambridge University Press.

Laibman, D. (2000), 'Value theory and the new orthodox Marxism', *Science & Society*, **64**, 310–22.

Lysandrou, P. (2000), 'The market and exploitation in Marx's economic theory', *Cambridge Journal of Economics*, **24**, 325–47.

Marx, K. (1970), *A Contribution to the Critique of Political Economy*, Moscow: Progress Publishers.

Marx, K. (1974), *Das Kapital*, Dietz-Verlag: Berlin. Bd. I–III.

Marx, K. (1841), 'Differenz der demokritischen und epikureischen Naturphilosophie nebst einem Anhange', Doktordissertation, reprinted in (1981a), *Marx Engels Werke, Ergänzungsband*, Berlin: Dietz-Verlag. pp. 257–373.

Marx, K., (1835), 'Betrachtung eines Jünglings bei der Wahl eines Berufes. Abiturientenarbeit – Deutscher Aufsatz', written between 10 and 16 August reprinted in (1981b), *Marx Engels Werke, Ergänzungsband*, Erster Teil. Berlin: Dietz-Verlag. pp. 591–4.

Marx, K. and F. Engels, (1985) *Über das Kapital*, Briefwechsel, Institut für Maxismus-Leninismus, Ausgen. u. eingeleitet von Hannes Skambraks, Berlin.

Meek, R. L. (1980), *Smith, Marx , and After*, London and New York: Chapman and Hall.

Meyer, D. (1984), *Labour Value and Utility*, Ph.D. dissertation in Hungarian, Hungarian Academy of Sciences, Budapest.

Morishima, M. (1968), *Marx's Economics*, Cambridge: Cambridge University Press.

Morishima, M. (1974), 'Marx in the light of modern economic theory', *Econometrica*, **42**, 611–32.

Prigogine, I. and I. Stengers, (1986) *La Nouvelle Alliance: Métamorphose de la Science*, Paris: Gallimard.

Runde, J. and P. Lewis, (1999), 'A critical realist perspective on Paul Davidson's methodological writings on – and rhetorical strategy for – Post Keynesian economics', *Journal of Post Keynesian Economics*, **22**, 35–56.

Spencer, D. A. (2000), 'The demise of radical political economics? An essay on the evolution of a theory of capitalist production', *Cambridge Journal of Economics*, **24**, 543–64.

Sraffa, P. (1960), *Production of Commodities by Means of Commodities*, Cambridge: Cambridge University Press.

Szentágothai, J. (1981), *Eigen – Winkler: A játék. Természeti törvények irányitják a véletlent*, foreword to the Hungarian edition of Eigen – Winkler, 1975, Budapest: Gondolat Kiadó.

Toms, M. (1988), *Der Gesraudiswert und seine Messung*, Berlin: Verlag die Wirtschaft.

Urena, E. M. (1977), 'Marx and Darwin', *History of Political Economy*, **IX** (4) 548–59.

Walters, B. and Young, D. (1999), 'Is Critical Realism the Appropriate Basis for Post Keynesians?', *Journal of Post Keynesian Economics*, **22**, 105–23.

Witt, U., 'Economics and Darwinism', *Papers on economics and evolution*, Max-Planck-Institute for Research into Economic Systems, Jena, Germany.

# 5. W. Sombart's system approach and evolutionary economics: a comparison

## Helge Peukert

### INTRODUCTION[1]

> The conception of capitalism as a historical formation with distinctive political and cultural as well as economic properties derives from the work of those relatively few economists interested in capitalism as a 'stage' of social evolution. In addition to the seminal work of Marx and the literature that his work has inspired, the conception draws on the writings of Smith, Mill, Veblen, Schumpeter and a number of sociologists and historians, notably among them, Weber and Braudel. The majority of present day economists do not use so broad a canvas, concentrating on capitalism as a market system, with the consequence of emphasizing its functional rather than its institutional or constitutive aspects. (Heilbroner 1988, p. 350b).

In his magnum opus, *Der moderne Kapitalismus*, Sombart (1863–1941) also tries to analyse (the development of) capitalism as a historical phenomenon with distinctive political, cultural and economic properties. The third volume of his work was completed in 1927 and is often considered as the most comprehensive synthesis of the research of the historical school. As the last major representative of the youngest historical school he stood in the tradition of 'theoretical historicism . . ., a synthesis between historical empiricism and theoretical economics . . . Sombart's principal interest was in the great tendencies of capitalist evolution, including the evolution of its institutions in time' (Chaloupek 1999, pp. 467 and 470).

In the last decades evolutionary economics (henceforth EE, also for evolutionary economists) developed as a distinct research tradition, often associated with Schumpeterian dynamics, that is, the development of industrial capitalism due to technological innovations. Sombart, who fits into the institutional research tradition mentioned above, is missing in Heilbroner's list, Schumpeter is not. In this chapter we will compare evolutionary and Sombartian economics and ask how far Sombart is a precursor of EE or if his research program is distinct. Therefore, we will first present basic principles of EE and then start the discussion from a Sombartian perspective.

# PRINCIPLES OF EVOLUTIONARY ECONOMICS

Evolution has become a fashionable word in economics.[2] Sometimes causal (physics), more often functional (biology), and intentional (social sciences) modes of explanation are used. EE is connected today with new institutionalist, post-Keynesian and Schumpeterian positions. They often include elements of biological evolutionary theory and apply the concepts of variation, selection and replication to analyse socioeconomic change from within the (economic) system.[3] A mechanism must exist to transmit the variations to offspring. Institutions and routines (rules) perform this function in social and economic evolution (Nelson and Winter 1982).

Most EE are explicitly oriented against orthodox neoclassical economic thought, their analogy of classical mechanics, the synthesis of optimization and equilibrium, and the reversible time concept. Instead, they focus on process and change and the crucial role of novelty as the main characteristics of modern economic systems. It is a theory of the forces of change, of variation exhibited by cultural artefacts. Sometimes, EE refer to the subjectivist branch of Austrian economics (Shackle 1992) which underlines the interpretative aspect of information gathering and processing and the uncertainty and volatility of future events which make maximization impossible. It can even be asked if H. Simon's idea of bounded or satisficing rationality is adequate to describe orientations in an open, evolving system with uncertain future states (Kubon-Gilke 1996, p. 732). In a broader perspective, the biological analogy is replaced in this tradition by the idea of spontaneous order (which originated in the Scottish enlightenment, see Adam Smith), where novelty can be explained by the unintended consequences of many individuals pursuing their own aims. Social orders are here the result of human action but not of human design (see also C. Menger and the works of his descendants like Hayek).

It is an open question how far evolutionary processes can be modeled mathematically and if EE will ever (or should ever, see Hodgson 1996) have a formal structure of a sophistication comparable to neoclassical economics. One perspective is to view a stochastic process with many dimensions and multiple equilibria. They may differ very much with regard to their attributes. The historically random cumulation of circumstances leads to locally stable equilibria which are destabilized if a critical mass is produced which leads the system to a deviation to another local equilibrium. The direction is lead by random effects. In the vicinity of bifurcation points the behaviour of systems is not predictable and fluctuations can lead to any state possible after the bifurcation point. In biology these phase transitions are often described as self-organizing phenomena (Prigogine). From biology, some researchers try to apply the concept of evolutionary stable strategies (Maynard Smith). Others apply catastrophe theory, replicator dynamics and the game-theory modelling à la Axelrod (see the general overview by Radzicki and Sterman 1994). The open question is however, if and how the emergence of novelty can be described in a formal way or if there is not a logical incompatibility because models have to refer to a given set of known variables and attractors. We have not very progressed much since the early Schumpeter and his analysis of rather unstable and dubious motivational forces and drives to generate inventions and push through innovations. Schumpeter's two main concepts, that discontinuous rather than continuous change (Marshall) should be at the centre of analysis (see also Dosi 1984, and Dosi et al. 1988) and that variations such as creative destruction are induced by entrepreneurs and that they are the essential push for natural selection among human artifacts, are shared by most EE. Another overlap exists between EE and research on the evolution of organizations, where the asset-specificity and the measurement-cost view in the Coase, Williamson, Alchian and Woodward tradition can be discerned. The first explains organizational structures by the hold-up problem, while the second relies on moral hazard. Both depend on a complex and partially unforeseeable environment, bounded rationality and opportunism (self-interest seeking with guile). The last assumption is more or less implicit in the epistemological rule of methodological individualism (on the connection between EE and methodological individualism see Witt 1987).

There are also warnings against a narrow borrowing of concepts from biology, for example, with which sociobiological concepts, the idea of the survival of the fittest and the parallel between genetic and cultural variation are concerned (see for example Witt 1992). In fact, the problem with the idea of selection and the survival of the fittest is – besides the question of the unit of selection (the gene, the organism or the group?) – that fitness is context-dependent and the selected economic unit can consciously (try to) shape and influence the selecting environment. The term 'adaptation' therefore becomes problematic and is often reduced to a Panglossian functionalism, in other words that survival implies efficiency and what exists is optimal. Often this idea is combined with political implications (as in Hayek): the selection mechanism of the market should not be interfered with by state intervention and central planning, a laissez-faire policy makes sure that the optimal solution survives. In a certain sense, this view is constructivist rationalism, because hypothetical or past designs are considered optimal.

> The true opposite of the constructivist rationalist is the evolutionary skeptic. Far from seeing what exists as optimal, the evolutionary skeptic sees it a central insight of evolutionary thinking that society is always necessarily an imperfect and unfinished edifice. But the skeptic also understands that improvement is inherently a matter of experiment not synoptic design. Thus the skeptic's proposal for 'intervention' will take the form not of a concrete picture of society but of a concern of the abstract structure of society – for its mechanisms for generating and selecting

variation; that is, the skeptic is concerned with processes, not directly with outcomes. It is for these reasons that many evolutionary social thinkers, from Smith to Hayek, have favored the background set of institutions so often derided as *laissez faire*. What Smith rather misleadingly called the obvious and simple system of natural liberty . . . recommends itself not for the wonderful *status quo* it produces but for its potential to change and improve society. (Langlois and Everett 1994, pp. 38–9)

We have presented this long citation because it spells out the major preanalytical 'vision' of EE and their market liberal policy implications.[4] It is dominant in many sentences, such as when the authors state that knowledge 'is the product of systemwide learning over time. It is not the product of design' (op. cit., p. 38).

Sombart may have asked the following questions of Langlois and Everett (see the citation above): why is learning not also a product of design, for example, of public education (see the Green Card debate in Germany)? If we are skeptics, how can we know and be sure that improvement is inherently and always a matter of socially unorganized experiment and not – at least sometimes – synoptic design? What does 'improvement' mean? Can we talk about improvements without having a picture of society in mind? Is a maximum of generating and selecting variation a rule or a value per se (the more the better)? If so, why? Can we not conceive an optimal balance or even a relatively low rate as best: what are the standards to evaluate it? Is the potential to change really equivalent with the improvement of society? Is it theoretically impossible that entrepreneurial innovation makes society more imperfect and unfinished and that maladaptive traits can be selected?[5] Can we state scientifically that there is an improvement in the long run like Nelson who notes that advanced industrial nations 'move in directions that have led to sustained economic progress' (1995, p. 83)?[6]

Sombart could argue here with the well known Arthur arguments of pathinefficient lock-ins if returns increase at different rates (Arthur 1989). Insignificant circumstances (history matters) may tip the system into the long-term inferior technology (the gasoline engine is sometimes mentioned as an example). In 'the increasing returns case laissez-faire gives no guarantee that the "superior" technology (in the long-run sense) will be the one that survives . . . a central authority could underwrite adoption and exploration along promising but less popular technological paths' (Arthur 1989, p. 127). Despite the recognition of lock-ins, externalities, ecological degradation, and so on, EE is mostly associated with the spontaneous order/laissez-faire vision (see our examples in the citations above). As we briefly tried to argue here, this is not necessarily so. Further, we can also imagine cases of creative destruction in which for example a public institution (the state) forces the private sector to innovate and adopt (for instance an obligatory certain percentage of electronic

cars in 2003). In this case the surprising arbitrary mutation is the new author-
itative legal rule. It can also be argued that the fastest rate of adaptation and
change is not the best one. An 'evolutionary system is necessarily "conservative" in the sense that it must possess a nonvolatile genetic memory' (Langlois
and Everett 1994, p. 38). We can imagine that without break mechanisms the
speed of change is too fast so that the system can no longer build up a sufficient genetic memory and loses orientation (this may also be a recent phenomenon in Western culture). An optimal mix would include islands of inertia
(such as bureaucracies).

Sombart may also have asked why competition is the only form of elementary interaction under consideration. In biology, the further strategies of
commensalism, predation and cooperation (members of a species cooperate
against a threatening environment) exist (see Gould, 1994, Chapter 22 on
Kropotkin). Depending on the circumstances, cooperation may be a superior
strategy to competition, predation may be a degeneration of competition
(Veblen). So there exists a possible alternative to competition (usually understood as innovation competition, the introduction of Schumpeter's new combinations) which should not be excluded per se, and competition has its dangers
and anomalies.

Another point of critical reference could be the concentration on explaining
only the sources of growth and qualitative changes in new products and
services by product, process, radical or incremental innovations and their
diffusion. The criticism made may be that progress is here reduced to changes
(improvements?) in man's material well-being, but Sombart would ask if man
really lives by bread alone. Implicitly, EE rejects the idea of a universe of
purpose and design, and a system of (transcendental or historically variable)
ethical values to which human nature is obliged or should conform. There is
no ultimate end, no goal or purpose for man in EE. What may be called the
spiritual aspect is totally neglected, but there are surely positive or negative
externalities of technological change with respect to the non-material dimensions. EE could be accused of reducing ends to means in not appreciating the
question of the *bonum honestum* of ethical progress versus simple material
progress (O'Brien 1992).

## SOMBART'S STUDY ON THE ROMAN CAMPAGNA: AN EVOLUTIONARY ANALYSIS?

Let us now have a closer look at Sombart's first relevant publication, his
dissertation (1888) on tenancy and labour relations in the Roman campagna.[7]
In our view, in 180 pages he delineates in a nutshell his complete further
research programme in an applied manner. In the introduction he states that the

functions of his work are not only to get some insights in theoretical agriculture and the historical development of a specific economy in time and space
but also – and this was relevant for him for general economic theorizing, see
1888, p. 6 – to extract some peculiar economic systems (his central notion of
*Wirtschaftssystem* is mentioned twice, on pp. 3 and 6).[8] Further, he wanted to
arrive at some practical social policy conclusions especially where the conflict
between personal and social interests is concerned. He was sure that the interests of the economically powerful may contradict the interest of the
national/local economy (p. 7).

Sombart tries to understand the campagna organism in applying the synthe-
sizing method of theoretical historicism. On the one hand he draws a secular
picture of the development of the campagna in the last centuries (pp. 132–40).
He further describes in detail the natural environment like climate, soil and so
forth (pp. 10–26), and the applied technical procedures in agriculture and
cattle breeding and its changes like machine use and forest culture over time
(pp. 27–50). He uses all statistical, empirical, and historical material available
(including government enquêtes, personal observations, interviews, and so on,
see p. 85). His description becomes very concrete and illustrative and is written in prosaic language. But he never loses track of his analysis: to delineate a
specific economic system, the 'campagna organism'.

This becomes most evident when he turns to the analysis of the social structure in terms of the property relations as the most relevant element. He analyses the change of property distribution and its size (50 per cent of the land is
owned by five per cent of the population), and develops a classification of
classes (the aristocracy, the church, the bourgeois, the workers). The basic
structure is that the landed non-functional aristocracy rents the land to the rich
tenants in the cities. They rent little plots to the final small tenants. His classification is developed along the lines of a social interest group model. But it is
not Marxist because Sombart includes, for example, the Church as an interest
group and he underlines the importance of small and capital intensive large
tenants and farmers which crosscuts class categories (see Part 3 of the book).
The different categories of workers (like wood-cutter, charcoal burner, herds-
man, daily paid land hands, itinerant worker, and so on) and their living conditions are analysed along the lines of what he later called personal types (1930,
p. 243). He has a social-functional (not a natural rights) theory of property and
therefore he always asks how far concentrated property (such as land in the
hands of the aristocracy which he severely attacked) is conducive in social,
political, cultural or economic respects. He does not reject the private possession of the means of production in general.

His interpretative frame is a regional economy in dissolution: the disappearance of the common field system, the decrease of small peasants, the
concentration of land ownership, the substitution of agriculture by farming,

the increase of a proletariat and the decrease in real wages due to overcompe-
tition are clear indicators for him that the working of free market mechanisms
(which he castigates, see for example pp. 80, 147–8) has social degenerative
impacts and invokes an ill organism (p. 93).

If we compare his analysis with basic principles of EE, we see that Sombart
does not ask how far free markets can be established and adaptive efficiency
be enhanced to increase GDP or other qualitative material changes by creating
non-attenuated property rights (for an attenuated version see North 1996) or
change can be induced by some (market) variation mechanism. His unit is not
the self-interested individual and his methodology is not methodological individualism but social groups and classes. The reference group for policy is the
nation. He shares with EE the conviction that the decision making of agents is
normally bound to rules, norms and institutions. But he asks about the impacts
of change for the culture of the nation or region under consideration. Not
economic performance per se but the social and cultural consequences of
changing social structures are important for him.

Sombart holds that in rural areas the familial peasant households and holdings are the regular and normal case and not the concentration of property and
proletarianization as a natural result of free competition. He has no narrow
concept of exploitation but an idea of a decent life which includes an acceptable wage, comfortable and hygienic conditions, no overwork, social embeddedness (for instance no long-term separation of families), existential security,
and a cultural minimum level (books and so on). Maybe the most important
point is that human action should be autonomous and not heteronomous, that
is, action under an extraneous will, for example the worker in a factory (see
1930, p. 225). As we will see in the next section this contradicts his understanding of the anthropological constitution of man.

The increasing cattle breeding and proletarianization is in the interest of the
powerful owners and large tenants. It will continue as the natural drift of
unregulated competition. Therefore, Sombart asks for a straight reform by the
state. It should act against this natural drift. His reflections are very modern
when he discusses the impact of the world market (p. 114), the existence of an
excess population due to machinery, and so forth. They remind the reader of
the problems of recent globalization and for example the non-regulated transformation in former socialist countries. For Sombart the big mistake was to
auction the immense property holdings of the Church without qualification so
that the economically more powerful became even more so (p. 152). His
proposition is to nationalize the big holdings (with recompense which will cost
a lot of money, see p. 162), and to redistribute it to small peasants in heredi-
tary tenure (see Sombart 1889) to support a more healthy agricultural
campagna organism. Positive state action is needed for social reform (pp.
160ff.) in an encompassing way to create a specific economic spirit (compare

1930, pp. 206–7) with an orientation of non-pecuniary satisfaction according to need and economic structures of self-sufficieny; an organism with specific goals, motives and rules of behavior (1930, p. 181).

Sombart's early work already implies his later threefold differentiation of spirit, organization and technique and is a fine example of the approach of the historical school (summarized by Betz 1994). His value judgment is against an untamed capitalist spirit and social structure. It is oriented against what he called the embrace of capitalist civilization. The campagna study tries to offer an agrarian alternative. Sombart holds that his ideal is not against economic logic and efficiency in the long run, because the aristocracy chooses large tenants and they choose cattle breeding mainly for reasons of convenience, not maximum yield. It is in the interest of society at large to choose a decentralized but intensive mode of agricultural cultivation instead of extensive stock farming to have a better product to finance imports (see pp. 114ff.).[9]

Sombart's early study shows that besides the organism metaphor he does not argue functionally and does not use the variation, selection and replication analogy. Like EE he rejects classical mechanics and neoclassical economics. Processes of change are non-deterministic and open-ended for him, but certain developments can be corrected so that his understanding of the irreversibility of time needs some qualification. Sombart uses a historical method; he never appreciated an applied mathematical modeling. Novelty and change are not his central concern but the living conditions and the social structure he considered *à la taille de l'homme*. The orientational mode of the ruling classes can be described with the concept of bounded satisficing rationality (Simon), but to the detriment of society at large. For Sombart their orientation is not a general description of man but more a historically specific disorientation. Sombart is an evolutionary skeptic, society is imperfect and an unfinished edifice. But he openly (and more radically then his mentor Schmoller) rejects the spontaneous order view (Smith, Menger, Hayek), for him human action can lead to an inferior or unacceptable constellation which necessitates human design, and state intervention. He rejects the survival of the fittest and the natural drift in the direction of a temporary market domination. In his campagna book the deco-ordinating tendencies in the long run outpace the coordinating tendencies of market mechanisms in the short run.

As a result of our discussion so far we will formulate a presumption here and test it in what follows. We will demarcate a fundamental difference between EE and Sombart's approach. Following Rutherford, the dynamic economic analysis of change and institutions faces 'some *general* problems inherent in any attempt to deal with institutions' (1996, p. ix). The problems can be formulated as trade-offs between five complementary but dichotomous research strategies and perspectives: formalism vs. anti-formalism, individualism vs. holism, rationality vs. rule following, evolution vs. design, and efficiency vs. reform. A more formal-mathematical proceeding for example has analytical rigor, 'but there is a trade-off between rigour and relevance'. The dichotomies mean in detail: 'i. The role of formal theoretical modelling as opposed to less formal methods, including historical and "literary" approaches. ii. The emphasis to be placed on individual behaviour leading to social institutions as opposed to the effect of social institutions in moulding individual behaviour. iii. The validity of rationalist explanations as opposed to those that place limits on the applicability of rationalist conceptions. iv. The extent to which institutions are the result of spontaneous or invisible-hand processes as opposed to deliberate design. v. The basis on which normative judgements can be made, and the appropriate role of government intervention in the economy' (Rutherford 1996, p. 174). Our guess is that EE is more situated on the first, Sombart more on the second expression of the dichotomies. Especially where the first dichotomy is concerned it should be stated that EE in general places greater dignity on formal models today but does not at all exclude non-formal reasoning (what Nelson and Winter called appreciative theorizing). It seems obvious to us that the other dichotomies clearly demarcate both approaches. EE puts an emphasis on individual behaviour, rationalist explanations (bounded rationality fits in here), invisible-hand processes, and the rejection of normative judgments (except growth and qualitative change) and in principle a negative view on government intervention.

## ON HUMAN NATURE AND SOCIAL ACTION: *GEIST* VERSUS NATURALISM

Sombart's last book was on anthropology (1938).[10] It should constitute and be a first step towards a general theory of culture. In the literature it was viewed as a more or less confused compilation of diverse thoughts without a unifying idea, the product of a disillusioned old man. In our view it is the key and heart and core to understand his thinking.[11] In 430 pages he tries to substantiate his view that man's distinguishing characteristic and human substance is to have 'spirit' (*Geist*, pp. 17–21, not identical with the more narrow concept of mind). Spirit materializes in religion, the state, the family, the economy, language, moral and esthetical maxims and norms (pp. 315, 417). Therefore, the social realm is constituted by culture as symbolic meaning systems (pp. 68, 77). It makes humans free to act and gives them responsibility for their actions (p. 288). But it also makes us a spiritually endangered species (p. 52).[12]

With *Geist*, human beings fall out of the realm of nature, they are creatures *sui generis* (p.109) and in so far not part of nature (p. 416). Sombart is arguing against the concepts of 'animalism' where the notion and reality of spirit are lost. Animalism exists in the two versions of physical–chemical mechanical materialism and Darwinian organic biologism (pp. 286–7). Both are aberrations (p. 109) and expressions of the power of natural science thinking over modern man (p. 93). There is always a close relationship between the image of man and scientific methods (p. 109). Sombart strongly emphasizes the basic dichotomy between an 'animalistic' and a 'hoministic' current (p. 99).

We see here a difference between Sombart and EE. Although we also find intentional explanations in EE, they are not so dominant as in Sombart. Further, Sombart explicitly rejects formal, causal and biological-functional explanations. Like Troeltsch (1922, see below) Sombart sees a great cultural and epistemological divide in the modern intellectual and scientific world between historicism on the one hand and mathematical models, and mechanical naturalism (biological and physical analogies) on the other hand. What Sombart has in mind is less self-interested bounded rationality and instrumental, cognitive goal-oriented standards and more culturally shared norms in the sense of Weber's value orientations as the essence of man. Sombart's human being is not naturally searching for the exploitation of arbitrage (Kirzner) or in search of novelty to generate profit.

Besides his basic dichotomy Sombart's construction is much more complicated because he introduces the soul (*Seele*) as an expression of the biological organism which is the vital centre of the human person and expression of life (motivation, desire and reproduction). Both independent parts, *Seele* and *Geist*, constitute man and we have to choose between vital nature (*Seele*) and spirit (p. 338). Animalistic concepts negate both (*Entseelung* and *Entgeistung*). Sombart's recommendation is not that *Geist* should substitute for nature (*Seele*), because *Geist* in its purest form has the tendency of self-alienation in the form of schematizing, bureaucratization, hyperorganization, the elaboration of formal taxonomies and so on (p. 20), which may remind the reader of Simmel's distinction between *Geist* and form. Sombart distinguishes between pure *Geist* (with no material correlation like the sentence of Pythagoras), bounded *Geist* (which depends on a material substratum) and living *Geist* (embedded in a human life history, see p. 79).

*Seele* may degenerate, for example, to pure mechanical drive satisfaction. Sombart leaves it open if *Seele* has in principle the vital constructive element in itself or if it depends in this regard on the influx of *Geist*. The more *Geist* develops, the greater is the danger of the form deviation of *Geist*. This may also explain why Sombart's book looks disorganized: he does not give any clear formal ('scientific') definition of *Geist* and he does not say exactly where it comes from (God, the brain, or whatever). Instead, he always cites literature, philosophy, and also scientific contributions in a cursory way and leaves the final answer open. In a certain sense this is necessary because a formal-mechanical-logical definition of *Geist* would be an expression of its own self-alienation (Veblen: self-contamination). So the playful and essay character of the work is the necessary *Seele* part of the reasoning. This is not to deny the problematic of many paradoxes in the book (see the fair criticisms in Vleugels' 1940, Wiese's 1940, and Klotter's 1988 reviews).

EE exactly formulates the claim to develop a scientific theory of motivation, behaviour and practical rationality (Witt 1987, pp. 101ff.). There is no recognition of the human dualism and the problem of self-alienation as Sombart sees it. In contrast, EE tries to understand how the conditions and ways of information gathering and processing and the accompanying learning processes operate to satisfy individual preferences. The aim is to formulate a cognitivist theory of preferences. The neighbouring sciences are behavioural psychology, experimental psychology, partially sociobiology, behaviourism, and so on. One strand is Simon's idea of aspiration levels and relative deprivation due to achievement insufficiencies which lead to learning behaviour. The general tendency of these approaches is as mentioned their instrumental and functional character to realize individual preferences.

Sombart's book ends with the remark that human existence consists of a constant conflict of our spiritual essence and our natural conditions (p. 432).[13] In his view there is an optimum of the balanced spiritual and natural portions in human action. Untamed and non-functionalized nature is important for this balance because it represents and strengthens our vital and natural component. This harmonious balance is disturbed in modern capitalism with its economic rationalism. This leads to Sombart's culture and deep ecological critique (especially pp. 324–39, compare Scaff 1988) which will be discussed later.

The idea of an optimal mix finds no place in EE. It does not question the commodification of all aspects of life and technical innovations as the main resource to solve human problems and to satisfy needs. The need for partially non-functionalized relationships with nature and other humans is not taken into consideration. Novelty always refers to new combinations in a market frame of reference.

Scheler's influence consists in the assumption of a formal hierarchical realm and stratification of value spheres (from the pleasant/useful, the vital feelings/health, the beautiful, the true and the truthful, truth, up to the holy and their respective opposites, see Scheler 1966, pp. 122ff.). The higher value sphere always has a natural preponderance over the lower ones. People always give meaning to their actions, they always have a subject of faith. The upheaval of values means that in modernity lower value spheres (such as the pleasant in utilitarianism) become more important then the higher ones or they are set as the Absolute (Allodi 1989, p. 469).

In Scheler's and Sombart's worldview, the neglect of questions of the *summum bonum*, at least the recognition of side effects of technical change on 'ethical progress' in EE, is an expression of the general wrong track of modern social sciences which only consider the potential to change and improve society in a goods and services maximizing way.

Sombart places in forefront of his neo-sociology the basic principle that all social life, and human beings are necessarily sociable, is (mediated by) *Geist*, that is, symbolic meaning transferred by language (1936, pp. 23–4). He distinguishes his sociology from natural rights (Hobbes), historical (Smith), metahistorical (Spann), formal (Simmel), 'German' (Freyer), and natural science concepts of sociology. The last concept is subdivided into physical (Pareto), biological (Spencer), and psychological (Giddens) approaches. All social units are to be understood as *Geistgebilde* (spiritual forms) which he calls associations (*Verbände*).[14]

Sombart distinguishes genuine and not genuine associations (1936 [1956], pp. 29ff.). In the latter category a spiritual connection is missing, for instance in language communities, statistical and affective groups. Genuine associations are subdivided into ideal (family, state/nation, religion), final (purposive and structured organizations like firms), and intentional associations (the *Geist* must be in the consciousness of the actors, such as interest groups without a permanent organization). The central notions in the three categories are ideas – goals – intentions. The purest social forms are ideal associations where a transcendental component dominates whereas in the goal type individual interests and rational nature prevail. In the family as an example of ideal associations, the eternal meaning is the completion and reproduction of human partial forms of existence (man, woman, child).

We see here again that in Sombart's anthropology and sociology the final essence of human beings and their self-realization are not defined by self-interest (seeking with guile) and the ensuing problems of hold-ups, moral hazard, *Trittbrettfahrerverhalten*, and so forth but consists in their commitment to shared values in a community where the realization of proper personal interests is of secondary importance.

## A METHOD CALLED *VERSTEHEN*

In his most pronounced contribution to method, Sombart (1930) distinguished three types of economic theories (in German the *richtende, ordnende* and *verstehende* approaches). They all consider themselves exclusive and universal. He rejects the first, orienting (*richtende*) type (Aristotle, the scholastics, Spann, Hegel, but he also includes the hedonist school and for example Adam Smith). It is normative and says what should be, for instance no chrematistics in the *polis*. For Sombart (like Weber), science implies the principle of value neutrality because different norms can be chosen. The *richtende* economics must be rejected because it cannot argue in favour of one norm instead of another. It is interesting to see that Sombart explains the emergence and existence of this approach by the overarching cultural value systems and social structures of the time (such as in the Middle Ages). Does this suggest that a meaning system produces the wrong intellectual superstructure?

The *ordnende* or ordering economics comprises mostly mainstream economics (1930, Chapter 9), subdivided into the objectivists (Marx), subjectivists (Menger) and the relationists (Walras). Despite all their disagreements they belong to the same fundamental type. Sombart chooses again an externalist explanation of its emergence. It came forth as a result of mainly cultural but also structural changes in the last 500 years: the secularization of the lifestyle, the decline of feudalism and its unitary culture, the disenchantment of nature and society, and so on. The aim of knowledge is now to control (natural) processes. The scientist has emotional distance; a depersonalization of knowledge generation takes place. 'The results of scientific inquiry have to be objective, separate from the person who does the inquiry; in this sense they can be proven, i.e. impressed upon an outsider' (1930, p. 96).[15] The external ordering in quantitative terms is at the centre, not the understanding of the substantial how and why of things and relations. Sombart's catalogue coincides with McCloskey's ten commandments of modern economics (1985). The greatest influence on economics was exerted by the ideal of the exact natural sciences and their practical success since the 18th century. It should be mentioned that his three basic types and his putting into boxes is all but self-evident: Smith could also be found in the *ordnende* economics, some would put Schmoller in the *verstehende* economics (henceforth VE), others Menger (see Leube 1994).

It is not easy to say if EE can be grouped under the heading of *ordnende* economics. On the one hand objectification and depersonalization are also values of method in EE, on the other hand some of McCloskey's ten commandments (such as predictability, the legitimacy of appreciative theorizing, and so on) are not totally shared by EE.

What is Sombart's criticism of the orienting program? Some minor points are the unclear notion of economic laws and the 'quantification only' principle (p. 130). But when he introduces his favourite VE in Chapter 10, he makes the strong assertion that VE is adequate to the subject matter which implies that *ordnende* economics is not (see for example pp. 140 and 292). This is a general statement, he does for instance not say that classical economics was right at the time of liberal capitalism and is wrong in late capitalism or that there is a division of labour between the approaches, depending on the respective scientific questions which constitute different objects of knowledge (for Amonn 1930 this would have been a more adequate line of reasoning). He does not explain the VE by an externalist culture approach as he did in his discussion of the *richtende* and *ordnende* economics. The ontological quality of his view is underlined by the fact that he rejects the typical heterodox criticisms of a lack of a national, social policy or ethical component or the allegations of atomism, chrematistics, statics, armchair theorizing, and so on (pp. 140ff.). The essential mistakes are the ten commandments of the natural science attitude (does this not imply atomism in the sense of decomposability of elements?). For Sombart, even Schmoller and Roscher fell into the natural science trap and into the aberrations of psychologism, historicism and teleology (pp. 154–5; in our view this is only partially correct, see Peukert 1998, Chapter 3). The foundations for VE were therefore laid by historians (Vico, Droysen), philosophers (Dilthey, Rothacker), sociologists (Cooley) and some few economists (Gottl, Spann).

To introduce VE he first explains the nature of economics and the economy. Economic theory deals with the need of subsistence (*Unterhaltsfürsorge*, p. 173), the provisioning of material goods. Secondly it is an empirical science (*Erfahrungswissenschaft*), it depends on reality in time and space. In our view, this does not exclude an approach according to Robbins's definition of the subject matter of economics. But thirdly economics is a cultural science, 'since body and soul find their purpose only in the spirit. They can be understood only by means of the spirit, they can become an object of "understanding" only in the context of the spirit' (p. 175). For Sombart this is the essential point (why not the other two?). Therefore, Korsch (1930) castigates his idealism. It can also be asked that if we assume the motive structure of Adam Smith's baker as given and the existence of markets and their mechanical price and quantity setting as near to the facts (as idealized in supply and demand diagrams), why should we care so much about motives and *verstehen*? Sombart chooses an ontological absolutist introduction of VE which does not convince us.

EE does not share Sombart's cultural bias. Instead, it focuses on the changes in the mode of production, techniques and accompanying consumption patterns. To understand the motives or typical motive constellations is not relevant for EE, it operates with the pattern assumption of self-interest.

One reason for Sombart's strategy is his commitment to the principle of value neutrality (see Landmann's arguments (1930) why in a VE perspective value commitments can hardly be excluded in research). In a certain sense he accepts the *ordnende* economics viewpoint only to say and describe 'what really is'. But if all knowledge depends on symbolic meaning structures there is no simple answering 'what really is'. He could have said that he has a specific image of man (anthropology – *Geist*) and a specific understanding of 'the social', formulated in his neo-sociology. It is the result of his interest analysing which type of human being (Weber's *Menschentypus* in Hennis's interpretation) is drilled in different economic systems. This is obviously not the central focus of EE who are essentially interested in the mechanisms of novelty and change in the economic sphere.

Sombart also introduces the concept of 'system' in an absolutist way in Chapter 12. For him, 'system' is a logical idea (Kant), a precondition of science and reason. The choice is again given by the nature of the subject, so we arrive naturally at the idea of the 'economy' and the three parts of the 'economic system': the economic spirit, the structural order and the technique (p. 181). No reasonable scientific argument is possible without this correct *Gestaltidee*.[16] If we understand his system in the general sense of systematic it is too general. But if we accept his threefold classification and dichotomies it is too specific because many other reasonable classificatory approaches (such as Spiethoff's) exist. They all depend on the researcher's predilections and questions, but none of them has an ontological dignity in our view. Many EE share Sombart's broad view in analysing technical change (for example Dosi), including organizational and legal conditions, and the influence of the state in their analysis. But usually they are more concentrated on changes in the narrower economic sphere and they hardly refer to mental frames or even put them at the top of the important variables in their investigations.

Sombart next introduces 'working ideas' as notions of reason (pp. 185ff.), as-ifs for research like a static or dynamic, an organic or mechanical way of analysing. He also includes in this epistemologically very constructivist part the ideas of an exchange economy versus a national economy (*Volkswirtschaft*, a living entity, p. 189). For Sombart both 'ideas' are valuable, depending on the economic system and the research question (p. 181). He even includes the relative validity of opposite value theories like Marx's objectivism versus the marginalist subjectivism in his functional argument. Having repudiated mainstream classical approaches in toto as *ordnende* economics in Chapter 9, he now puts his opinion in a context and accepts their relative validity.

But here Sombart falls into a certain relativist trap because he cannot hold both statements at the same time. The market/exchange models of his time implied that stability and welfare are brought about by the working of the objective market mechanisms. The opposite view is that we need strong social institution building, otherwise society will collapse and welfare decrease.[17] This was the quarrel between Schmoller and Menger and this was also Sombart's point against the Italian government in his campagna study. It is still the dividing line in the debate on globalization. It is not enough to say that an exchange paradigm is naturally only and partially good for capitalist exchange economies because we know that the exchange paradigm has – for good or bad reasons – been used for all types of economic structures (such as slavery as an implicit contract), even by the proponents of the historical school (Pearson 1997). In any case, we have the impression that Sombart shifts from an absolutist to a relativist view in a questionable way in Chapter 12.

In EE, causal, functional and intentional modes are used. Sombart too tries to broaden his arsenal and includes causal methods. At his time, functional evolutionary models did not exist and he does not consider including their rudimentary beginnings at his time. This inclusion of neoclassical mechanical models contradicts somehow his dynamic irreversible time and discontinuous change concept in his analysis of modern capitalism. At the same time he implicitly buys the spontaneous order paradigm with its policy implications.

Understanding (*Verstehen*) tries to grasp meaning, it asks 'why' do people act this or that way. We can understand, because the objective *Geist* (for example the meaning of a modern firm) obeys the same laws as our personal subjective *Geist* (individual actions). He differentiates three types of understanding. *Sinnverstehen* (understanding of meaning) refers to the timeless and ahistorical idea of the economy already mentioned with the elements of spirit, organization and technique. It is a priori. We already mentioned that others found different elementary categories and no methodological rule tells us how Sombart found the categories without historical studies. It is obvious that the dichotomies like traditionalism vs. rationalism, solidarism vs. individualism and satisfaction according to need vs. the principle of profit (*Bedarfsdeckungs-* vs. *Erwerbsprinzip*, see pp. 206–7) are closely linked to the transition from the Middle Ages to modern capitalism. They are not transhistorical principles.

EE would be highly skeptical vis-à-vis a relatively undefined concept of understanding. For them, modern capitalist or market institutions are taken for granted. For Sombart, the change from pre-capitalist to capitalist structures was the real *explanandum*. EE may doubt whether satisfaction according to need really existed in history. But the satisficing model (Simon) makes it appear less unrealistic because it entails (culturally) defined aspiration levels (see for example Witt 1993, p. 4).

Sombart's second category is *Sachverstehen* (understanding of circumstances), real historical understanding, comprising first the understanding of goals (this is in fact the behavioural logic of mainstream economic man). In addition, there is the understanding of objective interrelations, for example that if the corn harvest in the US perishes, more will be produced in Argentina due to the expected price increase. With *Sachverstehen*, Sombart brings back the basics of (neo)classical macro-economics (see for example Samuelson and Nordhaus 1989). It is not clear how far his listing under *Sachverstehen* makes a methodological or substantial difference to mainstream economics. After having thrown out the mainstream theories and toolboxes under the heading of *ordnende* economics in the first place, Sombart now restores the basics of mainstream economics (Schams 1930, pp. 469–70) to present VE as all inclusive. But at the same time it becomes a less specific approach. It can even be stated that neoclassical economics is fully based on *Sachverstehen*, Sombart's economics primarily on *Sinnverstehen*, so that the basic opposition *ordnende* vs. VE simply vanishes.

The third category is *Stilverstehen* (understanding of style), for example how far the behaviour of economic agents is oriented to the spirit of capitalism. It is perplexing to see that he negates the modern economy as a connection in style (*Stilzusammenhang*). He argues that there exists no meaningful relationship between average human economic behaviour and an underlying meaningful style (p. 217). If this is the case we may ask if his construction of the spirit of an economic system as the primordial principle in *Sinnverstehen* is not obsolete in capitalism. This would be a pleasant argument for mainstream economists as well as for EE to be content with *Sachverstehen* in capitalism.

His last category is the understanding of individual motives, called *Seelenverstehen*. All action has to be reduced to human intentional motives, the free will is a necessary assumption of VE (which has no developed logic, see p. 235). The basic notions are understood in an essentialist manner. We understand 'hammer' not by some categorical abstractions (for example, made of wood), but by understanding its function: to hammer. He distinguishes between heteronomous vs. autonomous, traditional vs. rational and goal vs. value oriented (p. 225) action. But usually we are not interested in individual motives but in real average motives in typical constellations, exemplified in his analysis of the different types of 'bourgeois'. The limits of 'understanding' are the unconscious, nature, the transcendental, and mental illness. Again we can say that EE is not interested in this form of *Verstehen*, because it is beside the main research questions.

Sombart's edifice becomes more and more complex and resembles the following of a maze where the arrangement of more and more VE elements gets out of hand and the general view is lost. But Sombart continues and introduces next the *Sinngesetze* (laws of meaning), that is, meaningful necessary relations. First come the mathematical laws of size like the quantity theory of money, the market law (the size of the markets determines the degree of specialization, see pp. 254–5), and so on. We see that Sombart once again tries to cannibalize elements of orthodox economics. Next are the structural laws of part and whole, for example capitalism can only expand if the proletariat increases (p. 257). Finally we have the functional laws, the rational means-ends calculations. It is not so easy to see the difference of this form the aforementioned *Zweckverstehen*. They are rational schemes. They imply what Sombart calls fictional laws. The prime example is the classical law of supply and demand (p. 261). His only criticism is, that the classics thought these were natural laws, but they in fact depend on specific conditions. The noteworthy point is that Sombart accepts that abstract knowledge without reference to the attribution of natural values (*Bedeutungszuschreibungen*) generates interesting and relevant insights as an elementary and the first step to understanding the real world. Here, he would also have to accept formal dynamic models in the tradition of game theory, catastrophe theory, and so on as generic models to start relevant research.

Next he asks why uniform actions of many actors occur. His answer includes common human nature and environment, rational behavior in systemic constraints, imitation, climate, soil, and so forth. Here Sombart is on slippery ground because VE implies that human motives are the final bedrock where causal investigations have to stop. Otherwise he himself would walk into diverse traps (like behaviourism). Here Sombart switches and hesitates between some fundamental choices which also show up in EE: determinism vs. purposeful behavior, determinism vs. indeterminacy, environment dependent vs. environment independent behavior.

The last section of Sombart's book is dedicated to the distinction between economic philosophy including ethics, economic science and economics as an art (*Kunstlehre*). There are many interesting and controversial aspects to his part. We will only mention his ambivalence towards mainstream theorizing and focus solely on his example of the transfer problem (p. 301). He argues that the quantitative theoretical mainstream scheme is not helpful because there are so many disturbing psychological, political and other elements in reality that the lawlike assumptions cannot really work out, so that the disturbing noise, the deviation from the scheme is what VE is about. But this is a problematic argument because neither Keynes nor Ohlin doubted the noise and Sombart seems to accept the rational scheme (in fact there were diverse transfer problem theories) as a starting point. He seems to have no alternative frame of analysis except to ask for empirically realist investigations. This is not enough. Probably Sombart's VE has a different fundamental task in the division of scientific research. Indeed, on the last pages he comes back to the proper field of VE, as part of the humanities, with strong ties to philosophy and culture. Practical utility plays a minor role and the answering of the question of the cultural meaning and basic structure of the economy is at the centre. This could also be a hint for a certain division of labour between Sombart who focuses on intentional explications including the broader social and cultural horizon, while EE focuses more narrowly on the economic sphere and causal and functional modes of analysis.

As a result we see that the problems in Sombart's book on method depend on two polar dichotomies which cannot be fulfilled at the same time: on the one hand the commitment to value neutrality (p. 289) and the formulation of an all embracing economic approach vs. a very specific understanding of economics in the sense of VE, which depends on his image of man. On the other hand we find the polarity between realism and constructivism in his book.[18] This is not to deny the legitimacy and possibility of a hermeneutical *verstehens* approach (Peukert 1998). We only suggest that Sombart's importance for VE is less in the methodological (ambiguities) than in the applied field, for example his studies on the campagna or on modern capitalism. Therefore it cannot be recommended to EE to adopt Sombart's explicit methodology.

But the methodology practised by Sombart had been summarized by E. Troeltsch in his formal logic of history (1922, pp. 27–67). He explains that in historicism the category of individual totality is the basic unit. This may be groups, religious communities, nations, or whatever. They are unique and have a qualitative specificity. Their essential components are value and meaning configurations, which may also be unconscious. These constellations show up in history at random, as an expression of liberty in history. They have the element of creativity and novelty, in that their composing elements set free an evolution which is more than an addition of its parts. Another principle is the concept of irreversible time and finally the dependence of the researcher upon the contingencies of his or her time, in other words, whether we like it or not, research is value dependent. We see here that Sombart's historicism and EE have some parallels (irreversible time, variations at random, systematic self-transformations), but that meaningful cultural systems are the basic unit for historicism, but not for EE. They choose firms, technological trajectories and so on in a more naturalist perspective.

## MODERN CAPITALISM[19]

Compared with the first, the second edition of *Modern Capitalism* (1916–1927) has worked up more empirical material and more influences which lead to capitalism have been considered. In addition, the distinction between historical and empirical parts is made more clear (I, XIII).[20] But the basic approach and aim are the same: to write a general history of the common economic (but also, social, cultural and political) development of European societies since Carolingian times.[21] The method is distinctively historical-theoretical (I, XV), the exposition genetic-systematic. It is distinguished from normal historical research by the long time horizon (almost one thousand years, in fact a *longue durée*), the level of abstraction and inclusiveness (common properties of all European societies), and the ideal-type method of systemic analysis.[22] Compared with the usual research topics of EE this is a pretentious goal. There may be no example in the EE literature with such a broad subject.

The introduction deals with the familiar essentials of the need of subsistence, the social character of work, the dimensions of the environment, the people and their culture, the concept of the economic system and the three building blocks of spirit, technique and organization (I, 13–21). The subcategories of these are spelled out in the following way (see also 1930, pp. 206–7, and 1927, pp. 14–32): The difference in the dimension of the economic spirit between the Aristotelian principle of satisfaction according to need and the principle of profit (*Bedarfs- vs. Erwerbsprinzip*) is related to the purpose of economic activity: the satisfaction of specific needs or as much money as possible. The second spiritual category deals with the subjective mode of the choice of the means of the activity: traditional vs. rational, that is, the means are used because they are traditional and usual or they are constantly and critically checked. The third category, individualist vs. solidary, deals with the relations among people. It is the orientation of pure self-interest vs. the inclusion of the interests of the larger community. In EE we do not find the spirit (dichotomies) as a distinct research subject. This has to do with the fact that EE take the modern orientations (the *Erwerbs*principle, rational, and individualist) for granted because their research is concentrated on changes within modern capitalism and less with the transition to it.

The second broad category, the form or organization of the economy, is first divided into bound vs. free rules. Bound means orientation to supraindividual norms, free means that only specific actions are forbidden, and what is not forbidden is allowed. The next category is private vs. public orientation, in other words, is the economic structure based more on private or public enterprises (note: a private economy can also operate in a bound rule system). Democratic vs. aristocratic refers to the question whether many people are decision makers or if most people are decision takers (for instance in capitalism or medieval feudalism). The difference closed vs. dissolved concerns the question whether the economic units perform all economic activities themselves or not. Next is the economy of satisfaction according to need vs. the market economy (*Bedarfsdeckungs- vs. Verkehrswirtschaft*), it refers to the objective constellation (not the subjective spirit), in other words, whether goods are produced for the market or if the producing are also the consuming units (for example in socialism or self-sufficient systems). Satisfaction according to need can also prevail in exchange systems (such as the crafts system[23]). The last organizational category is individual vs. communal firms (in communal firms the working process is divided among the workers). The organizational aspects are also a central subject for EE. A difference can be seen in the fact that for Sombart there are no pattern assumptions of a general superiority or inferiority of specific forms (there exists for example a certain inferiority assumption of democratic forms in EE).

Finally, the principles of technique can be based empirically (practical, personal, historical knowledge) or scientifically (systematic search for empirical rules and laws). Next comes the difference between the stationary (techniques change only over long periods) vs. the evolutionary (permanent change). Last, we have the difference between organic vs. non-organic, that is, the dependence on living organisms (plant, animal, humans) and their growth processes or not. If they are not dependent they can be mechanical if production and transport do not depend on humans or animals as means but on mechanisms or chemisms. The procedure can also be inorganic, if respective

resources like coal, minerals and so on are used or inorganic power like electricity. For EE this classification will look very rudimentary and not very helpful and needs further distinction, especially as a taxonomy of technologies,
innovations and strategies is missing. Innovations can be classified as product
or process, incremental or radical, innovation strategies can be classified as
defensive, offensive, imitative, dependent, traditional or opportunist, and so
on. But we should not forget that Sombart had a secular perspective of system
changes in mind.

All in all, we arrive at three subdivisions of economic systems (spirit, organization, technique) and 12 polarities. One implication of Sombart's system is
that – as mentioned – it does not make sense to think about a general superiority of systems and their variables because the measuring rod depends on the
spiritual orientation.[24] It also does not make sense to think about 'welfare
effects' or 'efficiency' without specifying the system under consideration.
Efficiency considerations beyond specific economic systems (for instance the
hypothesis of a general superiority of private over public enterprises) are
meaningless for Sombart but not for EE because the natural measuring rod is
a growth perspective and the inducements to change, novelty and variation.

In principle, Sombart distinguished the following economic systems: the
early self-sufficient types of (1) the tribal societies, and (2) the peasant village
economy. To exemplify: in the village economy the principle of satisfaction
according to need, traditionalism and solidarism dominate; the technique is
empirical, stationary and organic. Next we have the aristocratic self-sufficient
types, (3) the *oikos* economy in ancient Greece and Rome, and (4) the manored
farm *(Fronhof)* economy in the European Middle Ages. Sombart mentions (5)
the craft system, and (6) the socialist type. It is opposed to (7) capitalism (see
the precise description of all types in 1927, pp. 20–30). For Sombart they
constitute different symbolic worlds with fundamentally diverging goals.
Compared with modern systems, the older ones can be seen in an EE perspective only as deficient modes of less novelty generating societies.

The systematic aspect in Sombart is the emphasis on the dominant
economic system in historical epochs and the thesis that history is composed
of clearly identifiable distinguishable systems (for example no one-way road
to reduce transaction costs in history, no self-interested individuals all the
time, not only more or less growth). Further and in agreement with his metaphysics, 'the basic message of this work is that a different economic spirit has
dominated at different times, and that it is the spirit that seeks its adequate
form and in this way creates economic organization' (I, p. 25). For EE this may
sound dubious because we here have a bounded rational actor who always
tries to explore growth and profit opportunities. In the same vein, the following arguments will also be received skeptically by EE.

Pre-capitalist societies follow the Aristotelian idea of nourishment

(*Nahrungsidee*, I, p. 34), a socially defined and limited standard of material living, the principle of the need of subsistence and the principle of satisfaction according to need (*Bedarfsdeckungsprinzip*), embedded in moral and legal rules and customs (I, p. 32). It dominates in all pre-capitalist societies and it is opposite, for example, to the spirit of capitalism (the profit principle). Another important feature is behavioural traditionalism. The prior early medieval economic system in primitive and rural Europe is the system of self-sufficiency (*Eigenwirtschaft*, I, pp. 45ff.) in the peasant village communities (democratic type) and on the manored farms (*Fronhöfe*, the aristocratic type) which were based on politically different forms of feudal dependency (including slavery). Until the 13th century (I, p. 87), both were oriented to the self-sufficient mode of production and the principle of satisfaction according to need. They were organized in a communitarian way in the case of the villages which distributed land collectively and shared the principle of satisfaction according to need.

Sombart's historically rich and multifaceted analysis is far from self-evident. Not only EE may and have asked: Did little villages and a village solidarity among the peasants really prevail, did they not try to make money? Did they accept a modest standard of living? Was trade absolutely underdeveloped? Did the landlords conform to the principle of satisfaction according to need (he mentions that they always wanted to have more means for ostentation, see I, pp. 62–3)? F. Oppenheimer (1929), a contemporary critic who doubted that markedly different spirits existed in history,[25] argues that the profit principle was no goal in itself for the capitalists, the function was to increase luxury, security, power, and so on (see also Harnisch 1928). Conversely, the medieval craftsman also searched for the best increase of his money earnings. This may not be chrematistic because the motive could be security for the family, and so forth.

Sombart's essential line of reasoning is to highlight the contrast to capitalism as an epoch-making difference. Therefore, he follows a 'primitivist' tradition,[26] that is, he is leaning on the left hand side of his dichotomies and tries to show – like K. Polanyi (1977) – that exchange is an historical but not an elementary category of economic behaviour which came up relatively tardily in economic history. So he explains that exchange activities began relatively late (between the tenth and 13th centuries), and were locally confined. In his absolutely unorthodox theory of the emergence of cities (I, Chapter 9, see the definition on p. 128) he argues that the founders of the few small consumption cities were kings and landlords who could buy the necessary agricultural foodstuffs of the environing agricultural land and pay with taxes or feudal interest revenues. This contradicts most theories on the subject[27] which say that the city is the basis of trade, production and the new spirit of freedom and enterprise which undermines self-sufficiency and feudal bonds (see also

Mackensen 1970, Schäfers et al. 1976, and Berndt 1977). Chapter 11 explains that the cities were ruled by the idea of community and economic self-sufficiency and the principle of satisfaction according to need. Again, EE may put some question marks after these assertions.

But the city saw the emergence of a new economic system or mode of production and economic idea: the craft system, that is, legally and economically independent, traditionally acting craftsmen (see I, p. 188 for the definition). They followed the principle of satisfaction according to need but in an exchange nexus. The craftsman produces for the market but the idea of 'craftsmanship' corresponds to the dominating principles in the peasant villages because the market is in every respect tamed and non-competitive by the solidary self-regulation of the guilds and cooperatives of the craftsmen (stable and fixed demand and prices). It is further oriented to traditional and non-profit principles and empirical-organic techniques. In the little craft shops the *Seele* principle could survive. The pride in creating unique products in which the personality of the craftsman is incorporated was a safeguard against cold economic rationalization. Also the little traders lived and operated in a crafts-like environment (I, p. 291). Sombart tries hard to substantiate this claim empirically against the many opposing views which may also be found among EE.

The second book deals with the historical foundations of modern capitalism. A completely new economic system and idea of the economy emerges (I, pp. 319ff.). It is an exchange economy, with two major groups, those who own the means of production and those who do not. The principles of economic rationalism (vs. traditionalism) and the principle of profit (vs. *Bedarfsdeckung)* begin to work. The capitalist enterprise is characterized, and the functions of the entrepreneur are contrasted (organizing, trading, calculating, I, pp. 322ff.). The essence of capitalism is the new spirit which came up from the deep underground of the European soul (I, pp. 327–33). 'It is the same spirit which creates the new state, the new religion, the new science, the new technique and in all this the new economic life. We know that it is a spirit which is secular and based in this world, a spirit which with enormous power can destroy natural formations, can destroy old bonds and old barriers; and with the same strength it can reconstruct new forms of life, both ingenious and artistic functional forms. It is the same spirit which since the declining Middle Ages has pulled man out of his quiet organically grown forms of love and community and which has propelled him onto an orbit of the restless search for self-determination and individual gain' (I, p. 327). In contrast to Sombart EE is much less ambivalent towards the new spirit which unleashes the search for novelty and variation; it may also doubt that it is really predominantly a spiritual and less a technological revolution which took place at the origin. EE may as well see problems with the sudden emergence of a new spirit as an 'uncaused cause'.

It is not only Sombart's feelings about the new spirit that are ambivalent, but also this spirit itself has a polar orientation which distinguishes Sombart's from Weber's spirit concept.' It is the spirit of Dr Faustus: the spirit of inner doubt and restlessness which has taken possession of the people . . . Shall we call it the quest for the sky that we see manifesting itself again and again. We can do this with a certain measure of truth because the goals have been pushed to the limit. All the natural standards of organic bonds have become wanting, restrictive and narrow . . . With this Faustian spirit a new spirit has found an alliance; this is the spirit which grants economic life a certain order, a measure of numerical exactitude, which has come about by defining purposes in exact terms; this is the spirit of the bourgeois . . . Where the entrepreneurial spirit wants to conquer and acquire, the bourgeois spirit wants to create order and protect' (I, pp. 327–9). It is interesting to see that the difference from Weber[28] who highlights the spirit of the bourgeois and of order is more in line with EE because the Faustian drive can be seen as the motivational background for constant change and a need for novelty.

In the following pages Sombart describes the modern state (I, pp. 334ff.) and its policies (currency, and trade policy, and so on) and the reasonable aspects of a mercantilist policy for capitalist dynamic development (I, pp. 362ff.). The next lengthy chapter traces the development of technique. A lot of inventions and discoveries were made until the 18th century but the assumption of *Seele* in nature was an impediment to 'progress'. The new spirit, the Faustian will to knowledge, the desire for making money, research for the military, and the transition from the empirical-traditional to the scientific-rational mode of investigation changed the way of technical research and implementation. In a secular perspective, Sombart's exposition is also valuable for EE to grasp the basic change in technological orientation. The finding and production of precious metals (I, pp. 513ff.) are considered as a major and very important 'accident'. The inflow of species eased the establishment of capitalism and Sombart investigates the relationship between specie inflow, prices and production over the centuries. His ambiguous statements concerning the quantity theory of money are interesting and – as we saw – typical of him (I, pp. 543–7). He sounds more orthodox than EE in these paragraphs.

In conformity with his primitivist position he explains the first phase of the concentration of fortunes (not capital) as a precondition of early accumulation not by referring to merchants and trade (I, pp. 608ff.) but to the increase of the land rents (I, p. 619) and the earnings in the mining industry. The third important source was simple robbery, including the plundering of the later colonies (I, pp. 668ff.), the reintroduction of slavery and colonial exploitation (robbery of natural resources and general environmental degradation, see I, p. 709).

He then turns to the demand side and analyses the demand shift in luxury goods (I, pp. 719ff.). The next topic is the labour market, the oversupply and misery of the new proletariat (including a critique of Marx's historical view on the first phase of accumulation). He discusses the problem that the new spirit was missing because the proletarians were 'natural', 'lazy' people with a clear idea of the virtues of leisure. They also held a sufficiency standard for income, a *Bedarfsdeckungsprinzip* (I, p. 807, compare E.P. Thompson), so that the mercantilist state was inventive in motivating them to work more (I, Chapter 54). These passages underline Sombart's conviction that there exists no transhistorical *homo oeconomicus* who tries to make the best (income) possible; an assumption which may be induced from EE.

The other side is the birth of the capitalist entrepreneurs, the class whose ingenuity, will power and creative imagination are the major force in the winds of change (I, p. 836). As strongly as Sombart points out the situation of the *misérables*, he emphasises the qualities and deeds of the emerging capitalist class. He distinguishes early merchant, conqueror and founder types (I, pp. 872ff.). He identifies the social groups which they mainly come from: foreigners, Jews, heretics and chrematistic landlords (I, Chapter 57). But they also come from former small merchants and other categories of citizens (I, Chapter 58). The first volume ends with these ideal type characterizations of types and descent groups of early entrepreneurs. In these paragraphs we really have one of the origins of EE and the Schumpeterian tradition because Sombart clearly and forcibly identifies the role of the entrepreneurs for variation, novelty and the introduction of new combinations (Schumpeter 1911).

Volume II analyses early capitalism in Europe in which the old and the new spirit and organizational forms existed side by side. Different principles fight for supremacy, it is a period of transition dated from the 15th to the middle of the 18th century. The first local beginnings can be found in the 13th century (Siena). The material driving forces are multifold: the emergence of nation states, the discovery of America, the religious persecutions, modern military systems (see the discussion in Wachtler 1985), the system of double accounting, and so on. The general evolutionary path is from traditionalism to rationalism, from a static to a dynamic economy, from organic to mechanical ways of human interaction (II, Chapters 1–3).

In less then 40 pages Sombart describes impressively the new spirit of early capitalism. It is a prime example of the *Verstehen* method in practice which Sombart handles in a masterly way (II, pp. 25–64). He contrasts the 'romantic' element in which force intrudes and where the roles of merchant, pirate and adventurer are hard to distinguish (II, p. 26). The oversea companies combined elements of medieval solidary communities and freebooting. The other part is the bourgeois, civilian aspect (*Bürgergeist*), including methodological, rational goal-oriented behaviour and an ideal of contract loyalty with religious and philosophical roots. Commenting on the debate on the just price Sombart shows that the principle of honourable and honest acquisition was more important than maximum gains and cutthroat competition. 'Even when conducting business, the individual would not get absorbed by the noise and ado of business affairs. He remained true to himself. He retained the dignity of an independent man who will not compromise his honour to personal gain. In trade and commerce, personal pride remained dominant' (II, p. 62). Sombart shows here that self-interest and opportunism and the (organizational) problems of hold-ups, moral selection and so forth which are discussed in the asset-specificity and measurement-cost literature are not universal in capitalism. He demonstrates that in early capitalism business and morals intermingled so that self-interest seeking with guile may not have been the dominant character trait.

Sombart now comes to the organizational aspect of his classification. He discusses the mixed and transitory forms of firm organizations (like the single event corporations) and then analyses the modern capitalist firm, that is, the division of the personal and business, the rationalization of production, the rationale of making profit, and so on. His main example for the tendencies of objectification and mechanization is the history of double entry bookkeeping since Pacioli. In Chapter 11 he delineates the capitalist organizational forms (such as general partnerships). These parts of the book may also be found in contributions of the EE literature. But also in these detailed historical and empirical descriptions the emphasis is on cultural economics, such as when he shows that joint stock companies are alien to the spirit of early capitalism (II, p. 162). After a short digression on state companies he comes to the second main part of the book on the extension of the market due to population increases, and political and technical changes (Chapter 13). The new big armies and luxury demand are influences from the demand side (Chapter 14) which is in general less important then the changes on the supply side in Sombart's investigations.

He further describes the erratic–traditional modes of more or less subjective price setting, which depended on conventions, administrative influences, transport and informational obstacles. In a lengthy part (II, pp. 229–418) he describes the technical improvements in transport, travelling, the mail system and business publications which can also be found in EE literature. More and more the law of one price was effective as a result of the depersonalization and mechanization of the price setting process by, for example, institutionalized auctions and stock exchanges (Chapter 15). The same tendency holds good for the distribution of commodities from door-to-door salesmen to established regular markets, organized chains of distribution (II, p. 441), and the modes of payment (II, pp. 513ff.).

The modern business cycle did not exist, there were many crises but no rhythm, the boom phase is missing due to the dependency on organic techniques and the lack of fixed capital. The crises are simple sales crises

(Chapter 16). He then describes the mostly rural population. Agriculture remained self-sufficient and traditional between 800 and 1800, the trades in towns remained craft oriented (II, pp. 650–81). But changes took place in the crafts guild systems because the profit motive invaded the old system which degenerated and a polarization between master and journeyman occurred. But Sombart adds: not before the 19th century (II, pp. 692–3). Another major change refers to the new organizational forms of production, firms, manufactories, the putting out system and big industry (II, pp. 730ff.; for the changes from *Seele* to *Geist* see for example II, pp. 783 and 787). Later he discusses their advantages compared with the crafts system (mass production, uniformity and promptness of delivery, for example for the military, see II, pp. 841–86). Against Marx he argues that firms and manufactories went side by side for a long time and he describes their different types, the division of labour, the work process, and new techniques in specific branches. The craft system could also not adapt due to its particular spirit (II, p. 887) which again strengthens his emphasis on spirit in contrast to EE. After discussing locational aspects (immobilization and decentralization, see also II, pp. 901–6), he comes to the slowly changing working conditions.

He defines the ideal-type scheme of the capitalist-worker relationship. The conditions are:

> 1.   A pure capitalist entrepreneurship is confronted by wage earners without any property or any other means of subsistence; 2.   on both sides there is a determined capitalist economic spirit: the profit principle and the principle of economic rationality are shared both by the entrepreneur and the wage labourer. This implies that on both sides there is a will and determination to organize the labour contract with the view to maximize a) profits and b) wages; . . . 3.   the labour relationship rests on a free contract and is based on the strict contractual quid pro quo . . . The purposes that follow from this economic spirit can best be realized with: a) short term; b) money-based labour contracts; . . . 4.   labour is being utilized without any regard to the personal circumstances of the laborer (II, pp. 811–12).

From Sombart's point of view, the work contracts (short-term, outsourcing, and so on) and rationalized production processes of turbo capitalism correspond with the ideal type of capitalism compared with typical contracts in the social market economies (long-term, and so forth), and socially regulated working conditions. He goes on to summarize the real social position of the workers, their mentality, the content of the contracts in early capitalism, the organization of labour in the factories, and child and women labour (II, pp. 813ff.).[29] The difference from EE literature is that he somehow organizes the description from the viewpoint of labour, whereas EE usually chooses the perspective of the entrepreneurs.

Sombart then turns to the economic macro process. The first part describes mercantilist theory as a reasonable concept for practical policy which will surely not find approval by EE or public choice theorists (see Ekelund and Tollison 1981). Against the static-mechanical exchange paradigm of the British (he could not suppress some awkward chauvinist remarks here) mercantilist theory is a dynamic-organic theory of production with active idealism. This part is an original and informative digression on the history of economic thought (II, pp. 913ff.). Next come the changes in international economic relations (II, pp. 943ff.), and trade balances, balances of payments, and so on are surveyed. Again he gives a primitivist account, he asserts that only (and mainly consumption) goods in excess supply in the countries and almost no means of production are traded. The main component is colonial goods (II, pp. 1029, and 1036). In EE literature we would expect a stronger leaning to a modernist view. He further describes the new stratification of early capitalist societies, its old and new classes and the estates, including the new middle class and the new power of money (bourgeoisie) besides the old powers of kings and feudal lords (II, pp. 1085ff.). The development of economic forces in early capitalism took place in the national dimension, this immensely increased the power of the nation states (Chapter 65). Higher taxes were a natural result of higher national income, but also due to increased productivity (for the reasons see II, p. 1059) which nevertheless had been slowed down by wars, the influence of the Church, psychological factors, and transport conditions. For Sombart the traditional industrial code was no important impediment. This opinion has surely to do with the fact that the existence of markets is not an essential feature for him as a driving force for increased productivity because he holds the industrial and not the market paradigm (see Boltanski and Thévenot 1991) which is more at the centre of EE as we have seen above.

Two aspects are salient at the end of the second book. The first is his summary statement on the beginning of mechanization, depersonalization, banalization, and contractualization of society in the tradition of his cultural economics (II, pp. 1076–84). The second is his emphasis on the fundamental ecological break at the end of early capitalism which could have brought the new development to an early end: the overuse of wood as raw material, combustible and general organic source of energy since the early Middle Ages and its severe shortage since the 16th century which escalated in the 18th century (II, 1137ff.; see also Sieferle 1982). Both aspects play an important role in the EE discourse. Sombart's analysis testifies, to a high level of ecological consciousness long before a modest recognition of the natural restraints of capitalism has set in.

Four features are outstanding in Sombart's outline so far: first the rich empirical details, second the arrangement according to his threefold distinction, third his emphasis on cultural economics ('rationalization')[30] and fourth his primitivist bias.[31] He deviates from EE in his broad analysis by his threefold classification, his critical emphasis on cultural economics and his primitivist bias. The references for his investigation were scientific literature of all kinds, statistical investigations (but no regression analysis or econometrics), monographs, personal observations, statements of accounts, biographies, literature, laws and official declarations, travel reports, and so forth (see, for example, II, pp. 421–35). While not using formal methods proper, the dominant methodological strategy in EE today, Sombart shows how many interesting insights can be gained by his empirical strategy, and that EE may consider broadening its horizon in method.

Volume III which was first published in 1927 captures the phase of high capitalism from 1760 to 1914 when capitalism dominated all other partial economic systems. In contrast to EE, it is a unique and strange historical episode for him. He thought that after the First World War capitalism would never recover in full again (an assertion which may be doubted today). The driving force is the search for profit, for Sombart an uneconomic and in some sense irrational goal because it has nothing to do with the need of subsistence (*Unterhaltsfürsorge*) as such.[32] In the preface, he further mentions how much he owes to Marx (despite his book on proletarian socialism). But Marx lived in the early stages of capitalism so that it is no surprise that he made wrong predictions and was a cultural optimist. In Sombart's view, capitalism has produced nothing valuable in the cultural sphere. Capitalism should be rejected today (III, p. xxi). Sombart here makes a value judgment which is opposite to the EE view. EE would also stress the functional character of extra profit and temporary monopolies as a motivational power to innovate.

Like Schumpeter (for a comparison see Chaloupek 1995b) and against Marx he stresses that 'capital' is not the major driving force but human beings and their motives, in capitalism especially the entrepreneurs (III, Chapter 1). He stresses again the intentional instead of the causal or functional mode of analysis. But he also describes the function of the differentiation from the ownership of the means of production, and the different types (the merchant, financial and the expert type). He stresses the democratization of their recruitment, disentangles their motives (vanity, power, money, drive for activity, and so on, but he also mentions the sense of responsibility, see III, p. 36). He highlights the mixture of bourgeois rationality and calculation and the Faustian drive for infinity (III, pp. 14–23). The spiritual difference from early capitalism lies in the disembeddedness and independence of the capitalist spirit and profit motive from religion, customs, family, and so forth. Now a spirit of progress, the dominance of the achievement values, love for the business (and cultural ignorance), and the profit motive take the lead (Buss 1995, pp. 21–2). Without using their terminology, he comes close to the Coase, Williamson et al. tradition. Transpersonal and non-economic value commitments decline, the behavioural mode of self-interest (seeking with guile) comes to the fore, holdup and moral hazard problems consequentially emerge.

In a very short part he deals with the now much less powerful modern state. It comprises an ambiguous composition of liberal principles and political power aspects. The modern state is secular, individualist, and has to recognize the interests of capital (taxes). Germany has the bureaucratic-legal style (III, p. 57). The general exterior policy is despite all liberal phraseology neo-mercantilist. Imperialism plays a role but the origins are in the political sphere. Chapter 7 deals with the changes in the technical domain from a very general but impressive perspective. The Faustian motive and rational empirical research are now combined with the disenchantment of nature as a precondition. Applying his basic dichotomies of technique, the fundamental change lies in the scientific and rational character, which substitutes for the empirical and traditional mode. Discoveries are an essential component for economic growth. Modern man lives in a technical social atmosphere where everything technical is admired. Innovations and inventions are imposed, the final consumer is seen as a passive innovation taker (III, p. 95). In contrast to EE studies, he offers a history of technological change in a cultural and universal historical framework which complements EE.

Due to the inorganic nature of modern technical progress, an emancipation from the boundaries of organic nature takes place. The coke procedure is a major precondition and basis of modern capitalism. We see that Sombart stresses once again cultural economics but at the same time does not neglect the material preconditions of change at all. In earlier times, man lived from the yearly income of solar energy. 'And all of a sudden mankind had at its disposal the energies of the sun as treasures in the interior of the earth which had been accumulated there over millions of years through radiation down from the sun. A wealth had been found which mankind was not able to consume through the inventions of modern technology . . . We now live in an age in which mankind can consume its wealth in energies and substances and can in this way show off an unheard of glitter and wealth. What we call high capitalism is easily explained in the sudden increase in the wealth of mankind . . . By breaking the piggybank of earth and spending with both hands he succeeded in showing off an unheard of wealth' (III, pp. 122, and 272). Efficient allocation and the markets are not for Sombart the essential origin of wealth, but the exploitation of the earth, formulated in a neo-physiocratic and deep ecological way (compare Georgescu-Roegen 1971; on the importance of minerals and inorganic production techniques, and the extinction of species see for example III, pp. 263–8). It is distinguished from EE by the very critical connotations of this mega-trajectory in that Sombart castigates this process not (only) as a technological advance but as simple exploitation and he plays down the role of optimal or satisficing allocation by the market mechanism. According to Sombart, the richness of our society is based on theft.

The second main part deals with the structure of capital, its different types, like money capital, the mobilization of the commodity world (increase in goods, transport and so on, which also depended on the state infrastructure), and the essential function of a rationalized credit system for an expanding economy. Modern credit increased the depersonalization, denaturalization and minute classification of (economic) life (*Dekonkretisierung,* see the list in III, p. 222). All these aspects are discussed in a descriptive, taxonomic and empirical way (III, pp. 127–303), in other words he applies Nelson's and Winter's appreciative mode of theorizing but in contrast to them with a strong emphasis on culture economics. Sombart does not include the early debates on capital theory and monetary theory, probably a weakness in his project to describe modern capitalism. It is at least an omission in the light of his book on method (1930) which argued that *verstehende* economics should include relevant laws and insights of *ordnende* economics.

He asks next where the labour force came from and distinguishes and criticizes naturalist, economic, and sociological hypotheses (see III, pp. 304ff.). He stresses first the importance of forced labour (coloured slavery, III, p. 325), second the free excess population due to the dissolution of the old village communities and the agrarian reform, and third the simple increase of the population (III, p. 354). He also describes the new personality and behavioural ideal of the man in town (III, p. 348). Before discussing the internal and external distribution (III, pp. 470ff.), he highlights the necessity and ways to socialize the workers into the new spirit (Chapter 26). 'The new economic order needed such partial men bereft of their personality, reduced to spirit, happy and able to function as tiny wheels in a big and complicated clockwork' (III, p. 424). Force, drill, the religious spirit (Weber), the educational force of machine work, and so forth are presented. This part resembles as mentioned the research of E.P. Thompson, but also of Foucault and for example Bourdieu and their matrices of discipline. It further shows that for Sombart cultural economics not only means the harmonious socialization and functioning of norms but that culture also may have a power and force component. Let us notice again that his view from below and his interest in the necessary changes of mental attitudes is not thematic in EE.

It is surprising that Sombart calls the capacity of markets to regulate the economic activities by price setting through supply and demand a wonder (III, p. 519). Specific markets can be analysed according to the spirit, organization and technique scheme (III, p. 527). Sombart mentions the laws of price: supply and demand determine prices, price determines supply and demand, purchasing power has an autonomous influence on prices (see also his description of the mechanical emergence of an average price at the stock exchange as an example of the rationalization of price setting, III, p. 667). Also for the labour market the price laws hold, but it is only 'as-if', because labour is no commodity. On commodity markets the price is determined by the production costs

(III, p. 529). 'Artificial' intervention in the free markets can take place,for example by the state (taxes, but also tariffs, patents, laws, market orders, social security, and so on), which influences the free actions of the market participants. It is remarkable that Sombart's 'price theory' is less then elementary. He does not consider the 'theoretical' literature at all (see also the missing literature in the part on competition, III, pp. 551–3). As already mentioned at least as an additional aspect an evolutionary view of market dynamics would better fit into his general view of a discontinuous process of change over time. Maybe this is the theoretical missing link in his third volume so that he only comes back to the neoclassical standard static description of the function of markets and takes it as a historical fact.

Second he accepts the distinction between the free market as such in which intervention takes place. It would have been more in line with his general theoretical orientation to develop a concept of markets as instituted processes in the tradition of old institutionalism (see for example Hodgson 1988). It is a major weakness that Sombart never developed even a rudimentary alternative, institutional price and market theory. Today we can rely here on the institutional variant of EE to go beyond the free market-intervention simplifications (see also Samuels et al. 1994).

He goes on to discuss the influences on markets by labour (trade unions) and capitalist institutions (such as cartels, which are hereinafter discussed as legitimate and economically beneficial, see III, pp. 696–7). Later he also deals with the protection against risk (for example, insurance, Chapter 43). He distinguishes three forms of competition (Chapter 34): quality, surrogate and forced competition. Competition by quality (*Leistungskonkurrenz*) is acceptable, but it is an overvalued and secondary driving force of capitalism (III, p. 558). A surrogate means is advertisement, which he strongly rejects because it fools the customer with wrong or arbitrary nonsense (III, p. 559). This was often criticized as cultural elitism in Sombart. Forced competition means cutthroat competition to undermine competition and to establish monopolies. Technologically induced temporary monopolies as a result of innovative initiative are missing as a distinct category in Sombart's classification, but can be seen as a form of the competition of quality. In a later chapter he describes the rationalization of markets in the sense of greater uniformity and size (Chapter 36, and III, pp. 637ff.) which also depended on better transport conditions (III, p. 650). Speculation in the real and the monetary sphere has no productive function, it expresses the instinct for play (III, p. 664). Later he describes the joint stock companies (and their interdependent networks and the conglomeration of power in some few hands) as functionally and spiritually the best fit with high capitalism (III, pp. 712–47, see also Chapters 48, 49, and 50). He also subtly describes the spirit of high capitalist competition (III, p. 557).

Besides having discussed demand, and forms of firms (Chapters 31, 33, and

37), he delineates the emergence of the real, rhythmical, expansionary business cycle since 1825 (Chapter 35). The more recent stabilization of cycles is the first sign of capitalism becoming old (Chapter 45). Cyclical expansions are possible due to the inorganic production of goods. Slumps are the result of the disproportion between the expansion in the organic and the limits of expansion in the non-organic production spheres.[33] His cultural economics is manifest in his depiction of the spirit of demand (restlessness, nervousness, need for constant change, such as in fashion), its uniformization and would-be elegance (III, pp. 604–5, and 625–7). This corresponds with the depersonalization and *Vergeistung* of transactions, dominated by 'contractual forms in which the individual contracting partner enters into a system of objective conditions which rule the relationship from the very start, a relationship which he can use for his personal ends like a mechanism ... where there is no relationship between soul and soul but where the relationship is only realized through the mediation of an abstract legal concept' (III, p. 657). *Geist* here only appears in the self-alienated version and is defined as follows.

> The spirit is ... immaterial, what is not soul. Spirit leads its existence of its own without being alive. The soul is always tied to life, the soul of a being is tied to this being's life. The soul of a human being is bound to the life of this man. Spiritualization is then the process of moving from the soul to the spirit, to isolate and make objective the processes of the soul, a sort of 'reification'. (III, p. 895)

The *Geist* component should reduce costs, render possible accountability, and better control of the work force (III, pp. 925–6).

He rejects Marx's thesis of allover concentration, his empirical results show that concentration varies according to branches and depends on the optimal size of the firms (which hinges on production, distribution, and finance criteria, see III, p. 517). In most branches (except agriculture) the average size increased but only in very few branches have some big corporations extinguished small and middle sized firms; mergers are often due to prestige activities of managers (III, pp. 881ff.). Like EE Sombart does not hold the thesis of a general drift towards a specific market form, such as oligopolies, in most key branches. He comes back to the tendency of the abstraction of principles and rules, one example for these tendencies being the introduction of business economics (III, pp. 886ff.).

In the last part Sombart restates his aim to delineate the spiritual European background of the archetype of this wondrous greatest product of the civilized world called capitalism. It made it possible, 'to feed, cloth, and house a population which grew by the hundreds of millions, also ultimately to give them jewellery and fashion and to amuse them every night' (III, p. 952). We feel again his cryptic attitude and his difference from EE. He then asks how the older economic systems will fare. Self-sufficient economic structures still persist well. The crafts made up half of the working population, but they changed and most craftsmen became small bourgeois entrepreneurs (III, pp. 957 and 963).[34] The peasants were still holding a respectable margin of GDP but their average living conditions were depressed and the competitive spirit crept in (III, pp. 969–71). The cooperative system, defined as an association of non-wealthy economic subjects working to improve their economic situation and performance by large-scale enterprise (III, p. 896), differed in strength in different countries and might have had a great future, but it performed below its potential (III, p. 998). The public and semi-public sector was strong at Sombart's time but he thought that its future was open (III, p. 999). The last Chapter 60, on the future will be discussed in the next paragraph.

Sombart's third volume had been expected with much interest. Many readers were disappointed. There is no doubt that the book is less structured than the other two volumes and that sometimes a certain exhaustion can be felt. The spheres of law and politics are mostly missing. Sombart does not present an alternative theory of markets, competition and prices. Models and stylized fact theories of EE should have been presented. It is nevertheless one of the most impressive contributions to the social sciences where the broadness of the presentation, the application of his systems approach and his excellent application of cultural economics are concerned. This can be seen as the missing element in present day EE. Sombart was an applied methodological radical: he rejects pure theory in principle and *homo oeconomicus* as a universal phenomenon even on the level of ideal types (compare Weber). Not rational action but concepts of mind (spirit) are at the centre, historical-theoretical economics should replace mainstream economics, evolution is not Darwinist or economically rational but governed by idiosyncratic mentalities (see for these pattern variables Gislain and Steiner 1995). This demarcates common viewpoints with EE but also differences (which are summarized below).

## SOMBART AND EVOLUTIONARY ECONOMICS ON THE FUTURE

We will concentrate on four texts to summarize Sombart's discussion of the future (1916–1927, Chapter 60; 1928; 1932; 1934, pp. 160ff., see also Chaloupek 1994a, and 1996). In the last chapter of *Modern Capitalism* (III, Chapter 60), Sombart predicts the general persistence of the capitalist system and an adding of new and different economic systems, so that corporations, crafts, cooperatives, mixed public–private organizations, peasants, and other self-sufficient production systems will exist side by side. Sombart thought that the capitalist elements will lose their preponderance. But there will be no shortage of energy and many mouths have to be fed. EE also believes in the persistence of the capitalist system, but less so in a more mixed economy; the market system prevails although there are usually no general hypotheses in the literature.

Further, capitalism will be more regulated by the state, subdued to normative ideas, and it will become more quiet, less turbulent, adult. Big firms will become ponderous machines (III, pp. 1012–13). Non-capitalist economic system elements will increase which implies a planning economic element which supersedes the profit principle. For the human condition, he sees no great difference in a stabilized capitalism or a rationalized socialism. The difference is, whether the economic systems in which the *Seele* element rules (self-sufficiency, farming, and handicraft) will have a chance in the future (III, pp. 1016–17). As we saw, the distinction between *Seele* and *Geist* and their dialectics plays no role in EE. But for EE the difference between socialism and a market system is essential, because novelty and entrepreneurial innovations do not take place in socialism or at least at a much slower rate as an impediment to growth and new products.

Inner colonization and the increase of the peasantry seems inevitable because the former colonies are or will become independent and so the cheap supply of foodstuff will end. His (wrong) estimate was, that the peasantry will increase significantly as a share of the population and GDP. He holds further, that farming can never be totally rationalized (*vergeistet*). Not only EE will wonder today how wrong Sombart was with this prognosis.

In his paper for the meeting of the *Verein* in Zurich on the changes of capitalism, Sombart (1928) confirms the main points of his view: the emancipation of the developing countries, the necessary increase of agriculture, the intensification of regulation and rationalization, the decrease of entrepreneurship, and the plurality of economic systems. His discussion is organized around the classification of changes in spirit, organization and technique, in other words the *Gestaltidee* (1930, pp. 206–7) of economic systems. We can only mention the main points here. He emphasizes that the developing countries in Asia and Africa will further advance but that the West has not enough capital to invest because capital accumulation will decline. The reasons are a stagnant population in the developed countries, and the decrease of the productivity of labour. He puts an emphasis on the concentration of capital and cartels (1928, p. 248), and the dominance of finance capital. The workers will live like public servants (fixed working hours, administered wages, see III, p. 251). For Sombart, capitalism becomes older, it is – since the war – in the season of fall, he calls it late capitalism. Studies in the tradition of EE and common knowledge show that capitalism has experienced a growing rate of innovations and the introduction of novelty and discontinuous change.

The next text is about the future of capitalism (1932). Now Sombart does not only ask how the future looks but how it should be shaped actively, which is a problem of will (1932, p. 394). He points out the plurality of systems, concentration, *Vergeistung,* administered prices by cartels and bargaining, and so forth. Then he proposes a planned economy but not the abolition of private property. It should be uniform planning on the national level but with many degrees of freedom, such as in the sphere of consumption, with a multitude of different economic systems and spheres and free competition. But also partial socialization is considered and other types of influence like subsidies, taxes, and so on (1932, p. 409). He actively supports autarky in the sense of a strictly controlled and diminished foreign trade and some import substitution. Further he asks for a partial return to an agrarian state (*Reagrarisierung*, 1932, pp. 415–17). Forty per cent of the population should work in the only moderately mechanized farming sector. To realize this programme of fundamental reform all depends for Sombart on the spiritual willingness of the population to realize an alternative economic style (1932, p. 418).

With this ideal Sombart is in sharp contrast to EE which supports the division of labour, open markets, free competition and a higher pace of innovation. Sombart favours a slowdown and control of innovative activity and a control of market processes. For him, growth and new combinations are not essential for a good society.

Practically, he formulated a strategy against unemployment which had been added to the full employment plan of the *Studiengesellschaft für Geld- und Kreditwirtschaft* for the German chancellor of the *Reich* in August 1932 (see Backhaus 1989, pp. 94–8). Sombart supported bilateral trade relations and an immediate massive deficit financed infrastructure employment programme by the state. The money should be strictly reserved for investments to augment the productive capacities in the organic part of the economy (where Sombart typically assumed the bottleneck to be). He proposed the implementation of peasant villages and agricultural cooperatives, drainage, canals, a certain rationalization of agricultural production (for example the consolidation of farmland), and so forth. We see here the Keynesian aspect of Sombart's thinking besides the institutional and the Schumpeterian component which he also shares with EE. At this time he did not believe in the self-regulating capacity of the market processes. But his point is not so much the working of the multiplier but the absorption of the workforce to solve the problem of bottlenecks and to let people live in vitally satisfying environmental conditions.

Further he supported smallholder do-it-yourself villages to further strengthen the self-sufficient mode of production. We see here a fundamental difference from EE which does not aim at a modest technology and the preservation of more natural surroundings but which values positively the introduction of more and better technological equipment. He rejected 'luxurious highway projects'. All these measures would absorb the unemployed, reduce the bottlenecks and reenergize economic activity. These or similar plans were not realized. When Hitler won the elections in 1934, the highway and rearmament variant was chosen. In 1939 the Germans were not living a peaceful life near to nature, but went to war.

Some points of Sombart's theoretical and practical ideas are repeated and specified in his *Deutscher Sozialismus* (1934, pp. 244ff.). Technical development should be tamed and controlled by a patent agency which decides according to the public interest. A more simple life style and the creation of peasant communities are his ideal. The opulence and sophistication of goods, too many cars, planes and noise are condemned. He pleads for a drastic reduction of the productive and transport superstructure of society and the creation of natural free areas where a simple and natural life is still possible. The strengthening of the middle class, the peasants, the self-sufficient producers and the craftsmen is proposed. A number of branches ripe for socialization are enumerated, among them the great banks, and transport (1934, pp. 300–1). Sombart does not look for the establishment of mechanisms for generating and selecting variation as EE does but he opts for intervention to realize a concrete picture of society. EE is concerned with processes, Sombart with specific outcomes. He wants to improve society by blocking and channeling the potential to change. Not a spontaneous order but an ordered value system was his goal.

Sombart's prognosis of calm late capitalism has proven more or less wrong (especially in the last years). But we should note that for Sombart no objective laws exist, so everything depends finally on the free will of the economic actors. His prediction that regulation of capitalism will increase and that a plurality of economic systems will coexist side by side (craft system, capitalist firms, and so on) has some supporting evidence.

Despite all criticism, in our view Sombart's systems approach still has relevance. Countries in transition like China or Malaysia can be analysed in an encompassing way with his classification. In general what is missing today are interdisciplinary analyses which overcome the specialization of professions and disciplines. Another impressive point in Sombart is his formulation of strong hypotheses, for example on the influence of the Jews on capitalism (1911). Even if he overstated his cases, they were the starting point of highly relevant debates and what Popper would have liked: strong theses with a high potential of falsification.

In our view Sombart's primitivism is another convincing point against the tide (including some EE literature): because we live in a capitalist society, its origins and behavioural codes are retrospectively assumed to have existed since the dawn of man and will persist forever. Sombart's assumption of clearly distinct systems and styles includes the possibility that there may never be an end of history and that we will see another major distinct system in the future (based again on the principle of satisfaction according to need?). His work is also a counterpoint against the new orthodoxy in modern economic and evolutionary historical research, not only in cliometrics, only to be interested in the forces of growth and its impediments in a transaction costs, adaptive flexibility and property rights framework. From that perspective, capitalism and non-attenuated private property are the yardstick of success and failure in a historical unilateral perspective in which world history converges on capitalism. For Sombart, capitalism was more a strange and exceptional surprise. In the EE framework, alternatives to a high powered change and novelty system are not really conceivable in a meaningful way.

Sombart also posits another image of man in his anthropology against the opportunist pleasure and pain self-interested utility maximizer, our beloved *homo oeconomicus* who can also be found in the EE literature. A further point concerns his basic criticism of capitalist society, whereas today we have an almost uniform approval which sometimes seems to come close to ideological legitimization and where the EE literature usually only analyses the forces which enable technical change and does not reflect on the possible negative side effects in the political, social and cultural sphere.

Another aspect worth mentioning is his ecological and energy component (wood, coke, the exploitation of minerals, and so on), the plundering of nature as a precondition of capitalism. Today we have the economics of the environment as a clearly separated, and often highly formalized field of research. For Sombart, the ecological dimension has to be taken into consideration in *any* consideration of capitalist development. His critical remarks are more true than ever, the extinction of species increases, the hothouse effect leads among other things to the melting of the Arctic ice. The visible end of fossil energy (oil) is taken notice of in the oil producing countries (for instance in the Emirates). Will solar energy be accompanied by a completely different economic style? Henceforth the ecological dimension and its secular importance is not a major critical topic in the EE literature. The question of a new energy technological trajectory does not take into consideration the cultural aspects of such a change.

A certain principle of autarchy is discussed in the debate on the EU where some support a certain economic closure to hold environmental and social standards and fight against social and environmental dumping and beggar-my-neighbour policies. Sombart's support of a stronger agrarian basis and a careful inner colonization could certainly find an open ear in the green, back-to-nature movement. Again, the problems of social and ecological dumping play no important role in the EE writings.

Sombart's cultural criticism, which has been mostly left out of this chapter, seems to be relevant today.[35] There is an extensive and critical recent debate on the rationalization of all aspects of human life, including politics, in the social sciences.[36] It surely grasps an element of modern life. Whether rationalization in the sense of Sombart is the unequivocal tendency in modern firms and business relations may nevertheless be doubted. But his emphasis on the unnatural loss of *Seele* which was an often neglected but existing component of human interaction in big organizations (state bureaucracies, firms, and so on) and the relative degeneration of *Gemeinschafts*structures in them in the last years due to rationalizations is one major distinguishing criterion in the definition of postmodernity in the original and creative approach of Galtung on the costs of modernization (1997, pp. 43–92).

It can be argued that Sombart's negative vision of capitalism and the essence of it came genuinely to the fore only after the breakdown of the so-called socialist countries and in the process of the globalization of economies, in other words a certain income polarization in society, the inferiority of politics, the increasing abstraction of the money economy with joint stock speculation as the new pop culture, the decline of trust, the *Auto*-mobilization and commercialization in all parts of the world, the depersonalization of the work process due to computers, the decline of natural rhythms, the reduction and subjugation of all human interactions to the individual revenue maximizing principle, and so on. Sombart brings to light side-effects of modern innovative capitalism which are usually ignored in the EE literature but which seem necessary to consider to get a more complete picture of the benefits and costs of technological change.

In a very interesting and informative book on global capitalism by Luttwak, consultant and Senior Fellow at the Center for Strategic and International Studies in Washington DC, we read:

> (T)he logic of turbo-capitalism is that nothing should stand in the way of economic efficiency, neither obstructive government regulations nor traditional habits, neither entrenched interests nor feelings of solidarity for the less fortunate, neither arbitrary privileges nor the normal human desire for stability . . . The human consequences of turbo-capitalism are both liberating and profoundly disorienting. The loss of individual authenticity that Friedrich Nietzsche predicted is now upon us in full force. This process of depersonalization is visibly complete in the modern television politician. (1999, pp. 222 and 224)

Like Sennett, Bellah and others Luttwak (who does not know Sombart)[37] meticulously describes how the 'revenue-maximizing spectacle' intrudes upon all spheres of social life, the family, sports, medicine, and firms (for Germany see on a more journalistic level Kurz 1999). All these authors conform with Marx and Sombart in saying that capitalism is unique in history, that it is the fundamental shaping force in society and that it has non-acceptable social, political, cultural and ecological costs.

We arrive at the paradox that Sombart may be right because he was wrong. His diagnosis of the end of high capitalism and its further bastardization after

1914, the low impact of technological improvements in the confines of the coke paradigm, the necessary decrease of foreign trade and productivity, and so on were obviously wrong predictions in the longer run (but not where the available data of his time were concerned). But with the description of the pure logic of what he called capitalism and its consequences, including the cultural sphere, was he so wrong? Does his negative vision not at least complement the positive vista of EE and is it not in so far conducive to scientific truth?

A first step in a forward looking direction and application of Sombart was presented by Boltanski and Chiapello (1999).[38] In the conscious tradition of Weber and Sombart their book analyses the third ideological configuration of the capitalist spirit which emerged in the 1980s. The empirical basis of their description is the hermeneutical comparison of some 60 books of the managerial literature in the 1990s. The key element is what they call the metaphysics of the network pattern, including the positive judgment of adaptation, change, flexibility, teamwork, communication, creativity, and so on. This necessitates a charming, autonomous, flexible, communicative, opportunist and light (vis-à-vis passions and values) character and a permanent mental radar screening of the environment. Besides the social (unemployment, income polarity), their cultural critique formulates the personal and mental problems of the flexible networker, his anxiety to be disconnected (handymania), the exhaustion due to forced autonomy, the divide between flexible adaptation and the need for authenticity. The Sombart tradition here complements EE in that it asks which changes take place in the so-called subjective or mental attitude factor.

Sombart's relevance today could lie in the application of his approach to an analysis of the third industrial revolution with the information techniques as the material basis, after the breakdown of capitalism, the acceleration of globalization and deregulation; an analysis including all of Sombart's dimensions (the new economics business cycle, the organization and restructuring of international firms, the empirical distribution of capital flows, the exhaustion of non-renewable resources, and so on) under the guidance of his spirit, organization, technique systems idea with the strong emphasis on changes of 'spirit' as the ultimate driving force. This could be a starting point for further research in the Sombart tradition and complement and enlarge the more micro or meso focus of EE research.

Let us conclude. Compared with Sombart's historicism the evolutionary research programme is relatively young. As we mentioned, a physical, a biological-functional and an intentional concept as in other social sciences are in use. Nevertheless, we found some parallels between the two: both are concerned with the self-transformation of structural patterns and Sombart influenced Schumpeter in his view of the entrepreneur. The use of non-linear stochastic differential equations leads to a common perspective of irreversible processes in time. History matters (increasing returns, lock-ins and so forth) and is to some degree unpredictable. Some formal concepts, for example in chaos theory, have the paradoxical implication that the more determined and dependent on initial conditions they are the more they behave as if they were undetermined. Both hold that unique equilibria are very rare or nonexistent (multiple equilibria and so on).

Both are in principled disagreement with neoclassical economics and the mechanical model (but see the qualifications in the part on Sombart's method). A major difference lies in Sombart's rejection of the market liberal view of the market as a self-regulating system. In contrast, he supports state intervention, mixed economies and even a planning system as probable and desirable. They can also generate potential to change and improve society and may be necessary to solve lock-in problems. Another difference consists in the focus on cultural meaning systems in Sombart, and the focus on the endogenous permanent technical progress in EE. On the other hand, rules, norms and institutions play an indispensable role in EE. But Sombart puts meaningful cultural symbol systems at the centre whereas March and Simon's model of bounded rationality concentrates on the limited capacity to process informations by the human brain. But both share the impossibility theorem of an optimal gathering of information (Arrow's information paradox). Both approaches underline a kaleidic view of Austrian subjectivism, but Sombart would reject the accompanying methodological individualism and the idea of the survival of the fittest. Instead, he would underline that cooperation is another elementary interaction and that his units of selection are above the individual organism (groups, nations and so on). Sombart does not share either the view of the self-interested individual (seeking with guile) and opportunism as human constants which necessarily lead to hold-ups and moral hazard.

Furthermore, EE increasingly uses formal modelling and biological analogies (variation, mutation, selection) to describe innovation processes. Sombart rejects both under the category of misplaced naturalism. But a branch in EE is the previously mentioned appreciative type of theorizing (Nelson and Winter), which is applied in industrial economic studies.

Another divergence refers to economic growth as a self-evident aim of economic systems. One of Sombart's main points is to show that the growth goal is historically an exception. He points also out that untamed innovation and change has a high cultural price. His vision for the future is a limited or tamed capitalism and a social or political control of innovative activities. But Sombart accepts that technical development is a precondition for cultural development.

If we come back to the Rutherford dichotomies at the beginning it is fair to say that some basic orientational differences exist between Sombart and EE which can be put in the five dichotomies above (formalism vs. anti-formalism, individualism vs. holism, rationality vs. rule following, evolution vs. design, and efficiency vs. reform). But there are also some overlapping points which make both approaches to some degree complementary, in that a more historicist correction of the present evolution of EE is warranted, 'less in formal modelling and more in economic philosophy . . ., economic history, empirical enquiry' (Hodgson 1995, p. 484). So historicism would strengthen more intentional, context dependent, complex motivations including orientation of EE, which may be useful for the analysis of single firms but also up to structural and normative macro conditions as in the concept of economic style which may be relevant for the understanding of changes of technological paradigms. This includes reflections on the *bonum honestum* and normative deliberations on the future course of the global world society and economy. In a Sombartian perspective we could for instance ask if the increasing consumption of energy, matter and bio mass is sustainable in the future. If not, we would have spare time again to think about ethical progress.

## NOTES

1. Many thanks to J. Backhaus for discussions and translations and to H. Bruhns for discussions and a grant from the CNRS (Maison de l'Homme) in Paris to write this chapter.
2. See the overviews of the relevant literature in Nelson 1995, Saviotti 1996, Chapter 1, Foster 1987, Hanusch 1988, Andersen 1994, pp. 1–25, and for example the textbook by Arndt 1994.
3. As to how far the notions of mutation, selection and adaptation make sense to describe market processes see Vanberg 1996.
4. Witt notes for example, that Hayek's concept of competition as a discovery process 'reproduces the classics' view of the markets as a self-regulating system' (1993, p. 12). He also mentions that an evolutionary approach has to take into account both the coordinating tendencies and the de-coordinating tendencies of market allocation, but he then states again that this reproduces, despite the vague allocative implications, the classical philosophy of the market as a self-regulating system (Witt 1991, p. 99).
5. See the critique of Darwinism by Hallpike 1996 and his example of feuding in the Middle Ages.
6. Against the view of an abstract ideal of progress, for example in the sense of an increase in structural complexity or increasing heterogeneity see Gould 1977, 1996 from a biologist's background. He also argues against a strict adaptation/selection model in stressing that the natural environment is lax and that breeding capacity, luck, and so forth play a major role. Less radical is Mayr 1988.
7. In the following we will not deal with the background stories and the personal and biographical connotations of his works, but see the profound work of Lenger 1994.
8. Sombart in fact established the notion of economic system as a scientific notion not only in Germany, see Ritter 1999, p. 123.
9. We cannot discuss the validity of Sombart's empirical hypotheses here. He states for instance that Italy will never become an industrialized country 1888, p. 114, and in one of the few critical reviews, Dietzel 1889 doubts that Sombart has proven the antagonism between private and social interests, that the campagna is typical for Italy, further that he could not empirically show the income disparity between capital and labour and the long-term superiority of farming compared with cattle breeding.
10. Besides the necessarily dialectical way of reasoning the book contains in fact many departures from the main road; we will leave out examples like his reflections on Goethe, his elitist threefold classification of mankind, see 1938, p. 150, his meditations on merchants,

heroes and saints and the undercover arguments against race theories, see 1938, pp. 133, 137ff.

11. We cannot discuss the common thesis of Sombart's change from socialism to idealism in the secondary literature here, but see Peukert 2003.

12. It is interesting that he excludes technique. He argues that its function is always and in all culture spheres to relate means to pre given ends, see 1938, p. 82.

13. This view has surely to do with Sombart's position vis-à-vis his own erotic ambivalence, see 1930, p. 220.

14. In König's view, 1983, p. 49, and 1987, p. 267, this is a misnomer which simply means 'group'. For Sombart's highly skeptical assessment of sociology as a discipline in 1934 see Sombart in Käsler 1985, pp. 98–101.

15. All German references are our translations.

16. See also the intriguing hermeneutical interpretation of Sombart's methodological ideas in Weippert 1953.

17. The problem here has to do with the fact that the *ordnende* economics implies what Sombart calls *Wesenserkenntnis*, a general interpretation of the world, even if it is only formulated in mathematical language, see Schams 1934.

18. We cannot review the intensive debate on Sombart's book, maybe the best review is still the short article by Löwe 1932.

19. In the following, the citations with Roman letters refer to the books of the second edition of Modern Capitalism. For a brief overview of the structure of Modern Capitalism, see Backhaus 1992. We will leave out the discussion of all publications in the context of Modern Capitalism on the military, see 1913b, luxury consumption, see 1913c, the influence of the Jews, see 1911, and so on for reasons of space. These publications do not at all differ in orientation from the respective passages in Modern Capitalism. We even neglect Sombart's book on the bourgeois, see 1913a, a relatively disorganized but important precursor.

20. We will not discuss the rich literature on modern capitalism in detail, but see the reviews in Brocke (ed.) 1987, pp. 67ff., Appel 1992 and the contributions in Backhaus (ed.) 1996.

21. We cannot discuss the problem of continuity here, see Töttö 1996; for the opposite view see for example Breuer 1996, p. 234.

22. This research programme has survived for example in Braudel 1979.

23. For the most comprehensive critical discussion of the analysis of the craft system in the tradition of the historical school see Ehmer 1998.

24. We will not present Sombart's basic notions of production, consumption and so on, see Sombart 1960, which seem not to be peculiar or important.

25. The spirit concept was itself a nebular concept for him, see 1927, pp. 1135, and 1149–53; see also for example Weede 1990, p. 35. Most of the following criticisms of Oppenheimer were shared by the professional historians who mostly discussed partial aspects of his work in a very critical way, among them Dopsch, Brentano, and Below, see for example Below 1920.

26. In the debate on classical Greece modernists (Meyer, Beloch, Pöhlmann) and primitivists (Bücher, Hasebroek, Bolkestein) were distinguished according to their view on the social, economic and historical modernity of the Greek *poleis*. Oppenheimer was also very critical about Sombart's primitivism, see for example 1929, pp. 420, 824–7, 1075, 1094–5, 1116–17, 1142–3, on Sombart's thesis of the solidary (Teutonic) peasant communities, see 1929, p. 515. On Oppenheimer's critique of Sombart see Kruse 1996.

27. See for example Oppenheimer 1929, pp. 818–19, 854–5, 1144–7, also Nuglisch 1904.

28. For reasons of space we will not discuss the comparative 'Sombart-Weber-spirit of capitalism' debate, see for example Parsons 1928/1929, Fechner 1929, Leich 1957, Kraft 1961, Fleischmann 1981, Bruhns 1985 and 1987, Mitzman 1987, Rehberg 1989, Joas 1989, Töttö 1991, Fishman 1994, Tyrell 1994, and for a comparison and comment on Weber's thinking on Sombart in his Protestant ethics see Lichtblau and Weiß (eds) 1993.

29. See also his impressive handbook article in 1959, first published in 1931, on the historically changing arrangements of the labour contract, where in a masterly way he applies his historic–systematic ideal-type approach.

30. See his short discussion on method as *verstehende* sociology where the final causes are human motives in II, pp. 844–5.
31. He holds for example that there were no real commodity exchange markets before the 19th century and no commodity drawn bills until the 18th century, see II, pp. 499–500, and 525.
32. 'Through the pursuit of such an uneconomic goal as profit hundreds of millions of men . . . have been given a chance of life, culture has been restructured from the bottom to the top, empires have been founded and destroyed, the mystery world of technology has been created, the planet has been changed. And all this has happened only because a handful of people has been driven by the passion to make money' (III, p. xiv).
33. See Backhaus 1987a, 1987b, and 1989, Lowe 1989, Krohn 1977, pp. 58–65.
34. Sombart changed his opinion on the future of the crafts system in the face of the empirical data. In for example 1919, pp. 279ff., first published in 1903, he thought that crafts would more or less disappear.
35. As mentioned above, in his book on German socialism he speaks of the age of economics in the last 150 years. He criticizes the primacy of the economy, the profit motive in most human interactions, the population increase, agglomerations, the mechanization and depersonalization in production and everyday life, monotonous working conditions, the unification (of furniture, fashion, and so on), the deterioration of religious faith and lack of a common ethos, the destruction and functionalization of nature, the flooding of the world with commodities and motor vehicles, the dissolution of village communities and the disappearance of the cosy and restful personality instead of the nervous person with strong will and intellectual functions, the abolition of natural rhythms, the hurry up mentality and the ideals of meaningless bigness, quick and hasty movements, and the constant new, see 1934, Part 1. For the hurry up mentality and non-stop transmutations see Garhammer 1999.
36. One example is the highly interesting McDonaldization debate, see Ritzer 1993 and 1998, and for the critics Alfino et al. 1998, where hundreds of recent examples of rationalization are discussed.
37. For the parallels in the critical perspective see Mitzman 1987, pp. 6ff. The authors mentioned demonstrate that cultural criticism is not a strange extreme of old German conservatism and elitism. For Luttwak's remark on politicians compare Sombart 1907.
38. See our review in Peukert 2000.

# REFERENCES

Alfino, M. et al. (1998), *McDonaldization Revisited,* London: Praeger.
Allodi, L. (1989), 'Die Analyse des modernen Menschen bei Max Scheler und Werner Sombart', *Annali di Sociologia,* 5, 458–93.
Amonn, A. (1930), 'Die drei Nationalökonomien', *Schmollers Jahrbuch,* 54, 193–284.
Andersen, E.S. (1994), *Evolutionary Economics,* London and Munich: Pinter and Duncker & Humblot.
Appel, M. (1992), *Werner Sombart – Historiker und Theoretiker des modernen Kapitalismus,* Marburg: Metropolis Verlag.
Arndt, H. (1994), *Lehrbuch der Wirtschaftsentwicklung,* Berlin: Duncker & Humblot.
Arthur, B. (1989), 'Competing technologies, increasing returns, and lock-in by historical events', *Economic Journal,* 99, 116–31.
Backhaus, J. (1987a), 'Werner Sombart's theory of the business cycle', working paper Faculteit der Economische Wetenschappen, Rijksuniversiteit Limburg, Maastricht.
Backhaus, J. (1987b), 'Werner Sombarts Konjunkturtheorie', research memorandum, Faculty of Economics, Limburg University, Maastricht.
Backhaus, J. (1989), 'Werner Sombarts Konjunkturtheorie', in B. Schefold (ed.), *Studien zur Entwicklung der ökonomischen Theorie VII,* Berlin: Duncker & Humblot. pp 77–98.

Backhaus, J. (1992), 'Sombart's modern capitalism', in M. Blaug (ed.), *Gustav Schmoller (1838–1917) and Werner Sombart (1863–1941)*, Aldershot: Edward Elgar, pp. 93–105.

Backhaus, J. (ed.) (1996), *Werner Sombart*, Three vols. Marburg: Metropolis Verlag.

Below, G. (1920), 'Die Entstehung des modernen Kapitalismus', in *Probleme der Wirtschaftsgeschichte*. Tübingen: Mdv, pp. 399–500.

Berndt, H. (1977), 'Identität und Formwandel der Stadt', *Die Alte Stadt*, 4, 165–82.

Betz, H.K. (1994), 'From Schmoller to Sombart', *History of Economic Ideas*, 2, 331–56.

Blaug, M. (ed.) (1992), *Gustav Schmoller (1838–1917) and Werner Sombart (1863–1941)*, Aldershot: Edward Elgar.

Boltanski, L. and E. Chiapello (1999), *Le nouvel esprit du capitalisme*, Paris: Gallimard.

Boltanski, L. and L. Thévenot (1991), *De la justification*, Paris: Gallimard.

Böttcher, S. (1996), *Ostasien denkt und handelt anders: Konsequenzen für Deutschland*, Schriftenreihe des Ifo-Instituts für Wirtschaftsforschung. Berlin.

Braudel, F. (1979), *Civilisation matérielle, économie et capitalisme: XVe au XVIIe siècle*, Three vols. Paris: Colin.

Breuer, S. (1996), 'Von Tönnies zu Weber: Zur Frage einer "deutschen Linie" der Soziologie', *Berliner Journal für Soziologie*, 6, 227–45.

Brocke, B. (ed.) (1987), *Sombarts 'Moderner Kapitalismus': Materialien zur Kritik und Rezeption*, Munich: Dt. Tarchenbuch Verlag.

Brocke, B. (1992), 'Werner Sombart (1863–1941): capitalism – socialism – his life, works and influence since fifty years', in *Jahrbuch für Wirtschaftsgeschichte*, 1, 113–82, Berlin: Acadam Verlag.

Bruhns, H. (1985), 'De Werner Sombart à Max Weber et Moses I. Finlay: La typologie de la ville antique et la question de la ville de consommation', in P. Leveau (ed.), *L'origine des richesses dépensées dans la ville antique*, Aix-en-Provence: University of Provence, pp. 255–73.

Bruhns, H. (1987), 'Economie et religion chez Werner Sombart et Max Weber', in *L'éthique protestante de Max Weber et l'ésprit de la modernité*, Groupe de la Recherche sur la Culture de Weimar, Paris: Ed. de la Maison des sciences de l'homme, pp. 95–120.

Buss, E. (1995), *Lehrbuch der Wirtschaftssoziologie*, Berlin: de Gruyter.

Chaloupek, G.K. (1994a), 'The concept of maturity and the transformation of economic systems', *Review of Political Economy*, 6, 430–40.

Chaloupek, G.K. (1994b), 'Von Sombart zu Schmoller? [Review Appel 1993 und Backhaus (Hg.) 1993]', *Wirtschaft und Gesellschaft*, 20, 314–21.

Chaloupek, G.K. (1995a), 'Glanz und Ende der historischen Schule: Werner Sombart 1863–1941 [Review Lenger 1994]', *Wirtschaft und Gesellschaft*, 21, 352–9.

Chaloupek, G.K. (1995b), 'Long-term economic perspectives compared: Joseph Schumpeter and Werner Sombart', *European Journal of the History of Economic Thought*, 2, 127–49.

Chaloupek, G.K. (1996), 'Werner Sombarts "Spätkapitalismus" und die langfristige Wirtschafts-entwicklung', *Wirtschaft und Gesellschaft*, 22, 385–400.

Chaloupek, G. (1999), 'Werner Sombart (1863–1941)', in J.G. Backhaus (ed.), *The Elgar Companion to Law and Economics,* Cheltenham: Edward Elgar, pp. 466–71.

Dietzel, H. (1889), 'Sombart: Die römische Campagna [Review]', *Archiv für soziale Gesetzgebung und Statistik*, 2, 676–9.

Dosi, G. (1984), *Technical Change and Industrial Transformation*, New York: St. Martins Press.

Dosi, G. et al. (eds.) (1988), *Technical Change and Economic Theory*, London: Pinter.

Ehmer, J. (1998), 'Traditionelles Denken und neue Fragestellungen zur Geschichte von Handwerk und Zunft', in F. Lenger (ed.), *Handwerk, Hausindustrie und die historische Schule der Nationalökonomie*, Bielefeld Verlag für Regionalgeschichte. pp. 19–77.

Ekelund, R.B. and R.D. Tollison (1981), *Mercantilism as a Rent-Seeking Society*, College Station: Texas A & M University Press.

Fechner, E. (1929), 'Der Begriff des kapitalistischen Geistes bei Werner Sombart und Max Weber', *Weltwirtschaftliches Archiv*, 30, 194–211.

Fishman, A. (1994), 'Religious socialism and economic success on the orthodox kibbutz', *Journal of Institutional and Theoretical Economics*, 150, 763–8.

Fleischmann, E. (1981), 'Max Weber, die Juden und das Ressentiment', in W. Schluchter (ed.), *Max Webers Studie über das antike Judentum*, Frankfurt: Suhrkamp. 263–86.

Foster, J. (1987), *Evolutionary Macroeconomics*, London: Allen & Unwin.

Galtung, J. (1997), *Der Preis der Modernisierung*, Vienna: Promedia.

Garhammer, M. (1999), *Wie Europäer ihre Zeit nutzen: Zeitstrukturen und Zeitkulturen im Zeichen der Globalisierung*, Berlin: Ed Sigme.

Georgescu-Roegen, N. (1971), *The Entropy Law and the Economic Process*, Cambridge MA: Harvard University Press.

Gislain, J.-J. and P. Steiner (1995), *La sociologie économique,* Paris: Presses Universitaire de France.

Gould, S.J. (1977), *Ever Since Darwin*, New York: Norton.

Gould, S.J. (1996), *Full House*, New York: Norton.

Hagemann, H. und M.A. Landesmann (1991), 'Sombart and economic dynamics', Diskussionsbeiträge aus dem Institut für Volkswirtschaftslehre, Universitaet Hohenheim. Stuttgart.

Hallpike, C. (1996), 'Social evolution', *Journal of Institutional and Theoretical Economics*, 152, 682–9.

Hanusch, H. (ed.) (1988), *Evolutionary Economics*, Cambridge: Cambridge University Press.

Harnisch, L. (1928), Darstellung und Kritik der Sombart'schen Auffassung vom Unternehmen und Unternehmertum als Kernpunkt seiner Stellung zu dem System des freien Wettbewerbs, Frankfurt.

Heilbroner, R. (1988 ), 'Capitalism', *New Palgrave Dictionary*, J. Eatwell et al. (eds), London: Macmillan, Vol. 1. pp. 347–53.

Hodgson, G.M. (1988), *Economics and Institutions*, Philadelphia: University of Pennsylvania Press.

Hodgson, G.M. (1995), 'The evolution of evolutionary economics', *Scottish Journal of Political Economy*, 42, 468–88.

Hodgson, G.M. (1996), 'The challenge of evolutionary economics', *Journal of Institutional and Theoretical Economics*, 152, 697–705.

Joas, H. (1989), 'Die Klassiker der Soziologie und der Erste Weltkrieg', in H. Joas und H. Steiner (eds), *Machtpolitischer Realismus und pazifistische Utopie: Krieg und Frieden in der Geschichte der Sozialwissenschaften*, Frankfurt: Suhrkamp, pp. 179–210.

Käsler, D. (1985), *Soziologische Abenteuer: Earle Edward Eubank besucht europäische Soziologen im Sommer 1934*, Opladen.

Klotter, C. (1988), 'Bausteine des Menschen: Werner Sombarts "Versuch einer geisteswissenschaftlichen Anthropologie' ", in Gerd Juttemann (ed.), *Wegbereiter der Historischen Psychologie,* Munich: Beck, pp. 162–8.

König, R. (1983), 'Die analytisch-praktische Doppelbedeutung des Gruppentheorems: Ein Blick in die Hintergründe', in F. Neidhardt (ed.), *Gruppensoziologie: Perspektiven und Materialien*, F. Neidhardt (ed.), *Kölner Zeitschrift für Soziologie und Sozialpsychologie*, Sonderheft 25, Opladen, pp. 36–64.

Korsch, K. (1930), 'Sombarts "verstehende Nationalökonomie"', *Archiv für die Geschichte des Sozialismus und der Arbeiterbewegung*, 15, 436–48.

Kraft, J. (1961), *Das Verhältnis von Nationalökonomie und Soziologie bei Franz Oppenheimer, Werner Sombart, Max Weber und in der sozialwissenschaftlichen Systembildung des 19. Jahrhundert*, dissertation, Göttingen.

Krohn, C.D. (1977), 'Zur Krisendebatte der bürgerlichen Nationalökonomie in Deutschland während der Weltwirtschaftskrise 1929–1933', *Gesellschaft: Beiträge zur Marxschen Theorie*, Frankfurt, pp. 51–88.

Kruse, V. (1990), 'Von der historischen Nationalökonomie zur historischen Soziologie: Ein Paradigmenwechsel in den deutschen Sozialwissenschaften um 1900', *Zeitschrift für Soziologie*, 19, 149–65.

Kruse, V. (1996), 'Entstehung und Entfaltung des modernen Kapitalismus: Zur historischen und allgemeinen Soziologie Franz Oppenheimers', in V. Caspari und B. Schefold (eds.), *Franz Oppenheimer und Adolph Lowe*, Marburg: Metropolis Verlag, pp. 163–93.

Kubon-Gilke, G. (1996), 'Institutional economics and the evolutionary metaphor', *Journal of Institutional and Theoretical Economics*, 152, 723–38.

Kurz, R. (1999), *Schwarzbuch Kapitalismus*, Frankfurt: Eidborn.

Landmann, E. (1930), 'Wissen und Werten', *Schmollers Jahrbuch*, 54, 95–111.

Langlois, R.N. and M.J. Everett (1994), 'What is evolutionary economics?', in L. Magnusson (ed), *Evolution and neo-Schumpeterian approaches to economics*, Dordrecht: Duncker & Humblot. pp. 11–47.

Leich, H.G.R. (1957), *Die anthropologisch soziologische Methodik bei Karl Marx, Werner Sombart und Max Weber*, Cologne.

Lenger, F. (1994), *Werner Sombart (1863–1941): Eine Biographie*, Munich.

Leube, K.R. (1994), 'Begreifen und Verstehen: Bemerkungen zur methodologischen Position der österreichischen Schule der Nationalökonomie innerhalb der Geisteswissenschaften in den 20er Jahren', in K.W. Norr et al. (eds), *Geisteswissenschaften zwischen Kaiserreich und Republik: Zur Entwicklung von Nationalökonomie, Rechtswissenschaft und Sozialwissenschaft im 20. Jahrhundert*, Stuttgart: Steiner, pp. 321–37.

Lichtblau, K. und J. Weiß (eds) (1993), *Max Weber: Die protestantische Ethik und der 'Geist' des Kapitalismus*, Bodenheim: Athenäum.

Lowe, A. (1989), 'Konjunkturtheorie in Deutschland in den Zwanziger Jahren', in B. Schefold (ed.), Berlin, pp. 75–86.

Löwe, A. (1932), 'Über den Sinn und die Grenzen verstehender Nationalökonomie', *Weltwirtschaftliches Archiv*, 36, 149–62.

Luttwak, E. (1999), *Turbo Capitalism*, London: Europa Verlag.

Mackensen, R. (1970), 'Verstädterung', *Handwörterbuch der Raumforschung und Raumordnung*, ed. Akademie für Raumforschung und Landesplanung, Hanover: Janicke, pp. 3589–600.

Mayr, E. (1988), *Toward a New Philosophy of Biology*, Cambridge: Beknap.

McCloskey, D.N. (1985), *The Rhetoric of Economics*, Madison: University of Wisconsin Press.

Mitzman, A. (1987), *Sociology and Estrangement: Three Sociologists of Imperial Germany*, New Brunswick: Transaction Books.

Mommsen, W.J. et al. (eds), (1996), *Kultur und Krieg: Die Rolle der Intellektuellen, Künstler und Schriftsteller im Ersten Weltkrieg*, Schriften des Historischen Kollegs, Munich: Oldenbourg.

Nelson, R.R. (1995), 'Recent evolutionary theorizing about economic change', *Journal of Economic Literature*, 33, 48–90.

Nelson, R.R. and S.G. Winter (1982), *An Evolutionary Theory of Economic Change*, Cambridge MA: Harvard University Press.

North, D.C. (1996), *Institutions, Institutional Change and Economic Performance*, Cambridge: Cambridge University Press.

Nuglisch, A. (1904), 'Zur Frage nach der Entstehung des modernen Kapitalismus', *Jahrbücher für Nationalökonomie und Statistik,* 28, 238–50.

O'Brien, J.C. (1992), 'Evolutionary economics: the end of it all?', *International Journal of Social Economics*, 19, 8–33.

Oppenheimer, F. (1929), *Abriss einer Sozial- und Wirtschaftsgeschichte Europas von der Völkerwanderung bis zur Gegenwart*, First part, Jena: Fischer.

Parsons, T. (1928–1929), 'Capitalism in recent German literature: Sombart and Weber', *Journal of Political Economy,* 36, 641–61 and 37 (1929), 31–51.

Pearson, H. (1997), *Origins of Law and Economics,* Cambridge: Cambridge University Press.

Peukert, H. (1998), *Das Handlungsparadigma in der Nationalökonomie*, Marburg: Metropolis.

Peukert, H. (2000), 'L. Boltanski and E. Chiapello: Le nouvel esprit du capitalisme', *Economic Sociology: European Electronic Newsletter*, 1, Part 2, 19–21 (http://www.siswo.uva.nl/ES).

Peukert, H. (2003), 'Werner Sombart', in J. Backhaus (ed.), *Sombart in Perspective*, Marburg, (forthcoming).

Polanyi, K. (1977), *The Livelihood of Man,* H.W. Pearson (ed.), New York: Academic Press.

Radzicki, M.J. and J.D. Sterman (1994), 'Evolutionary economics and system dynamics', in R.W. England (ed.), *Evolutionary Concepts in Economics*, Ann Arbor: University of Michigan Press, pp. 61–89.

Rehberg, K.-S. (1989), 'Das Bild des Judentums in der frühen deutschen Soziologie: "Fremdheit" und "Rationalität" als Typusmerkmale bei Werner Sombart, Max Weber und Georg Simmel', in E.R. Wiehn et al (eds), *Juden in der Soziologie*, Konstanz: Harteng–Garre Verlag, pp. 127172.

Ritter, U.P. (1999), 'Das Wirtschaftssystem', in F. Helmedag and N. Reuter (eds), *Der Wohlstand der Personen*, Marburg: Metropolis, pp. 121–51.

Ritzer, G. (1993), *The McDonaldization of Society*, Thousand Oaks: Pine Forge Press.

Ritzer, G. (1998), *The McDonaldization Thesis: Explorations and Extensions*, London: Sage.

Rutherford, M. (1996), *Institutions in Economics,* Cambridge: Cambridge University Press.

Samuels, W.J. et al. (1994), 'An evolutionary approach to law and economics', in R.W. England (ed.), *Evolutionary Concepts in Economics*, Ann Arbor: University of Michigan Press, pp. 93–110.

Samuelson, P.A. and W. Nordhaus (1989), *Economics*, 13th edn, New York: McGraw Hill.

Saviotti, P.P. (1996), *Technological Evolution, Variety and the Economy*, Cheltenham: Edward Elgar.

Scaff, L.A. (1988), 'Das Unbehagen im Weber-Kreis', in H. Maier et al. (eds), *Politik, Philosophie, Praxis, Festschrift für Wilhelm Hennis zum 65. Geburtstag*, Stuttgart, pp. 174–88.

Schäfers, B. et al. (1976), 'Zur Entwicklung der Stadt-, Gemeinde- und Regionalsoziologie in Deutschland: Ein Überblick nebst einer in Auswahl kommentierten Bibliographie', *Soziologie*, 2, 57–77.

Schams, E. (1930), 'Die "zweite" Nationalökonomie', *Archiv für Sozialwissenschaft und Sozialpolitik*, 64, 453–91.

Schams, E. (1934), 'Wirtschaftslogik', *Schmollers Jahrbuch,* 58, 1–21.

Scheler, M. (1966), *Der Formalismus in der Ethik und die materiale Wertethik*, Bern: Francke.

Schumpeter, J.A. (1911), *Theorie der wirtschaftlichen Entwicklung*, Düsseldorf: Verlag Wirtschaft u. Finanzen.

Shackle, G.L.S. (1992), *Epistemics and Economics*, New Brunswick: Transaction Press.

Sieferle, R.P. (1982), *Der unterirdische Wald*, Munich: Beck.

Sombart, W. (1888), *Die römische Campagna*, Leipzig: Duncker & Humblot.

Sombart, W. (1903), *Die römische Campagna*, 4th edn, 1919.

Sombart, W. (1907), 'Die Politik als Beruf', *Morgen*, vom 26. Juli, pp. 195–9.

Sombart, W. (1911), *Die Juden und das Wirtschaftsleben*, Leipzig: Duncker & Humblot, 1988.

Sombart, W. (1913a), *Der Bourgeois*, Reinbek: Rowolt Taschenbuch Verlag: Duncker & Humblot.

Sombart, W. (1913b), *Krieg und Kapitalismus*, Munich: Duncker & Humblot.

Sombart, W. (1913c), *Luxus und Kapitalismus*, Munich: Duncker & Humblot.

Sombart, W. (1916–1927), *Der moderne Kapitalismus*, Three Vols., Munich: Duncker & Humblot, 1987.

Sombart, W. (1928), 'Die Wandlungen des Kapitalismus', *Weltwirtschaftliches Archiv*, 28, 243–56.

Sombart, W. (1930), *Die drei Nationalökonomien*, Berlin: Duncker & Humblot.

Sombart, W. (1931), 'Arbeiter', in A. Vierkandt (ed.), *Handwörterbuch der Soziologie*, Neudruck, Stuttgart: Enke, 1959, pp. 1–14.

Sombart, W. (1932), 'Die Zukunft des Kapitalismus', in B. Brocke (ed.), *Sombarts 'Moderner Kapitalismus'*, Munich: Deutscher Taschenbuchverlag, 1987, pp. 394–418.

Sombart, W. (1934), *Deutscher Sozialismus*, Berlin: Duncker & Humblot.

Sombart, W. (1938), *Vom Menschen*, Berlin: Bucholz & Weisswange.

Sombart, W. (1960), *Allgemeine Nationalökonomie*, W. Chemnitz (ed.), Berlin: Duncker & Humblot.

Töttö, P. (1991), *Werner Sombart*, Tampere: Vastapaino.

Töttö, P. (1996), 'In Search of the U-Turn', in J. Backhaus (ed.), *Werner Sombart (1863–1941): Social scientist*, Marburg, pp. 227–39.

Troeltsch, E. (1922), *Der Historismus und seine Probleme*, Tübingen: Mohr.

Tyrell, H. (1994), 'Protestantische Ethik – und kein Ende die Neuausgaben der "Protestantischen Ethik"', *Soziologische Revue*, 17, 397–404.

Vanberg, V. (1996), 'Institutional Evolution Within Constraints', *Journal of Institutional and Theoretical Economics*, 152, 690–7.

Vleugels, W. (1940), 'Auf dem Wege zur Lehre vom Menschen als wissenschaftlicher Grundlegung der Geisteswissenschaften [Review]', *Jahrbücher für Nationalökonomie und Statistik*, 151, 625–50.

Wachtler, G. (1985), 'Militärsoziologie und Gesellschaftsstruktur', in S. Hradil (ed.), *Sozialstruktur im Umbruch, Karl Martin Bolte zum 60. Geburtstag*, Opladen, pp. 235–46.

Weede, E. (1990), *Wirtschaft, Staat und Gesellschaft: Zur Soziologie der kapitalistischen Marktwirtschaft und der Demokratie*, Tübingen: Mohr.

Weippert, G. (1953), *Werner Sombarts Gestaltidee des Wirtschaftssystems*, Göttingen: Vandehoeck & Ruprecht.

Wiese, L. (1940), 'Das Problem einer Wissenschaft vom Menschen', *Zeitschrift für öffentliches Recht*, 20, 1–19.

Witt, U. (1987), *Individualistische Grundlagen der evolutorischen Ökonomik*, Tübingen: Mohr.

Witt, U. (1991), 'Reflections on the present state of evolutionary economic theory', in G.M. Hodgson and E. Screpanti (eds), *Rethinking Economics*, Aldershot: Edward Elgar, pp. 83–102.

Witt, U. (1992), 'Evolution as the theme of a new heterodoxy in economics', in U. Witt (ed.), *Explaining Process and Change*, Ann Arbor, MI: University of Michigan Press, pp. 3–20.

Witt, U. (1993), 'Evolutionary economics: Some principles', in U. Witt (ed.), *Evolution in Markets and Institutions*, U. Witt (ed.), Würzburg: Physica, pp. 3–16.

# 6. Reconstructing the early history of path-dependence theory[1]

## Staffan Hultén

## INTRODUCTION

Had Joseph A. Schumpeter never written 'Add successively as many mail coaches as you please, you will never get a railway thereby' or dared to suggest that it is possible to write the economic history of the United States in the second half of the 19th century in terms of railroad construction and its effects, the path-dependence theory would perhaps never have emerged.[1] Path-dependence theorizing is path-dependent on the evolution of thought in the social sciences and it so happened that Schumpeter's grand example triggered intellectual developments that had direct influence on path-dependence thinking.

Path-dependence theory continues to develop and to some extent there exist different visions of what we mean by path-dependence theory. In my mind path-dependence theory proper is the theory codified by P.A. David and W.B. Arthur during the 1980s. One of the most renowned claims of this path-dependent theory is that a winning technology may not be the best choice because small historical events can give an initial advantage to an inferior technology. The initial advantage creates a snowballing effect, based on learning-by-doing and learning-by-using and a rapidly expanding installed base that attracts investments in production, R&D and marketing. The technology is locked in.[3] A very common source of lock-in in a dynamic setting is that the actors 'prematurely' select a technology without giving sufficient time for the competing technologies to develop. The short term gains from internal production economies and often from external economies defeat the long term advantages of letting the market repeatedly figure out which is the best technology. This vision of the market process shows a strong resemblance to Marshall's notion of the survival of the fittest in the economy.

> This leads us to consider the main bearings in economics of the law that the struggle for existence causes those organisms to multiply which are best fitted to derive benefit from their environment. This law is often misunderstood; and taken to mean that those organisms tend to survive which are *best fitted to benefit* the environment. But this is not its meaning. It states that those organisms tend to survive which *are*

*best fitted to utilize* the environment for their own purposes. Now those that utilize the environment most, may turn out to be those that benefit it most. (A. Marshall, 1899, p. 140, original emphases)

In this chapter I will present an interpretation of how path-dependence theory developed from the perspective of developments in economic history. When reflecting on this development I have been trying to capture the process in a simple philosophical model. First I was inclined to think that it was a case of Hegelian evolution driven by a process of thesis, anti-thesis and synthesis. Schumpeter's remark inspired economic historians like Jenks (1944) to regard all economic evolution in the 19th century as basically driven by the railways. Fogel, who was a student of Schumpeter's student Kusnetz, reacted to this extreme position by taking another equally extreme position: let us imagine what a world without railways would have looked like in terms of GDP per capita. Paul David, who as I will demonstrate later on in the text, became heavily influenced by Fogel, noticed some contradictions in Fogel's approach, most importantly the dealing with history and not seeing the historical process. David in his critical appraisal of Fogel writes: '. . . we ought not to concern ourselves with the absolute size of the consequent social savings or their relationship to the aggregate volume of production. Rather, we should insist on knowing whether this particular innovation afforded opportunities for utilizing resources in a manner that yielded higher rates of return than those obtainable through investments in other directions' (David, 1969, p. 521).

However, not to get trapped in extremism I will regard the development of path-dependence theory in the less dramatic Popperian search for better and truer theory through a process of conjectures and refutations which permits a stepwise evolution of knowledge.

If we use the measuring stick of Mark Blaug (1980), path-dependence theory qualifies today for being on track to become a new bold economy theory. First, it presents us with refutable predictions about technology evolution that enables us to make predictions of novel facts that are capable of discriminating between the old and the new theory. The path-dependence theory has since its origin developed in many directions and been tested in many different settings. A further fact, not discussed by Blaug, is that the theory is grand enough to open carrier opportunities for academics like Liebowitz and Margolis; see for example their paper from 1990, specializing in efforts to refute it.

## DIFFERENT VISIONS OF PATH-DEPENDENCE THEORY

The notion of paths can be found well before the path-dependence theory emerged. The path notion is evident already in Schumpeter. 'It is interesting to note that such absence of friction [friction refers to an old sphere which tries to secure prohibition of the new ways of doing things or to discredit them] does not always make the path of progress smoother' (Schumpeter, 1939, p. 108). In totality Schumpeter saw economic evolution as being constituted among other things of entrepreneurs following a first entrepreneur 'in the path of innovation, which becomes progressively smoothed for successors by accumulating experience and vanishing examples' (Schumpeter, 1939, p. 131).

Hodgson (1993, pp. 112–13 and 203–10) finds many pre-David and pre-Arthur examples of path-dependent theorizing. He traces path-dependent ideas back to the 19th century, claims that Kaldor saw the possibility in the 1930s, and gives a couple of examples from the 1970s. In the 1980s he finds numerous examples of path-dependence theorizing; he mentions studies of how small-scale firms or labour-managed firms could have contributed more to the industrialization process had institutions and so forth been different. He also cites a study by Best from 1982 on how investments in the motor car system blocked investments in competing transport technologies. One of many path-dependence models in Hodgson is hyperselection. In this category of path-dependence models we find the David-Arthur model. It refers to a process whereby strong positive feedbacks freeze a given attribute or structure making further amendment difficult, even if the original configuration is imperfect (Hodgson, 1993, p. 206).

In Lawson (1997) the David-Arthur model is the centrepiece of the path-dependence approach. He writes that the path-dependence model is the approach that most straightforwardly overlaps with his own at the level of suggesting how social science might actually proceed. Lawson is in particular, like many others, interested in the QWERTY story. What Lawson finds so attractive with path-dependence is that this approach demonstrates how we can integrate history into economics. But, he has reservations about how the QWERTY case is presented. It can result in the view that 'once a technology or social structure is in place it can be treated as locked-in for good, that the past is not only ever present but also all determining' (Lawson, 1997, p. 251). Lawson also makes a distinction between path-dependency and path-dependence. He suggests that the former is closer to the mainstream approach without demonstrating exactly how this is the case.

Antonelli (1997) is basically affirming the importance of the David-Arthur path-dependence model to create a codified path-dependence theory that can be tested and further formalized. But, similarly to Hodgson, his reading of the economic literature has presented him with numerous examples of path-dependence thinking. He finds such ideas in Rosenstein, Rodan and Abramowitz in the 1930s, and his interpretation of the industrial organization field leads to the conclusion that path-dependent processes have been an important research agenda for many decades. In Arthur's article in the

*Scientific American* from 1990 (reprinted as Chapter 1 in Arthur, 1994a) references are also given to antecedents to path-dependence theory. Myrdal and Kaldor are mentioned because of their positive feedback models, Schumpeter for his discussion of multiple equilibria, and so on.

## COUNTERFACTUAL HISTORY AND PATH-DEPENDENCE THEORY

When looking at the references of David and Fogel from the 1960s it is evident that they read and reflected over the same books. However, David's early work shows (David, 1975, Chapters 4 and 5) that he wanted to add insights to the then fashionable literature on economic development of Rostow, Hirschman, Habakkuk and others while Fogel (1964) wanted to attack established ideas on economic growth.[4]

An illustrative study by David is his article on the mechanization of reaping in the antebellum Midwest (David, 1975, pp. 192–232). In this article David tried to show how the agricultural sector in the ante-bellum economy contributed to the industrialization process. By doing this he wanted to mitigate Hirschman's (1958) claim that agriculture shows a lack of stimulus to setting up new activities through linkage effects, or Rostow's idea that modernization of the agricultural sector constituted a temporal precondition for rapid industrialization in USA. David arrives at showing that agricultural modernization and industrialization were interrelated. The farmers' decision to adopt mechanical reapers was found to depend on farm size, relative wage levels, and so forth. A key finding was the threshold function for the adoption of reapers. With hindsight this study didn't present David with much material on the dynamic effects of innovation. By looking at the total amount in 1859–60 of the industry and craftsmen producing farm equipment he finds that this production represented four per cent of the value added of the nation's industry. To further enhance the importance of the sector he points to the case of Illinois where farm equipment production represented eight per cent of total value added in the industry. In this early work of David we notice some ideas that will develop and form part of the path-dependence theory: (1) the study of a historical process, and (2) the modelling of adoption as a process determined by economic factors, technical factors and geography.

Compare this with Fogel's approach. He decides to show that the role of the railways was not as substantial as was generally presumed. Fogel chose to test this by conducting a comparative static analysis of the contribution of the railway sector to American economic growth. Fogel's and to some extent Fishlow's (Fishlow, 1965) calculations of the measurable economic effects of the railways were criticized by many other researchers. But the new economic history approach was also hailed by many economists and economic historians; eventually Fogel's studies gave him a Nobel Prize in Economics.

Two observations can be made concerning the critique of Fogel's research. First, all attempts to make Fogel change his basic result – the railways had in total a single digit percentage impact on GDP per capita in 1890 – were always rejected by Fogel, see for example Fogel (1979). He either found that the factual objection was incorrect or too small to matter.

Second, methodological objections tended to be disregarded by Fogel. However, some types of theoretically oriented critique he could easily handle. This was the case with researchers wanting to find a moral in the history derived from 'what was'. One of the most prominent of these economic historians was E. D. Genovese who disliked the overemphasis on economic matters in the new economic history reinterpretation of the Southern slave economy. From a moral point of view it is possible to understand that Genovese was disgusted by findings showing that the slave economy was profitable and probably sustainable.[5] The general problem with this type of attack, trying to cope with the new methodology by making remarks on how it was and what was in the data made a counterattack easy for Fogel. Because as Fogel (1966) writes: '. . . reliance on counterfactual statements is a long-standing practice of economic historians, both these statements and the theories on which they rest are rarely made explicit'. Genovese's study from 1962 (Chapter 7 in 1967) of 'The significance of the slave plantation for Southern economic development' is shown by Fogel to contain a set of hidden counterfactual assumptions that are not properly treated.

The difficult methodological issues were those that pointed to the limits of the counterfactual research programme. When re-reading Fogel's texts on the social savings of railroads and other similar studies one of the most striking features is what is being omitted from the counterfactual comparison. As von Tunzelman (1978, p. 42) puts it, 'There are further problems in envisaging a counterfactual world in which only the invention we are interested in is bombed out of existence.' Knowledge or other cumulative externalities are the principal facts missing. Fogel and others are of course aware of the fact that they are only telling part of the story when they measure the social savings of major innovations. What is beyond the pure measurement is speculation or extremely difficult to disentangle. Fogel (1966, p. 43) writes: 'The development of spacecraft, unlike the railroad, thus offers man access to knowledge that cannot be obtained in any other way. The knowledge gained from space exploration may have enormous consequences for the biological and physical sciences'. In Fogel (1979, p. 38) he acknowledges the existence of a vast literature on 'the proposition that the specific inputs required for railroad construction and operation induced the rise of industries, productive techniques and management and labor skills that were essential to economic growth. To review this literature adequately would require a separate paper'.

Rostow's (1960) 'lateral' effects that reinforce the industrialization process on a wider front were excluded by Fishlow (1965, p. 16, original emphasis) in his study of railroads in the antebellum economy because the lateral effects 'are so general as to constitute the very process of industrialisation and are a *consequence* of the other effects (the effects measured by Fislow) rather than an additional route of influence'. The exclusion of measuring the impact of the innovations induced by a major innovation was consequently not a mistake but a conscious decision to avoid measurement problems and other complications.

Von Tunzelman (1978) noted that it was unrealistic and problematic to assume that all other innovations would have developed in the same way as they actually did. The notion of a counterfactual world with *coeval changes* in the environment occurring in the hypothetical absence of a major invention is an extreme assumption as one might expect that the more significant the invention the greater the irreversible innovations might be. But the convenient assumption of there being no irreversible derived innovations in related industries is an extreme *one*, as historians such as Professor David have emphasized (von Tunzelman, 1978, p. 42).

From our point of view a remark by David (1969, p. 508, original emphasis) is particularly interesting as it points to a major weakness in Fogel's approach that could be solved if another methodology were used. David wrote: 'The task of reckoning the direct social savings attributable to railroads in 1890 would seem to afford a splendid occasion for a thorough examination of the technical and economic aspects of late nineteenth-century transport and distribution arrangements in the US. An undertaking of that undoubtedly would shed much light upon elements of interrelatedness among methods of shipping, handling and storing goods. It would, moreover, be particularly germane to the thesis that the appearance of isolated "great innovations" is less consequential for economic progress than the rate at which clusters of interlocking mutually supporting techniques can be brought into use. Regrettably, the opportunity to pursue such an inquiry has not been seized in Fogel's book'.[6]

David (1969) is silent on the type of approach that could be used to handle this type of problem but some ideas appear in the text. In retrospect David seems to have taken significant steps towards the future path-dependent model. 'It is no doubt salutary for us to be thus reminded that economic questions arise, by definition, only when there is more than one way to skin the same cat. ... So long as possibilities exist for substituting other goods and techniques in order to fulfill material wants, can any single alternative truly be held to be indispensable? The state of the arts typically offers an array of production and distribution options among which may be found some method that is not a *dismally* inferior alternative to the best-practice solution under consideration.'

David (1975) deals with methodological issues that can handle complex problems like these. In the introduction entitled 'Technology, history and growth' David stresses the historical character of economic growth and the role of technological learning, indivisibilities, and irreversibility are identified. All of these ideas appear and in fact take centre stage in the path-dependence literature if in 1975 they were not put into a formal verbal or mathematical model. With hindsight it is also possible to regard the formal modelling of technological change along compulsive sequences (David, 1975, pp. 84–6) as being an early example of path-dependence. Another revelation in David (1975) is his identification of the path-dependence mathematical toolbox to be – he discusses Markov chains and Polya turns as possible ways of treating the data. So to a significant extent the David-Arthur path-dependence model existed already in 1975, as has been suggested by P.A. David himself (1992, p. 135.): 'See for example David (1975, pp. 6–16, 50–91) . . . for formulations of the underlying view of the nature of the stochastic process that generates path-dependent technological progress'. However, still absent were the jargon and cases bringing home the abstract theory, and specific ideas on how to exactly use the mathematical tools.

Others also saw that the counterfactual methodology used by Fogel opened up possibilities for comparisons of competing technologies. When discussing the history of the steam engine von Tunzelman (1978, p. 22) remarks: 'Development along each of these paths continued through the first sixty years of the nineteenth century'. Stoneman (1983, p. 235) came even closer to the language of path-dependence: 'When calculating rates of return a comparison of actual social welfare with that on some counterfactual path (that without technological change) must be employed. , , . The construction of counterfactual paths is notoriously difficult and the greater the technological shock the greater the difficulty. Partial equilibrium analysis allows one to limit the problem of constructing the counterfactual, but if one considers an innovation such as railways the widespread repercussions must make a partial-equilibrium approach to calculating the counterfactual rather inappropriate. . . . Moreover, technological change may be considered cumulative. One technological advance lays the basis for further advances; . . .'.[7]

Even Fogel (1979, p. 7) came close to regarding social savings problems as problems of competing technologies and behavioural lock-ins: 'Alternative specifications also permit the historian, with his advantage of hindsight, to be able to identify errors made by planners and investors in the past because certain of their assumptions regarding the future technological or market developments turned out to be wrong. For example, the set of decisions that led to a 94 percent increase in the density of the US railroad networks between 1890 and 1914 were based, to an extent that has yet to be evaluated, on a failure to take adequate account of the rate of improvements in motor vehicles. If the speed of advance in motor transportation had been known, some of the extensions of railroads would not have taken place'.

## DAVID MEETS ARTHUR

The crucial next step in the codification of the path-dependence theory according to David and Arthur is when they start to exchange ideas. This happens in the early 1980s, Arthur manages to advance the mathematical models that make path-dependence theory credible in economics; they both struggle with the QWERTY case but David (1985) writes the better story.

Suddenly path-dependence theory is a tangible theory with conjectures and testable and refutable hypotheses. The QWERTY case proved to be a marvel and nearly as attractive as Fogel's railway case and this success should perhaps be studied in a separate paper. Why were economists and social scientists so taken by a reinterpretation of the work tool of secretaries? I think that the QWERTY case appeared when it did because of societal changes. More and more scientists were forced by computerization to type all day long and at their finger tips they had this enigma of technology.[8] As Lawson (1997) puts it any configuration of keys except ABCDEFGHIJ would have been intriguing for a social scientist on the hunt for an illustrative case.

There existed 'competing cases'; some were more provocative than the QWERTY like Arthur's attempts to question the success of the internal combustion engine over steam and electric motors as a tractive force for cars.[9] Others could certainly stand the test of being refuted better than QWERTY like Cowan's nuclear power research (Cowan, 1990)[10]. Even railways re-entered the stage with Puffert's study of gauge competition. Computer designs and VCR standards were other early cases that despite entering the path-dependence case book weren't snazzy enough to make everyone sit up and stare. In total Foray (1997) lists seven major empirical research fields for path-dependence theory.

To conclude it must be stressed that the function of the cases isn't necessarily to survive all counterattacks and particular refutations. Our examples of cases taken from the theoretical development of path-dependence theory demonstrate that *cases aren't innocent* when scientific research is conducted in the spirit of appreciative theorizing.[11] The primary role of cases is to permit expansions or explorations into new theoretical perspectives. One case can prove to be a better tool to advance knowledge than another case. Paul David in Carter (1999, p. 27) talks about the rhetorical force of the QWERTY case. The revelatory capability of a case is measured by its capacity to provide insights applicable to theoretical analysis and synthesis.

The theory is not in the words of Popper 'immunized' by an empirical example but by the staying power of its concepts and predictions. Just look at this quote from Fogel (1979, p. 48) where as a last *tour de force* he makes new economic history an integral part of economic history.

> It is in the nature of debates that points of disagreements and discontinuity are exaggerated, while the points of agreement and continuity are slighted. . . . I wish to report that when, in preparation for the writing of this paper, I reviewed both the old and the new literature, *I was struck more by the elements of continuity than by those of discontinuity* [my emphasis]. . . . Certainly the new economic history has done little to change our perception of the sequence of events that constitute the history of modern transportation. Nor has it eroded the proposition that the collective impact of advances in transportation technology during the 19th century was of such a magnitude as to warrant the title of a 'transportation revolution'. Nor has it contradicted the belief that this transportation revolution accounts for a considerable part of the growth in per capita income during the 19th century.

## NOTES

1. I would like to thank Robin Cowan, MERIT, for helpful comments on a preliminary version of the chapter and to the participants of the seminar 'The History of Evolutionary Thought in Economics' at Max Planck Institute in Jena 26–28 August 1999 for suggestions and critical observations.
2. A. Fishlow (1965), p. 13 and Schumpeter (1939), p. 341.
3. R. Cowan (1990, pp. 543ff).
4. In Susanne B Carter's interview with Paul David he says: 'Although its [Walt Rostow's book *The British Economy of the Nineteenth Century*] explanation of the Great Depression did not leave me convinced . . . , I liked the methodologically pioneering side of that book and in my paper I tried to suggest ways of taking it further. From that point onwards, I was firmly "hooked" on what I took to be a new and more useful approach to writing economic history.'
5. As a graduate student Paul David was already confronted with new economic history and the slavery issue. In Carter (1999), p. 10, Paul David says: '. . . it was exciting to be associated with doing something new and slightly daring, like talking dispassionately about slavery'.
6. David (1969), pp. 506–25 reprinted in P. Temin (ed.), *New Economic History. Selected Readings*, Harmondsworth: Penguin Books, 1973, pp. 267–68.
7. Compare the following quote from David (1992, p.167): 'Meaningful global evaluations of efficiency are difficult if not impossible to make between alternative technological systems whose influences ramify so widely and are so profound that they are capable of utterly transforming the economic and social environments into which they have been introduced'.
8. Arthur (1994b, p. 15) 'It need not be the case that the number of technologies competing for a given purpose is few. If we consider the arrangement of the 40 or so keys on a typewriter as a technology, then in principle 40-factorial or $10^{48}$ possible keyboards compete with the standard QWERTY keyboard.'
9. See Arthur (1994b, p. 27) originally published in 1983 and in revised versions 1985 and 1989. 'Gasoline's superiority over steam as the propulsion device for automobiles, for example, we take for granted. But among engineers it is still in dispute, just as it was in 1900.'
      The competition between different car traction technologies have been discussed by others, see for example Cowan and Hultén (1996) and Foray (1997).
10. In Carter (1999) p. 28 Paul David suggests that the nuclear reactor case perhaps is more interesting than QWERTY, a 'manifestly minor illustration'.
11. See Nelson (1995) for a discussion of this concept.

# REFERENCES

Antonelli, C. (1997), 'The economics of path-dependence in industrial organisation', *International Journal of Industrial Organisation*, **15**(6), 643–76.

Arthur, W. B. (ed.) (1994a), *Increasing Returns and Path Dependence in the Economy*, Ann Arbor: University of Michigan Press.

Arthur, W. B. (1994b), 'Competing technologies, increasing returns, and lock-in by historical small events', in *Increasing Returns and Path Dependence in the Economy*, Ann Arbor: University of Michigan Press.

Carter, S. B. (1999), 'An interview with Paul David', *The Newsletter of the Cliometric Society*, July, 3–10 and 25–30.

Cowan, R. (1990), 'Nuclear Power Reactors: A Study in Technological Lock-in', *Journal of Economic History*, 50, 541–67.

Cowan, R. and S. Hultén (1996), 'Escaping Lock-In: The Case of the Electric Vehicle', *Technological Forecasting and Social Change*, 53(1), September, 61–80.

David, P.A., (1969), 'Transport innovation and economic growth: Professor Fogel on and off the rails', *Economic History Review*, 22, 506–25 reprinted in P. Temin (ed.), *New Economic History. Selected Readings*, Harmondsworth: Penguin Books, 1973, and also reprinted in David (1975).

David, P.A. (1975), *Technological Choice, Innovation and Economic Growth*, London: Cambridge University Press.

David, P.A. (1985), 'Clio and the Economics of QWERTY', *American Economic Review*, Vol. 75:2, 332–9.

David, P.A. (1992), 'Heros, herds and hysteresis in technological history: Thomas Edison and "The Battle of the Systems" reconsidered', *Industrial and Corporate Change*, **1**(1), 129–80.

Fishlow, A. (1965), *American Railroads and the Transformation of the Antebellum Economy*, Boston, MA: Harvard University Press.

Fogel, R.W. (1964), *Railroads and American Economic Growth: Essays in Econometric History*, Baltimore, Md.: The John Hopkins Press.

Fogel, R.W. (1966), 'Railroads as an analogy to the space effort: some economic aspects', *Economic Journal*, P. Temin (ed.), 16–43, reprinted in *New Economic History. Selected Readings*, Harmondsworth: Penguin Books, 1973.

Fogel, R.W. (1979), 'Notes on the social saving controversy', *The Journal of Economic History*, **39**(1), 1–54.

Foray, D. 'The dynamic implications of increasing returns: technological change and path dependent inefficiency', *International Journal of Industrial Organisation*, **15**(6), 733–52.

Genovese, E. D. (1967), *The Political Economy of Slavery*, New York: Vintage Books.

Hirschman, A. O. (1958), *The Strategy of Economic Development*, New Haven: Yale University Press.

Hodgson, G. M. (1993), *Economics and Evolution*, Cambridge: Polity.

Jenks, Leland H. (1944), 'Railroads as an economic force in American development', *The Journal of Economic History*, IV, 1–20.

Lawson, T. (1997), *Economics and Reality*, London: Routledge.

Liebowitz, S. J. and Margolis, S.E. (1990), 'The fable of the keys', *Journal of Law and Economics*, 3, 1–25.

Marshall, A. (1899), *Elements of Economics* (Third edition), London: Macmillan.

Nelson, R.R. (1995), 'Recent evolutionary theorizing about economic change', *Journal of Economic Literature*, 33, March, 48–90.

Rostow, W. (1960), *The Stages of Economic Growth*, Cambridge: Cambridge University Press.
Schumpeter, J. A. (1939), *Business Cycles*, Volume I, New York: McGraw-Hill.
Stoneman, P. (1983), *The Economic Analysis of Technological Change*, Oxford: Oxford University Press.
Tunzelman von, G. N. (1978), *Steam Power and British Industrialization to 1860*, Oxford: Clarendon Press.

# 7. Adolph Wagner's contributions to public health economics[1]

## Ursula Backhaus

## INTRODUCTION

Adolph Wagner (1835–1917),[2] the public finance theorist and advocate, was interested in the limits of the state and the likely long-term development of the tasks of the state. He studied jurisprudence and political science at the Universities of Göttingen and Heidelberg. For five years, he was a professor at the Commercial Academy at Vienna (1858–1863), where he devoted himself to the theory of public finance. From Austria, Wagner proceeded to Hamburg, and held chairs at the universities of Dorpat, Freiburg and from 1870 until his death in 1917 in Berlin. His major works are *Grundlegung*[3] and *Finanzwissenschaft*.[4] He was a member of the Royal Statistical Bureau of Prussia, and from 1882 to 1885 a member of the Prussian Lower House for the German conservative party. Although Wagner was one of the founders of the Verein für Socialpolitik, he did not actively participate in its research and debates. As a 'Socialist of the Chair' he wanted to promote social freedom and thereby overcome class friction and prevent class struggle, but in his efforts to create the possibility for social progress and elevation, he was also concerned with the proper limits of the state.

Embedded in the analysis of the Austrian state budget,[5] Wagner (1863) provided a forecast for the long-term behaviour of the state, which is now known as Wagner's Law:

> On the whole, the realm of the state's activities has become ever more extensive, as the concept of the state developed, as people achieved higher and higher levels of civilization and culture, and the more demands were consequently addressed to the state. This has also led to a continuous increase in the required state revenues, an increase which was generally even higher relative to the increase of the extent of state activity. The cause for this relative difference lies in the means employed by the state: these have become ever more complex, comprehensive and costly as one and the same need required an ever more perfect, higher and refined way of being satisfied. Consider by way of example the educational system! The phenomenon has the character and importance of a 'law' in political economy, the requirements of the state are constantly rising as people progress. (English translation by Jürgen Backhaus)[6]

In subsequent writings, several areas of application tempted his interest, among them, and of particular interest in this chapter, was the application to health care.[7] Wagner's analysis of the state budget and the limits of the state led to insights so far neglected in health economics. In this chapter, I try to place his analysis in the context of the modern body of research on health economics. However, tension[8] remains in confronting the politically charged and applied issues of modern health economics with Wagner's Law and the conditions he gave for intervention of the state, as he was more concerned with economics as a science of enhancing the understanding of economic behaviour and in particular the behaviour of the state than with providing inputs for directly applicable policy research.

## WAGNER'S LAW

Wagner predicted in 1863 (op. cit.) that the state will become more influential with an increase in the cultural and technical development and general sophistication and interconnectedness of a complex society. As he was concerned about the impact of the development which we today call Wagner's Law on the status of civil liberty, he distinguished between primarily indirect and primarily direct state[9] services and expected that both types of services would have a different effect on the economy. Primarily indirect state services would allow private and small political entities to remain independent and thus facilitate free market exchange, while primarily direct state services would lead to centralization. Wagner argued that provision through primarily direct state services will occur when in relation to marginal costs average costs are very high. This case of increasing returns to scale, however, is important from the point of view of civil liberties, too. Because of high average costs, a central provider of a service or product can realize economies of scale and economies of scope[10] and faces therefore lower production costs than smaller entities, but the central provider may have difficulties in absorbing the relevant information from the base. Wagner, an advocate of minimum state influence, preferred indirect to direct state influence, as the former would leave civil liberties more intact.

When writing on the Austrian state household, Wagner foresaw an increase in the tasks of the state with respect to measures of law and order, state defence, and primary education (1863, op. cit., p. 31). In his later writings (1911), he also expected an increase in the share of publicly delivered and financed health care measures and measures of public hygiene leading to better health:

> The conditions leading to health or sickness of people, animals, and plants involve light, air, water, food, housing etc., as well as infective agents and means of precaution.

The scientific progress of natural sciences with respect to these conditions of health and sickness is among other things in many respects an important influence that the public, the state purposes will continue to expand in the interest of everyone in order to ensure welfare conditions of this kind.[11]

The quote shows that health care in Wagner's view encompassed the progress in natural sciences leading towards better health, healthy animals and plants, and the environment is in general crucial to human health. Wagner expected the state to implement the insights and new knowledge developed through natural sciences. This is also the underlying idea which led to Wagner's forecast that over time prevention would become more important than cure: 'The principle of prevention with extensive institutions to prevent legal distortions and other evils (for instance in the area of health care) . . . will more and more be applied, so that the system of cure will become less important . . . .'[12]

In order to provide better prevention, more complex organizations in society would be needed. Wagner thought that in the modern state public services would be delivered in a different way with capital and human knowledge becoming more important. Large institutions and organizations would emerge requiring highly qualified labour. Well educated civil servants would be employed in complicated organizational structures in areas such as law, defence, and health care (1911, op. cit., p. 737).

Could civil servants fulfil the requirements posed by a modern society? Wagner compared the performance of public and private employees and found that civil servants were hampered in their work by unavoidable state controls and lacked the incentive to make profits, as they did not have a share in the outcome. Wagner considered continuous profitability a measure of efficiency for private businesses. However, the state could offer other than monetary rewards to civil servants such as honours (ranks, titles and decorations) and give them a better standing through greater security of office and better prospects of promotion. Therefore, Wagner (1883) wrote that 'the state often has at its disposal a quite exceptionally competent body of employees and, at equal salaries, a more efficient one than can be found anywhere else'.[13] Due to the extra incentives the state can offer Wagner concluded that civil servants would be better employees than those in the private economy.

The state as a provider would become more important, as civil servants are better employees than private ones, and a more capital-intensive way of production[14] would be chosen. As consequences of more preventive measures of the state Wagner predicted an increase in costs, as well as a more even distribution of costs and benefits in the form of taxes in the long run. He considered a more equal distribution as a favourable outcome of the preventive system (1911, op. cit., p. 737).

Although Wagner's Law (an increase of state tasks over time in a well-developed and growing society, and the predictions it leads to, for instance that prevention will become more important over time), intuitively seem to be right, efforts in empirical testing have often been frustrated.[15] This is, however, not surprising since econometric methods have been devised for many, mostly deterministic models. Econometric theories suitable to evolutionary models are rare and far between. The difficulty lies in the openness of the Law as to the forms state involvement may take. For instance, invoking the subsidiarity principle,[16] the state may take on additional tasks while at the same time delegating responsibilities elsewhere; either downwards in a decentralizing way or laterally like charging or creating additional institutions.

## THE CONDITIONS FOR PUBLIC PRODUCTION

As guidelines for state intervention Wagner developed the following four conditions. The first three conditions refer to characteristics in the production process, the fourth condition relates to characteristics in the use of the good or service publicly produced:

1. Production should be guaranteed for a long time period.
   Wagner wanted the state to undertake large investments over a long period. He assumed that the bond rate must be lower than the private interest rate for borrowing, because the state is the better risk. This is only the case if budgetary discipline exists.[17] The state budget has to be balanced. Only under the condition of a balanced budget can the state refinance itself.
2. Production should extend over a wide area.
   Wagner assumed that local businesses can only reach a relatively small area. Consequences are differences in prices and quality, local monopolies, and unavailability of goods and services in certain regions. A state can intervene by creating a larger business area, which Wagner typically wanted to achieve with an improvement of the railroad.
3. Production should lie in one hand.
   Wagner had allocative questions in mind. He wanted make it impossible for a private company to create a monopoly and receive a large monopoly rent. Today, this condition is important as well. For redistribution, production has to lie in one hand, too.
4. Many consumers benefit and marginal utility cannot be measured.
   According to this condition, insurance companies should be allowed to introduce a variety of different contracts. This policy is frustrated if a government does not allow differentiations to that extent. Then, different marginal utility valuations can no longer be revealed, and hence they

become unobservable. In such a case, Wagner's fourth condition may be fulfilled.

When these four conditions are met, then Wagner considered it as likely that a good or service will be provided by the state (1911, op. cit., p. 738). Therefore, they form the basis of political consent.[18] Interest groups should not become important, but on the basis of the conditions formulated by Wagner participants of the political process should be able to come close to a unanimous vote in order to support provision of the service or good by the state.

## HOW CAN WAGNER'S LAW BE APPLIED TO HEALTH CARE?

Wagner foresaw a role for the state in the provision and finance of health care. His prediction and projection of 1863 was that the tasks of the state in a complex and developed society would and should grow over time. His law in application to health and health care means that when the cultural development in a society rises, the level of health will improve. As people strive for a better education and higher incomes, bad health carries higher opportunity costs and therefore, the demand for health care increases and preventive health care will become more important as well. According to Wagner's forecast, more state intervention will become necessary, because in his view, only the state will have the capital to finance medical research and provide new and expensive technology. The state intervention leads to a better health level of the population and to an additional cultural rise, which again increases opportunity costs of illness. Wagner recognized that through state intervention, the system transforms itself and requires further state intervention. The state is therefore part of the evolutionary process. Critical readers, who negate a role of the state in evolutionary economics, could pose the question, what is evolutionary about Wagner's Law, when government influence in the health care systems of developed Western countries is typically so strong? Critics typically suggest that by exerting power the state destroys the results of existing evolutionary economic growth.[19] According to this view, there is no role for state intervention in evolutionary economics. They misunderstand Wagner's Law, which starts out from the cultural rise in society and through a change in opportunity costs leads according to the process described above to an increase in the tasks of the state. From this it follows that Wagner's Law can be characterized as an evolutionary law.

Should the state take an active role in the finance and organization of health care? A look at the four conditions stated by Wagner shows the following:[20]

What is important for condition one, that the production should be guaranteed for a long time period? When applied to public health economics, this condition makes sense, as there are large capital investments, for instance in basic medical research. What is important with respect to condition two, that production should extend over a wide area? For health economics, this condition is important as differences with respect to access, price and quality of health care provision and services and the finance of health care among different regions and countries persist.[21] It is for instance politically desirable that people in rural areas have the same access to health care as people in metropolitan areas. What is important for condition three, that production should lie in one hand? Questions of equity and redistribution[22] are important in health economics. An example is the foundation of the British National Health Service, which has presumably been founded for reasons of altruistic externalities. Those people who formerly eschewed care, would consume more of it, if it is free.[23] In developed countries without a national health care system, the state either wants to guarantee equal access to health care for all persons, or at least provide a minimum level of health care provision for the poor and needy people. What is important for condition four, that many consumers benefit and marginal utility cannot be measured? In health care, differentiation of insurance contracts is typically politically restricted. People with serious illnesses tend to be treated financially in the same way as people who are less seriously ill. As a consequence of the political restriction moral hazard[24] can occur, a change in a person's behaviour leading towards an overutilization of medical services due to health insurance or any other reduction of the risk of illness. Wagner proposed that the citizens should pay small fees for state services. Imposing patient cost sharing could restrict moral hazard in health insurance.

All four of Wagner's conditions are met in the case of health care services and we can therefore conclude that there is a role in the finance and provision of health care for the state.

## WAS WAGNER RIGHT?

Wagner was right under the presumptions he made. We can understand his thinking best by assuming a simplified model with two basic assumptions. First, the cultural rise and measures of improvement of health are not imposed on a population, but come from within the population. This is plausible, because the rules or conditions under which the state should take over certain tasks according to Wagner come close to forming a consensual basis. Secondly, capital markets have not been developed yet, therefore the state plays an important role in providing capital. The state finances medical research, which presumably leads to new innovations and further progress of society. In the health economy today, the first assumption is not always fulfilled and the second assumption, a lack of capital markets, is simply no longer a given. Therefore, while the underlying principle is true, we can only cautiously interpret our reality with Wagner's Law.

The following example illustrates what happens, when the first assumption is not being met. When Roman Catholic priests of the order of St. Edmund and nuns of the order of St. Joseph came to Alabama's Black Belt in the 1930s to help relieve poverty, high infant mortality and other conditions that led to a low life expectancy especially among the black population, they found a local health care system in place. 'When we first came to Selma, there were cottages and other small buildings used to treat black people . . . We used them until we were able to begin building our own facilities.'[25] A federal grant through the Hill-Burton Program of $800 000 allowed the construction of a hospital in 1963, which replaced the small local health care facilities. Only 20 years later, this hospital had to be closed due to mounting debts leading to debt payments of $1 million annually. Additional health policy measures by the state were required to ensure the provision of health care in the area.

In this example, the state gave a federal subsidy to the Church to build a hospital and thereby destroyed the local health care system. When the Church failed with the state financed health care facility, new state intervention was required. A well-meaning effort by the Church thus led to the destruction of small local self-help groups as the quality of health care these groups delivered was not considered acceptable. Instead of giving incentives to provide better service in the same small local environment, a new state funded central hospital was built, which soon became financially unbearable. Not only was the ability for self-help destroyed, but also transmission of information with respect to prevention, nutrition and other lifestyle factors important to health. The cottages and small buildings used to treat blacks had been centres of communication, which served to transfer health related information not only to patients, but to people living in the area.

This example shows that by interfering in an evolutionary process, the system transforms itself and new state intervention is necessary. The federal programme failed, and the state took on a new and additional task of setting up a health care system as the local system had been destroyed. Centralization occurred at the wrong place.[26] The effect would probably have been less distortionary, if one had tried to strengthen the existing informal organization, or if the move towards cultural rise, leading to a higher education, better incomes, and better health, had come from the black Alabamians living in that area themselves instead of imposing it on them. Then, Wagner's Law would have also led to government intervention and a transformation of the system requiring new government intervention, as described above, but in a less distortionary way. It was a main concern of Wagner that civil liberties would be kept intact.

Let us now turn to the second provision made by Wagner. He assumed that there were no capital markets and that therefore the state has to provide the capital necessary to undertake large investments. In a culturally rising society innovations would lead to more complicated and capital-intensive methods in the future, so that the tasks of the state will grow over time.[27] Major developments of economic theory have occurred in the area of capital markets in the meantime. Particularly relevant to explain the health economic context are developments of the theory of the firm and the Baumol-Bowen hypothesis,[28] which finds that economic growth is related to the capital-intensive sectors in the economy. The theory of the firm, a large body of literature, explains among other things the behaviour of large organizations in contrast to small privately owned companies. One major reason for the emergence of large organizations is the presence of capital markets. In large organizations, there is a potential conflict between management, employees and owners, which also plays a role in explaining conflicts of control in large health organizations.[29] The presence of capital markets is also important for the Baumol-Bowen hypothesis. According to this hypothesis, large organizations move towards more capital-intensive production methods in the future; those sectors which are labour-intensive and cannot realize major gains in productivity are called stagnant sectors of the economy. The forecast is the same as Wagner's Law: a move towards more capital-intensive production methods in the future, but, because of the presence of a capital market, these capital-intensive methods will not be provided by the state but by large private organizations. The state is typically to be found in the areas of the stagnant sectors of the economy.

## SUMMARY AND CONCLUSIONS

The relevance of Wagner's approach consists in two parts. On the one hand, we want to understand to what extent Wagner's Law can explain current trends in state involvement and expenditure with respect to health care. Here, our findings are that the explanatory power is limited. One does not do justice to Adolph Wagner, the public finance theorist, if one neglects his normative concerns. Here we strike a fertile mind.[30] His conditions can be used as a yardstick against current developments and may help in the formulation of policy.

## NOTES

1.  This material was presented at the Workshop of the Max-Planck-Institute for Research into Economic Systems on 'History of Evolutionary Thought in Economics' in Jena, August

26–28, 1999. I thank Mrs. Gabriele Brandt for her useful detailed critiques, the editor for much worthwhile advice, and the other workshop participants for their valuable suggestions, which helped to improve the chapter. Any remaining errors are my own.

2. See also my earlier (1997) work on Schmoller's and Wagner's contributions to a system of social security.
3. The *Grundlegung* (Foundations) is Wagner's own work and part of his (1892–94) which grew out of a revision of Rau's textbook on political economy.
4. See his (1877–1901).
5. Wagner (1863).
6. Wagner (1863), op. cit., p. 31. In note 3, p. 296, Wagner referred to a textbook by Umpfenbach as the original source of the Law. The original quote reads as follows:

'Im ganzen ist der Bereich der Staatsthätigkeit immer ausgedehnter geworden, je mehr sich die Staatsidee entwickelte, eine je höhere Stufe der Civilisation und Cultur ein Volk erreichte, je mehr neue Anforderungen in Folge dessen an den Staat gestellt wurden. Damit ist dann aber auch die Größe des Staatsbedarfes fortwährend gewachsen, und zwar relativ meist noch stärker als der Bereich der Staatsthätigkeit, weil das System der zur Erreichung der Staatszwecke dienenden Mittel complizirter, umfassender, kostspieliger wurde und ein und dasselbe Bedürfnis auf eine immer vollkommenere, höhere, feinere Weise seine Befriedigung verlangte. Welcher Fortschritt ist z.B. in dieser Beziehung im Unterrichtswesen eingetreten! Die Erscheinung hat den Charakter und die Bedeutung eines "Gesetzes" im Leben des Staates: der Staatsbedarf ist bei fortschreitenden Völkern in regelmässiger Vermehrung begriffen. Hiermit steht die bekannte Richtung der gegenwärtigen Zeit auch keineswegs in Widerspruch, wonach gerade jetzt in einer Menge von Lebensbeziehungen der Staatsbürger, besonders in der speciell volkswirthschaftlichen Sphäre, die befördernde, bevormundende, regulierende, in Alles sich einmischende Thätigkeit der Staatsgewalt wenigstens bei den germanischen Nationen vielfach beschränkt und beseitigt wird.'

7. Wagner (1911).
8. On the two missions of health economics as enhancing the understanding of economic behaviour on one hand and as input for health policy and health services research on the other, see Fuchs (1999).
9. In public finance, by 'state' is meant the best service provider for the task defined as a state task; for instance for canals, postal services, or electricity, the national level would most likely be appropriate; for more local tasks such as garbage disposal a regional or city level would be chosen (compare Wagner, 1901 (2) ).
10. When savings can be realized by producing more of a good or service, then economies of scale are present. When a broader range of goods or services leads to savings, then we speak of economies of scope.
11. Wagner (1911), op. cit, p. 736: 'U. a. sind die naturwissenschaftlichen Fortschritte in der Erkenntnis der Bedingungen von Gesundheit und Krankheit der Menschen, der Tiere, der Pflanzen in betreff von Licht, Luft, Wasser, Nahrungsmitteln, Wohnung usw., Krankheitserregern, Vorkehrungsmitteln dabei in vielen dieser Beziehungen von Einfluß darauf, daß die öffentlichen, die Staatstätigkeiten sich im Gesamtinteresse immer weiter ausdehnen, um Wohlfahrtsbedingungen dieser Art zu verbürgen.'
12. Wagner (1911), op. cit, p. 736: 'Das Präventivprinzip mit umfassenden Einrichtungen zur Prävention von Rechtsstörungen und anderen Uebeln (so auf dem Gebiete des Gesundheitswesens), ... wird immer mehr zur Durchführung gebracht, so daß das Repressivsystem zurücktritt.'
13. See Wagner (1883), p. 4.
14. Here, the link to the Baumol-Bowen hypothesis is obvious, which states that a culturally rising society will adopt more capital-intensive methods over time, and those sectors which succeed best in the adoption of these methods will be the most productive sectors in the economy.
15. An overview of the literature of empirical tests of Wagner's Law is provided by Demirbas (1999).

16. On the subsidiarity principle in a history of economic thought perspective, see for instance Jürgen Backhaus (1998).
17. Wagner's condition is of current importance if we look at the example of the Euro. The Maastricht criteria of convergence have as their goal to achieve budgetary discipline.
18. The intellectual link to Wicksell (and therefore Buchanan) is obvious at this point.
19. This was suggested at the Jena Workshop of Evolutionary Economics. Another suggestion was to look at the work of Joseph Schumpeter, who saw a role for the state as a political entrepreneur, which would possibly fit into the context of evolutionary economics. I did not follow up on the latter suggestion, as it is not immediately connected to public health economics. There was, however, a consensus at the Workshop that the role of the state in evolutionary economics needs further attention.
20. Wagner did not explicitly apply his conditions to the provision and finance of health care.
21. For a discussion see for example Maarse and Paulus (1998).
22. For an in-depth discussion of the justification of equity and redistribution in health care see Williams (1997).
23. Buchanan tried to understand and solve the following dilemma of the British National Health Service: on the one hand people presumably should have an incentive to consume more care, because additional care is considered to be beneficial, on the other hand, taxpayers are not willing to finance all care that is being demanded at a zero price. In the NHS, the price mechanism cannot be used to equalize demand and supply, therefore, as a consequence of the dilemma described, other measures of rationing prevail, such as long waiting times, priority lists, exclusion of some forms of therapy, and so on. For a discussion of collective and market solutions of this dilemma see Pauly (1999).
24. Here we recognize a parallel between Wagner and Buchanan. Wagner realized that a collective decision is required when marginal costs cannot be differentiated. Buchanan went a step further in viewing the resulting additional cost due to moral hazard 'not as disembodied (or even specifically game-theoretic) individual or insurance-firm behaviour but rather placing it explicitly in the context of collective choice'. Pauly disagreed with the collective approach and rather suggested giving people a choice of highly differentiated insurance contracts. Pauly, op. cit., p. 2 (preliminary Internet version).
25. See the report by Alvin Benn, 'Saints of Selma'. *Montgomery Advertiser.* 28 July, 1999, pp. 1A, 4A.
26. In the long run, federal programmes tend to lead to agglomeration. This is one reason why people move from the countryside to the city, it is cheaper there. This effect is known as Brecht's Law. Another law, Popitz's Law, states that in the case of federal states, one can find a long-run tendency towards centralization in the development of the shares of the central state, of the single states and of the cities as part of all public expenditures. Compare Wittmann (1970).
27. Wagner did not investigate the process of economic development in detail. This task was left for Schumpeter, who focussed on the role of persons with leadership qualities, who pick up inventions and turn them into innovations. He considered those innovators as the driving force of economic development. Compare Schumpeter (1912).
28. For a discussion of the Baumol-Bowen hypothesis see my (2000).
29. Compare Fuchs (1986).
30. In comparison with his contemporary and leader of the Younger Historical School, Gustav Schmoller, Wagner's strength lay in his normative approach. Schmoller arrived at conclusions solely on the basis of empirical statistical material. See Jürgen Backhaus (1997).

# REFERENCES

Backhaus, Jürgen G. (ed.) (1997), *Essays on Social Security and Taxation. Gustav Schmoller and Adolph Wagner Reconsidered*, Marburg: Metropolis Verlag.

Backhaus, Jürgen (1998), 'Christian Wolff on subsidiarity, the division of labor, and social welfare', in *Christian Wolff, Gesammelte Werke, II. ABT. Bd. 45, Christian Wolff and Law & Economics,* Hildesheim: Georg Olms, pp. 19–36.

Backhaus, Ursula (1997), 'Historical approaches to health economics', in Backhaus, Jürgen (ed.), *Essays on Social Security and Taxation. Gustav von Schmoller and Adolph Wagner Reconsidered,* Marburg: Metropolis-Verlag, Marburg, pp. 445–71.

Backhaus, Ursula (2000), 'My family doctor is not a robot: an application of the Baumol-Bowen Hypothesis to health care', in G. Meijer, W. J. M. Heijman, J. A. C. van Ophem, B. H. J. Verstegen (eds), *The Maastricht ISINI-Papers,* Vol. I, pp. 25–34. The Netherlands: Shaker Publishing.

Demirbas, Safa (1999), 'Cointegration Analysis-Causality Testing and Wagner's Law: The Case of Turkey, 1950–1990', paper presented at the annual meeting of the European Public Choice Society, 7–10 April, Lisbon, Portugal.

Fuchs, Victor R. (1986), *The Health Economy,* Ch. 15: 'The Battle for Control of Health Care,' Cambridge, MA and London: Harvard University Press.

Maarse, Hans and Paulus, Aggie (1998), 'Health insurance reforms in the Netherlands, Belgium and Germany: a comparative analysis', in, Leidl, R. (ed.), *Health Care and its Financing in the Single European Market,* Amsterdam: IOS Press, (Biomedical and Health Research, Vol. 18). pp. 230–53.

Musgrave, Richard A. and Peacock, Alan T. (eds) (1958), *Classics in the Theory of Public Finance,* London: The Macmillan Company.

Pauly, Mark (1999), 'James Buchanan as a health economist', http://www.uni-duisburg.de/FB1/PHILO/Buchanan/files/pauly.htm. Forthcoming in: *Festschrift for Buchanan.*

Schumpeter, Joseph (1912), *The Theory of Economic Development,* Leipzig: Duncker & Humblot.

Wagner, Adolph (1863), *Die Ordnung des österreichischen Staatshaushaltes,* (The System of the Austrian State Budget), Androsch, Hannes, Haschek, Helmut, and Vranitzky, Franz (eds), with a preface by Knapp, Horst, Vienna: Verlag Christian Brandstätter.

Wagner, Adolph (1877–1901), *Finanzwissenschaft* (The Science of Public Finance), published in four parts, Leipzig and Heidelberg: C. F. Winter sohe Verlagshandlung.

Wagner, Adolf (1883), 'Three extracts on public finance', extracts from *Finanzwissenschaft,* Part I, (3), Leipzig 1883. pp. 4–16, 69–76, in: Musgrave, Richard A. and Peacock, Alan T. (eds) (1958), *Classics in the Theory of Public Finance,* London: The Macmillan Company, pp. 1–15.

Wagner, Adolph (1892–94), 'Grundlegung' (Foundations), a part of his *Lehr- und Handbuch der politischen Oekonomie* (Text- and Handbook of the Political Economy), Leipzig: Winter.

Wagner, Adolph (1901 (2) ), 'Der staat' (The State), in *Handwörterbuch der Staatswissenschaften.* Jena: Gustav Fischer, pp. 907–51.

Wagner, Adolph (1911), 'II. Staat in nationalökonomischer Hinsicht', (The State in Economic Perspective), in *Handwörterbuch der Staatswissenschaften,* Jena, Verlag Gustav Fischer, pp. 727–39.

Williams, Alan (1997), *Being Reasonable about the Economics of Health. Selected Essays by Alan Williams.* Culyer, A. J. and Maynard, Alan (eds), Cheltenham: Edward Elgar.

Wittmann, Walter (1970), *Einführung in die Finanzwissenschaft,* (Introduction to Public Finance). Stuttgart: Fischer, pp. 13–16.

# 8. The evolution of the economic principle and motive towards a creative homo agens

**Hans Maks**

## INTRODUCTION

The more or less received opinion equates neoclassical insights with those of Chicago School economists of the last half of the twentieth century. This equation, of course is a very dubious one. It is even to a large extent untenable. The neoclassical revolution as a reaction on the classical school around the 1860s has a much broader scope than Chicago. The development within neoclassical economics lead to a philosophy of the economic science that stands clearly in contradiction with Chicago with its essentially perfect rationality and its narrow economic motive.

In evolutionary economics the agents are bounded rational. In this paper the development of apriorism, the mainstream philosophy of economic science, towards bounded rationality is sketched. An essential element of apriorism is the idea that the economist should always start his or her analysis from a core of assumptions, in which he or she can have great confidence. The mainstream philosophy of economic science, at least until the 1950s, is apriorism, especially empirical apriorism.

A great number of economists, when writing about their philosophy of science, reveal ideas which are related to those of the classical author John Stuart Mill, the Neo-Classical and Austrian author Carl Menger and neoclassicist Lionel R. Robbins and the Austrian Ludwig von Mises. This applies, for example, to Senior, Cairnes, Dietzel, J.M. Keynes, Schumpeter and Nelson and Winter. In my seventh section this point is further developed. Therefore, to understand apriorism it is useful to give a fairly extensive and precise sketch of the ideas of Mill, Menger, Robbins and Mises. The second to sixth sections are an attempt to do this, by focusing attention on the arguments these writers give for their philosophies and to emphasize the restrictions they see in the applicability of their ideas. In the eighth section it will turn out that evolutionary economics with its bounded economic rationality, fits the ninth empirical apriorism in its modern Robbins-Mises form. Finally, the ninth section shows that economic theories built upon subjective, creative (evolutionary) apriorism can be falsifiable.

## THE CLASSICAL PHILOSOPHY OF ECONOMIC SCIENCE ACCORDING TO MILL

The title of Mill's essay, 'On the Definition of Political Economy; And on the Method of Investigation Proper to It', emphasizes the important relation that, according to Mill, exists between this definition and the appropriate method of analysis. The social sciences should concentrate on the 'principles of human nature which are peculiarly connected with the ideas and feelings generated in man by living in a state of society'.[1]

Moreover he states: 'When an effect depends on a concurrence of causes, those causes must be studied one at a time, and their laws separately investigated, if we wish through the causes to obtain the power of either predicting or controlling the effect.'[2]

And: 'In order to judge how he [that is, man in society] will act under the variety of desires and aversions which are currently operating upon him, we must know how he would act under the exclusive influence of each one in particular.'[3]

Given these statements Mill's description of the task of economics hardly contains a surprise. Economics, as a branch of the social sciences, is concerned with man in society:

> solely as a being who desires to possess wealth, and who is capable of judging of the comparative efficacy of means for obtaining that end. It predicts only such of the phenomena of the social state as take place in consequence of the pursuit of wealth. It makes entire abstraction of every other human passion or motive; except those which may be regarded as perpetually antagonizing principles to the desire of wealth, namely aversion to labour, and desire of the present enjoyment of costly indulgences.[4]

The first of the sentences in this quotation is, in Mill's view, an accurate description of the law of human nature whose consequences in various classes of circumstances economics has to study, and from which this science has its solid starting point. One may of course wonder on what grounds Mill bases this contention. In the first place he argues:

> The desires of man, and the nature of conduct to which they prompt him, are within the reach of our observation. We can also observe what are the objects which excite these desires. The materials of this knowledge every one can principally collect within himself; with reasonable consideration of the differences, of which experience discloses to him the existence, between himself and others.[5]

Hence introspection reveals the distinguishable desires: the pursuit of wealth is the subject for economics. The rest of Mill's argument follows from his conception of what a social science should do.

So, all economic analysis should start from an economic man knowing his economic goal and the relative efficiency of means to achieve it. This core is to be supplemented with assumptions specifying classes of circumstances. Next, analytically implied consequences are to be deduced from this conjunction of fundamental and specifying axioms. If the results of such specified theories are to be confronted with reality one has to investigate, firstly, with which class of cases the particular set of circumstances correspond.[6]

Secondly, one has to investigate what other circumstances are apparent. These may or may not 'operate upon human conduct through the economic principle [i.e. law] of human nature'.[7]

If they do, one may consider whether they are of a sufficient general importance to supplement the theory with additional specifying assumptions, or to replace some of the auxiliary assumptions, in order to arrive at a revised and specialized theory. If they work through the laws of nature of other social sciences, the case falls outside the province of economics.[8] Economics is applicable only to those 'departments of human affairs, in which the acquisition of wealth is the main and acknowledged end'.[9]

These conclusions must be supplemented in two aspects, both mainly originating in the complexity of the circumstances. The first concerns prediction, and the second those cases in which the acquisition of wealth is not the only main and acknowledged end. According to Mill, the social sciences cannot be sciences of 'positive predictions, but only of tendencies',[10] because 'observation in circumstances of complexity is apt to be imperfect'.[11]

The complexity arises from the 'extraordinary number and variety of the data or elements – of the agents which, . . ., co-operate towards the effect'.[12]

Hence one can only infer tendencies, that is, one can only conclude 'from the laws of human nature applied to the circumstances of a given state of society, that a particular cause will operate in a certain manner unless counteracted'.[13]

If an effect depends on different laws of human nature one should consider 'all the causes which conjunctly influence the effect and compound their laws [that is of the different social sciences concerned] with one another'.[14]

In such a case the complexity problem of the circumstances may worsen in such a way that the confidence in the results of the deduction process as well as in the comparison of these results with those observed 'diminishes in value, . . . , in so rapid a ratio as soon to become entirely worthless'.[15]

In such instances Mill recommends that one postulates laws obtained 'conjecturally from specific experience, and afterwards connect them with the principles of human nature by a priori reasonings, wich reasonings are thus a real verification'.[16] Mill refers to this method as the inverse deductive method.[17]

To summarize Mill's philosophy of science one can proceed as follows. Each of the branches of the social sciences should study the consequences of one law of human nature, considered in isolation. The formation of theories in a social science consists in the development of conclusions analytically correctly deduced from a set of axioms. This set has a core, consisting of the law of human nature of the particular social science concerned. In economics this fundamental postulate states that the sole end of mankind is to acquire wealth and that it knows the relative efficiency of means to achieve that end. Mill's definition of the task of economics contains this postulate. In addition economics should analyse the consequences of the fundamental axiom in various classes of circumstances.

Two arguments, basically, defend this method. Firstly, Mill sees it as the best way to understand and explain social effects. For we should know the effect of each law separately, before we are able to explain an effect from a conjunction of laws. Secondly, observation, but principally introspection, teaches what the different laws of human nature are. Hence, introspection also reveals the economic law of human nature.

The fundamental axiom has to be supplemented with assumptions, describing classes of specific circumstances, which influence the outcome of the analysis. Economists should develop specialized theories concerning relevant (that is, sufficiently general) classes of circumstances. Predictions can only be made in a conditioned sense, in other words if the auxiliary assumptions remain close enough to the circumstances of the particular case.

A posteriori confrontation of a specialized theory with the facts may indicate replacement or supplementation of the auxiliary assumptions. It may also suggest that other laws of human nature are involved. Then, one may consider combining the expertise concerning the principles of human nature involved in an effort to analyse their compound effects. Such analysis rapidly becomes too difficult a task, because of the complicating influence of the auxiliary axioms specifying the circumstances. Then, Mill recommends the use of the 'inverse deductive' instead of the 'concrete deductive' method.

## NEO-CLASSICAL AND EARLY AUSTRIAN PHILOSOPHY OF ECONOMIC SCIENCE ACCORDING TO MENGER

According to Menger theoretical science has and must have an exact and an empirically realistic branch.[18] These branches differ in two aspects, namely the amount of abstraction and the nature of the laws involved. In the empirically realistic branch one starts the analysis from 'real types'. These types describe the typical, characterizing features of the real phenomena. Within this there is some room for peculiarities.[19] The empirical laws related to these 'real types' are to be arrived at by observation of the regularities in subsequence and coexistence of the real phenomena. Menger sees as the most important property of this kind of laws that they cannot be guaranteed to hold without exception.[20] However, exact laws, which hold without exception, can be obtained by the exact method of theoretical science. The task of the exact social science is, as Menger states it, to analyse

> the phenomena of mankind from the most original and most fundamental forces and motives, and to investigate to what effects each basic, separate motive of human nature leads in a completely free behaviour not restricted by any factors, particularly not by error, ignorance of the situation or external compulsion.[21]

In this way we obtain a series of social theories: each taken apart gives only one aspect of human behaviour; taken together however they allow us to understand social behaviour.[22] Exact economics has to analyse the consequences of a very important motive, that of human self interest in its striving to satisfy its needs for goods in complete freedom and with full knowledge of all relevant facts.[23] The exact mode of inquiry is to be based on 'strict types', describing the strictly typical elements of the realities. For economics Menger lists as 'strict types': the human need for goods, goods directly offered by nature, including means of production, and the pursuit of the highest satisfaction of these needs.[24] Exact laws are related to these 'strict types'.

Menger's philosophy concerning the exact social sciences is obviously related to Mill's concrete deductive method. They use virtually identical arguments for the assumptions from which each instance of economic analysis has its solid starting point. First, one should analyse each tendency of human nature, taken in isolation. Then one should put them together to arrive at a full understanding of social behaviour. Economics is concerned with a very important motive, described in the solid core assumptions. These axioms are also very much alike for both authors. Mill defines his economic man 'as a being who desires to possess wealth and who is capable of judging the comparative efficacy of means for obtaining that end'.[25]

Menger's economic man strives to satisfy his needs for goods in complete freedom and with full knowledge. Mill is willing to confront the deduced results of an economic theory, specified with auxiliary assumptions with reality in cases where the economic end is the main and acknowledged one. At the same time he suggests that this is an important and large class of cases.[26] Menger is hardly prepared to confront the theoretical results with reality, being convinced that a theory with his core, economic man assumption accords with full reality only in very rare cases.[27] He classifies testing of exact theories against reality as a denial of the basic principles of the exact method.[28]

'Nothing is so certain' as Menger puts it 'as that the results of exact analysis seem . . . unrealistic to the norms of reality'.[29]

Menger thinks that this distinction between an exact and an empirically realistic branch applies to all sciences. To illustrate this point he states, as an example, that chemistry postulates the unrealistic laws that elements and their compounds exist in their full purity and that they are identical in their real phenomena for all times and places.[30]

Furthermore it is to be emphasized, in the most explicit way possible, that Menger warns against a one-sided use of only the exact method.[31] In his view the finding of empirically realistic laws is of great importance for the prediction and the control of phenomena in the real economy.[32] He also adds that the more complex the situation is, the more difficult the application of the exact method is.[33] So, again we find a parallel idea with Mill. He also sees application of the concrete deductive method as a more difficult task in more complex situations. Moreover, Menger's empirically realistic method obtains empirical laws in the same way as Mill's inverse deductive method. But since, in Menger's view, empirical laws can never be guaranteed to hold without exception, he cannot see Mill's connective reasoning to the principles of human nature as a verifying procedure.

Menger strongly criticizes the view of the Historical School.[34] According to the adepts of this school the economic phenomena should be studied in an inseparable relation with the social and political (*staatlichen*) development of the peoples.[35] Economics should not start its analysis from an unrealistic economic man assumption, because in reality many, sometimes conflicting, motives lead to human action. Menger acknowledges this principle as guideline for a historic understanding. History should teach all aspects of all phenomena.[36] As already pointed out above, theoretical sciences should study the consequences of each basic human motive in isolation, whereas a universal, full understanding of the social phenomena can only be obtained by a conjunction of social sciences. Moreover, the real types and the empirical laws of the realistic method also abstract from full reality. Without abstraction, one cannot obtain any law, as Menger puts it.[37] But empirical laws related to specified real types are, of course, influenced by the context of law, and so on morality, within which the real types concerned have been observed. Hence, Menger considers an attempt to imply non-economic factors in the empirically realistic branch as superfluous.[38]

In this connection one may observe the following. The critique of the Historical School did not and does not find any considerable momentum among economists. Hereto one can add that the work related to this school

has, with a few exceptions, been stuck into the collection of empirical data, of which the theoretical processing was postponed to a distant future. When they tried a theoretical reasoning, they usually used the just heavily criticized principles of the abstract economic theories.[39]

# NEO-CLASSICAL PHILOSOPHY OF ECONOMIC SCIENCE ACCORDING TO ROBBINS

Robbins also emphatically deals with the definition of the task of economics.[40] As in the cases of Mill and Menger the resulting concept is closely related to his philosophy of science. Economics has, as Robbins posits it, to analyse human behaviour purposively directed to ends with scarce means, which have alternative uses.[41] Scarcity 'means limitation in relation to demand'.[42]

He stresses that 'economics is entirely neutral between ends' and 'to speak of end as being itself "economic" is entirely misleading'.[43]

As is rather obvious this definition of the task of economics differs from the ones given by Mill and Menger. In Mill's concept there is clearly an economic end: the desire to possess wealth. This also applies to Menger, for whom the fullest attainment of satisfaction with goods is the economic motive. Hence, Robbins does not consider economics that part of the social sciences that concentrates on the economic motive, and abstracts from the other human desires, as Mill and Menger do. Furthermore, his definition does not imply the assumption of fully efficient or completely rational use of the given means to achieve the given end, whereas Mill and Menger assume something that is very much akin to this economic principle. It only implies purposive action.[44] So it is to be noted that Robbins' description of the task of economics does not contain his core assumptions, the consequences of which the economist has to analyse in various cases. This task, however, is precisely the nature of economic analysis as he sees it. That nature consists:

> of deductions from a series of postulates, the chief of which are almost universal facts of experience present whenever human activity has an economic aspect, the rest being assumptions of a more limited nature based upon the general features of particular situations which the theory is to be used to explain.[45]

Obviously this proposition is by and large in agreement with the philosophies of Menger and Mill. The subsidiary postulates concern 'the condition of markets, the number of parties to the exchange, the state of the law, *the minimum sensible* of buyers and sellers, and so on'.[46]

So these auxiliary assumptions may be drawn from 'historico-relative material'.[47] This does not apply for the main, core assumptions.[48] Robbins lists as examples of these universal axioms:

- 'the different things that the individual wants to do have a different importance to him, and can be arranged therefore in a certain order.'[49]
- the law of diminishing returns, i.e. the increase of the amount of one factor of production without increasing the amounts of the others leads to a less than proportional increase of the product.[50]

- the uncertainty with regard to the future availability of scarce good and scarce factors.[51]
- the existence of indirect change.[52]

As a third kind of premises Robbins adds 'approximative' assumptions such as perfect rationality and perfect foresight 'which are introduced into economic analysis at various stages of approximation of reality'.[53]

The purpose of this kind of assumption is:

> to enable us to study, in isolation, tendencies which, in the world of reality, operate in conjunction with many others, and then, by contrast as much as by comparison, to turn back to apply the knowledge thus gained to the explanation of more complicated situations.[54]

So, although Robbins rejects the economic principle (since he lists as universal axiom the uncertainty with regard to the future availability of scarce goods and scarce factors), he allows assumptions of this (third) kind as intermediate steps towards full reality. This point of view clearly differs from the insights of Menger and Mill.

However it must be stated that Robbins does not elaborate on this, for instance how these approximations must be improved and how the obtained results relate to other sciences. With regard to the confrontation of the conclusions of the deducted results with reality Robbins identifies three functions:[55]

- a check on the applicability of different types of theoretical constructions to given situations
- the suggestion of the auxiliary postulates
- the exposure of areas where pure theory needs to be reformulated and extended.

From given data the predictions of the economic theory follow logically and inevitably. So, if the circumstances and the auxiliary assumptions correspond, then the deduced conclusions are inevitable predictions. But, of course 'if the data change, the consequences predicted do not necessarily follow'.[56]

Moreover, as Robbins adds:

> the very fact that events in the large are uncontrolled, that the fringe of given data is so extensive and so exposed to influence form unexpected quarters, must make the task of prediction, however carefully safeguarded, extremely hazardous.[57]

These insights, regarding prediction and the confrontation of theory with reality, coincide largely with Mill's ideas.

Although Robbins acknowledges the value of applied economics related to index data for certain practical purposes, he emphasizes that the conclusions thus obtained do not follow from the laws of pure theory.[58] Moreover, he states very explicitly that attempts to obtain quantitative laws will not lead to results of a permanent value: not one quantitative law of permanent value has emerged, not in the studies of the Historical School, not from the Institutionalists and not from the applications of modern statistical techniques by adepts of 'orthodox' theoretical analysis.[59] They may, however, provide some guideline for short-term predictions.[60]

## MODERN-AUSTRIAN PHILOSOPHY OF ECONOMIC SCIENCE ACCORDING TO MISES

Finally, we will discuss Mises. He sees economics as a part of praxeology. This theoretical science is concerned with human action. To act means 'to strive after ends, that is to choose a goal and to resort to means in order to attain the goal sought'; or: 'Action is purposive conduct. It is not simply behaviour but begot by judgements of value, aiming at a definite end and guided by ideas concerning the suitability of definite means'.[61]

This purposive action should be done so that 'no less urgently desired end should be satisfied if its satisfaction prevents the attainment of a more urgently desired end'.[62]

Economics is, according to Mises, the only elaborated branch of praxeology and deals 'with all market phenomena, in all their aspects'.[63]

It is remarkable that the task Mises sees for praxeology coincides very much with the task Robbins defines for economics. So, economics in Robbins' sense can clearly be conceived of as a part of, or as identical to, Mises' praxeology. And their philosophies of science have more in common. It is obvious that his description of purposive action implies Robbins' ordered preferences assumption. Mises also emphasizes the uncertainty of the future,[64] which is Robbins' third basic postulate. For Mises states that 'the predictions of praxeology are, within the range of their applicability, absolutely certain'.[65]

But the value judgments concerning the ends of human action may change in the future, so it cannot be known in advance whether the anticipation of these future value judgments based on specific historical understanding will be correct.[66]

Moreover Mises acknowledges the auxiliary assumptions, as he states:

> Into the chain of praxeology reasoning, the praxeologist introduces certain assumptions concerning the condition of the environment in which an action takes place. Then he tries to find out how these conditions affect the result to which the reasoning must lead. The question whether or not the real conditions of the external world correspond to these assumptions is to be answered by experience.[67]

Notable related views also concern prediction. So, it turns out that one need not hesitate in placing Mises within the framework of empirical apriorism.

Finally we should emphasize two additional properties that are compatible with the subjective rationality concept of Robbins and Mises. As we have seen in the development of the *homo oeconomicus,* rationality becomes subjective in two aspects: it lacks an objective economic motive and it does not imply an objective economic principle. This supplies scope firstly for bounded rationality in the form of satisficing behaviour and secondly for creative, entrepreneurial behaviour.

About routine, satisfaction level driven behaviour Mises state the following:

> Most of a man's daily behaviour is simple routine. He performs certain acts without paying special attention to them. He does many things because he was trained in his childhood to do them, because other people behave in the same way, and because it is customary in his environment. He acquires habits, he develops automatic actions. But he indulges in these habits only because he welcomes their effects. As soon as he discovers that the pursuit of the habitual way may hinder the attainment of ends considered as more desirable, he changes his attitude.[68]

Next one should add to this subjective satisfaction level/maximizing aspect of economic behaviour the entrepreneurial element: 'In any real and living economy every actor is always an entrepreneur'.[69]

Moreover this entrepreneurship human action is 'seen from the aspect of the uncertainty inherent in every action'[70] and: 'Entrepreneur means acting man in regard to the changes occurring in the data of the market'.[71]

So, what we see is that both routine, satisfaction level driven behaviour and entrepreneurial action find their place in Mises' subjective, bounded rationality concept.

## CHARACTERIZATION OF MILL, MENGER, ROBBINS AND MISES WITH A FEW KEY WORDS

It may be useful to list a few keywords to characterize the essential features of the philosophies of science which have been discussed so far. These concepts are: economic motive, economic principle, empirical, exact and apriorism. 'Economic motive' means here that the author concerned believes that it possible to define an economic end. 'Economic principle' refers to postulates assuming that human action, directed to given ends, is capable of striving after these ends in an efficient way. The predicate 'empirical' refers to the idea that the results of economic analysis should be applied and confronted with reality in a way described for Mill, Robbins and Mises in the second, fourth and fifth sections.[72] The adjective 'exact' indicates Menger's view that the results of exact economic analysis should not be tested against reality. Finally 'apriorism' stands for the idea that all economic analysis should start from a basic set of axioms, a core in which the economist can have great confidence, supplemented with auxiliary assumptions specifying classes of circumstances.

With these concepts Mill's concrete deductive method can be characterized as 'empirical apriorism', in which the core contains an economic motive and an economic principle. The exact method of Menger can be referred to as 'exact apriorism' with again an economic motive and principle as core. Robbins' and Mises' philosophy can be called 'empirical apriorism', in which the universal axioms do not include an economic end and efficient action. They only assume 'purposive action' and have an eye open for uncertainty and future changes.[73]

## RELATED VIEWS WITH AN ECONOMIC MOTIVE AND PRINCIPLE

A great number of authors have ideas which can be conceived of as a kind of mixture of those of Menger and Mill. This applies, for example, to Senior, Cairnes, Dietzel, and J.M. Keynes. Senior lists four 'elementary' core assumptions. The first of these implies 'efficient action'.[74] Cairnes reports two 'paramount mental principles', implying an economic motive and an economic principle. Moreover he also points out two kinds of subsidiary axioms. Of these two kinds an economist should always use one in some specified form. They relate to propensities, determining the laws of population, and to the physical qualities of the soil and other natural agents.[75] Dietzel distinguishes between psychological 'core' premises and social 'subsidiary' postulates. The first two of his three psychological assumptions state an economic motive and efficient action respectively. As general 'core' assumptions of J.M. Keynes one may list:

> the principle that men desire to increase their sum of satisfactions with the smallest possible sacrifice to themselves, the law of decreasing final utility as amount of commodity increases, the law of diminishing return from the land, and the like, . . .[76]

As less general subsidiary assumptions he denotes the alternative hypotheses of free competition and pure monopoly. For the combination of all the assumptions he requires that 'all the phenomena at the period and place to which the investigator has primary reference'[77] be included. So, apart from the core the theory must contain adequate auxiliary assumptions.

# EVOLUTIONARY ECONOMICS: NELSON AND WINTER

The development we have sketched of the homo oeconomicus shows the following. One observes the disappearance of the economic motive. First we have Mill's economic motive: striving after wealth. This to a certain extent made more subjective by Menger: the agent pursues the highest satisfaction of the human needs for goods. But this goal can still be conceived as economic: it relates to satisfaction and goods. Robbins (the different things that the individual wants to do have a different importance to him, and can be arranged therefore in a certain order) and Mises (action is purposive conduct. It is not simply behaviour but begotten by judgments of value, aiming at a definite end) get rid of the economic motive: every motive behind the differences in importance or behind the judgment of value is acceptable. It may range from selfishness to altruism, from profit to sales or from power to prestige.

Moreover we see that the economic principle is replaced by the subjective belief that the action contributes to the goals striven for. First we see that Mill starts from the economic agent 'solely as a being who desires to possess wealth, and who is capable of judging of the comparative efficacy of means for obtaining that end'. So Mill adheres to the economic principle. Menger too states that exact economics has 'to investigate to what effects each basic, separate motive of human nature leads in a completely free behaviour not restricted by any factors, particularly not by error, ignorance of the situation or external compulsion'. One clearly notes the economic principle. But again this cannot be observed for Robbins (he emphasizes the uncertainty with regard to the future availability of scarce goods and scarce factors) and Mises (the value judgments concerning the ends of human action may change in the future, so it cannot be known in advance whether the anticipation of these future value judgments based on specific historical understanding will be correct). This implies that an economic agent may act purposively directed to his ends in the subjective perception that his or her action is effective. But it may turn out that this routine fails or innovative action does not lead to the desired effect.

So we have to analyse to what extent evolutionary economics adheres to this 'not founding its analysis on the economic motive and the economic principle'. This will be done on a limited basis. We will refer mainly to Nelson and Winter, because they can be considered as the seminal authors for evolutionary economics.

Nelson and Winter (1974) introduce the evolutionary framework. They criticize the Chicago approach. Against all tendencies in the development of neoclassical economics (as reflected in the works of for example Walras[78], Wicksell, Marshall, Schumpeter, Hicks, Hayek and many others, Chicago economists (among others Friedman, Posner, Muth, Lucas and Becker) returned to the old economic motive and principle method. Nelson and Winter rightly criticize the formal theories based upon this approach: in contemporary formal theory, the profit seeking subject is typically represented as the profit maximizing subject with choice sets precisely known and given.[79] They replace maximization decisions by routine behaviour as long as the aspiration levels are satisfied. If a firm fails to reach an aspiration level, a better action is searched for.[80] This coincides perfectly with Mises' subjective rationality: as soon as the subject discovers that the pursuit of the habitual way may hinder the attainment of ends considered as more desirable, he or she changes his or her attitude.[81]

The satisfaction level postulate is to be conceived as a specification of the subjective maximization principle reflecting the available information and the costs of information gathering and processing. The received routine will be replaced as soon as one expects that another course of action will perform better. Or as Nelson and Winter put it:

> Information imperfections, and informational differences among actors, are not complications of the basic structure, but are central to the Schumpeterian scheme. ... The gains obtainable by guessing better and acting sooner ... are the crucial motive power and adaptive mechanism of a system that is permanently in [intertemporal] disequilibrium.[82]

Evolutionary economics is typically concerned with modeling an intertemporal sequence of Hicksian or temporary Walrasian equilibria:

> Evolutionary economic models are, of course, intertemporal models. More specifically, they typically fall under the rubric of 'temporary equilibrium' models. Some economic processes are conceived as working very fast, driving some of the model variables to (temporary) equilibrium values within a single period. ... For example, in the model used in this paper, a short-run equilibrium price of output is established in every time period. Slower working processes of investment, and of technological and organizational change, operate to modify the data of the short-run equilibrium system from period to period.[83]

In this intertemporal disequilibrium consisting of a sequence of discoordinated temporary equilibria the role of entrepreneurial action is essential:

> And, because it arises from a continual unfolding of unanticipated possibilities, the disequilibrium is disequilibrium in the fundamental sense: expectations are not being realized, mistakes are being made and corrections attempted.[84]

Entrepreneurs make these attempted corrections. The better they perform the more chance they have to survive:

> Firms (and entrepreneurs) may seek profit, and may innovate or imitate to achieve higher profit. . . . . . The competitive environment within which firms operate is one

of struggle and motion. It is a dynamic selection environment, not an equilibrium one. The essential forces of growth are innovation and selection.[85]

Or:

evolutionary theory involves, finally, explicit analysis of the economic selection mechanism – the change in the weighing of different decision rules that comes about through the expansion of firms using profitable rules and the contraction of firms using unprofitable ones.[86]

From all these observations it seems safe to conclude that evolutionary approach adheres to subjective or bounded rationality very similar to the core assumptions of the empirical apriorism of Robbins and Mises.

The question remains however whether evolutionary economic action restricts itself to the economic motive of striving after profit. So far, the entrepreneurial quest for profit could clearly be observed in evolutionary economics. This may lead to the impression that evolutionary economics restricts itself to the economic motive of profit as the sole aim of evolutionary economic action. However, Witt (1985 and 1986) describes the evolutionary selection of preferences (or motives) especially in relation to the debate about altruism and self-interest. Although prima facie profit may win from sales or political power as an entrepreneurial firm goal, the type of preferences that may survive in entrepreneurial consumer behaviour may vary with the social and institutional context. Whatever the result of these selection processes on motives, it shows that in principle evolutionary economics is not to be seen as a priori restricted to the economic (profit or income) motive.

## FALSIFIABILITY AND SUBJECTIVE RATIONALITY

One might be inclined to conclude that this development towards subjective rationality ends in non-falsifiable theories. So it might be useful to analyse whether this is a point that diminishes the value of evolutionary apriorism as a starting principle and core assumption of economics. Of course, the seminal contributor to the falsifiability concept is Popper.

According to Popper a theory is not verifiable but it may be falsifiable or refutable.[87] A theory is part of empirical science if it is refutable, that is, if it has empirical content. The empirical content of a theory is equal to the set of basic statements that refute the theory: the potential falsifiers.

A few properties of an such a Popperian empirical, falsifiable theory deserve to be emphasized. From the definition of this concept as given above, it follows that an empirical theory contains at least one empirical law. However, it does not mean that every law used in such a theory must be empirical. A subset of the axioms and conclusions can be, and often is, entirely non-empirical. Or as Popper puts it: 'The point is that all physical theories say much more than we can test' and 'most of the concepts with which physics works, such as forces, fields and even electrons and other particles are . . . qualitates occultae'.[88]

It is also to be stressed that the empirical content of a theory is more than just a formal property. The potential falsifiers of an empirical theory must satisfy a material requirement, namely,

> a requirement concerning the event which, as the basic statement tells us, is occurring at place *k*. This event must be an observable event; that is to say basic statements must be testable by observation.[89]

Klant (1979) considers falsifiability or testability as being a merely logical, syntactical and semantic property. However, this view opposes rather essentially Popper's ideas and is a fundamental step back in the direction of the logical positivism of Neurath and Carnap (1936, 1937). For they also believe that these kind of rules can select the well-formed sentences belonging to the language of empirical science.

Returning to Popper's fundamental point that refutable theories say more than we can test brings us back to the question whether economic theories built upon subjective, creative (evolutionary) apriorism can be falsifiable. They may be as long as their aprioristic core assumptions are adequately supplemented with assumptions that specify classes of 'empirical' classes (see Mill, second section above), with auxiliary assumptions that are drawn from historico-relative material (see Robbins, fourth section above), with assumptions concerning the conditions of the environment in which an action takes place (see Mises, fifth section above) or with assumptions that specify the better guessing and acting sooner behaviour or the profit seeking and innovating actions (see Nelson and Winter, section eight above). These additional assumptions in conjunction with the core may constitute Popperian refutable theories.

## SUMMARY

In evolutionary economics the agents are bounded rational. In this paper the development of apriorism, the mainstream philosophy of economic science, towards this evolutionary bounded rationality is examined. An essential element of apriorism is the idea that economists should always start their analysis from a core of assumptions, in which they can have great confidence. Since most aprioristic thinkers reflect to some extent the insights of Mises, Robbins, Menger and Mill, the latter are considered rather extensively.

Menger and Mill have virtually the same arguments for their almost identical core assumptions. For knowledge of the consequence of the various motives influencing human action, we must first know the consequences of each of these motives separately. Observation and/or introspection reveal to us what these motives are. This amounts to the core assumption of an economic man striving efficiently towards his economic end.

Economics has, as Robbins posits it, to analyse human behaviour purposively directed to ends with scarce means, which have alternative uses. As is rather obvious this definition of the task of economics differs from the ones given by Mill and Menger. In Mill's concept there is clearly an economic end: the desire to possess wealth. This also applies to Menger, for whom the fullest attainment of satisfaction with goods is the economic motive. Hence, Robbins does not consider economics that part of the social sciences that concentrates on the economic motive, and abstracts from the other human desires, as Mill and Menger do. Furthermore, his definition does not imply the assumption of fully efficient or completely rational use of the given means to achieve the given end, whereas Mill and Menger assume something that is very much akin to this economic principle. For Robbins it only implies purposive action.

Mises sees economics as a part of praxeology. This theoretical science is concerned with human action. To act means to strive after ends, that is to choose a goal and to resort to means in order to attain the goal sought. Action is purposive conduct. It is begotten by judgements of value, aiming at a definite end and guided by ideas concerning the suitability of definite means. Mises, like Robbins, emphasizes bounded rationality caused by the uncertainty of the future. Notable related views also concern prediction. Mises states that the predictions of praxeology are, within the range of their applicability, absolutely certain. But the value judgements concerning the ends of human action may change in the future, so it cannot be known in advance whether the anticipation of these future value judgements based on specific historical understanding will be correct.

Evolutionary economists replace maximization decisions by routine behaviour as long as the aspiration levels are satisfied. If a firm fails to reach an aspiration level, a better action is searched for. This coincides perfectly with Mises' subjective rationality. It is also shown that in principle evolutionary economics is not to be seen as a priori restricted to the economic (profit or income) motive.

Economic theories built upon subjective, creative (evolutionary) apriorism can be falsifiable as long as their aprioristic core assumptions are supplemented with assumptions of an adequate empirical nature.

## NOTES

1. See Mill (1874), p. 134.
2. Ibid., p. 139.

3. Ibid., p.139, the text between brackets is mine.
4. Ibid., pp. 137–8.
5. Ibid., p. 149.
6. Ibid., pp. 150–1.
7. Ibid., p. 151, the text between brackets is mine.
8. Ibid., p. 151.
9. Ibid., p. 139.
10. See Mill (1851), p. 477.
11. See Mill (1874), p. 153.
12. See Mill (1851), p. 474.
13. Ibid., p. 477.
14. Ibid., p. 474, the text between brackets is mine.
15. Ibid., p. 476.
16. Ibid., p. 476
17. Ibid., p. 477.
18. See Menger (1883), esp.Chapter 4.
19. Ibid., p. 36.
20. Ibid., pp. 36–38, 58.
21. Ibid., pp. 77–8. Menger's quotations have been translated by the author.
22. Ibid., pp. 77–8 and 42–3.
23. Ibid., esp. pp. 73–5 and 78.
24. Ibid., p. 45.
25. Mill (1874), pp. 137–8.
26. Mill (1874), p. 139.
27. Menger (1883), esp. p. 54–7.
28. Menger (1883), p. 54.
29. Ibid., p. 54.
30. Ibid., p. 76.
31. Ibid., pp. 46 and 52.
32. Ibid., p. 54.
33. Ibid., p. 52.
34. Ibid., esp. Chapters 6 and 7.
35. See for example. Dietzel (1864), p. 52 and Knies (1853), pp. 29 and 109 ff.
36. See Knies (1853), p. 67.
37. Ibid., p. 68.
38. Ibid., p. 70.
39. See Hennipman (1945), p. 19. The translation is mine.
40. See Robbins (1932), Chapter 1.
41. Robbins, op. cit., pp. 16, 24, 93.
42. Ibid., p. 46.
43. Ibid., p. 24.
44. Ibid., esp. pp. 93–4.
45. Ibid., pp. 99–100.
46. Ibid., pp. 79. Robbins explains this on p. 99: A change in price must attain the minimum sensible to have an effect.
47. Ibid., p. 80.
48. Ibid., p. 80.
49. Ibid., p. 75.
50. Ibid., pp. 76–7.
51. Ibid., pp. 77–8.
52. Ibid., p. 78.
53. Ibid., p. 94.
54. Ibid., p. 94.
55. Ibid., p. 118.
56. Ibid., p. 123.
57. Ibid., p. 125.

58. Ibid., esp. pp. 63–70.
59. Ibid., pp. 114–16.
60. Ibid., p. 108.
61. See Mises (1962), pp. 4–5 and 34.
62. Ibid., p. 69.
63. Ibid., p. 77.
64. Ibid., pp. 65–6.
65. Ibid., p. 65.
66. Ibid., p. 65.
67. Ibid., p. 44.
68. Mises (1949), pp. 46–7.
69. Ibid., p. 252.
70. Ibid., p. 254.
71. Ibid., p. 255.
72. So 'empirical apriorism' in our context differs in meaning from Klant's, see esp. (1979), p. 88.
73. See the sections on Robins and Mises above.
74. See Senior (1938), esp. pp. 26 ff.
75. See Cairnes (1875), esp. p. 41.
76. See Keynes (1891), p. 227.
77. Ibid., p. 227.
78. See Witteloostuijn and Maks (1989 and 1990) for Walras' philosophy on subjective rationality and time.
79. Nelson and Winter (1980), p. 179.
80. Nelson and Winter (1974), p. 891.
81. See again Mises (1949), pp. 46–7.
82. See Nelson and Winter (1977a), p. 271.
83. See Winter (1984), p. 288.
84. See Nelson and Winter (1977a), p. 271.
85. See Nelson and Winter 1974, p. 890.
86. Ibid., p. 893.
87. See Popper (1972a), p. 41.
88. See Popper (1972b), p. 266.
89. Ibid., p. 387.

# REFERENCES

Cairnes, J.E. (1875), *The Character and Logical Method of Political Economy*, London: Macmillan.

Carnap, R. (1936, 1937), 'Testability and meaning', *Philosophy of Science,* Indianapolis: Bobbs-Merrill, 3, 4, 419–71, 1–40.

Dietzel, C. (1864), *Die Volkswirtschaft und ihr Verhältnis zu Gesellschaft und Staat,* Frankfurt am Main: Saverländer.

Hennipman, P. (1945), *Economisch motief en economisch principe,* Amsterdam: Noord-hollandsche vitgeres maatschappij.

Keynes, J.M. (1891), *The Scope and Method of Political Economy,* London: Macmillan.

Klant, J.J. (1979), *Spelregels voor Economen,* Leiden: Stenfert Kroese.

Knies, Karl (1853), *Die politische ökonomic vom Standpunkte der geschicht Methode,* Braunschweig: Schwetsenke.

Menger, C. (1883), *Untersuchungen über die Methode der Sozialwissensehaften und der politischen Ökonomie insbesondere,* Leipzig: Duncker & Humblot.

Mill, J.S. (1851), *A System of Logic, Ratiocinative and Inductive,* vol. 11, London: Parker.

Mill, J.S. (1874), *Essays on Some Unsettled Questions of Political Economy,* London: Longmans, Green, Reader and Dyer.

Mises, L. von (1949), *Human Action,* New Haven, CT: Hodge.

Mises, L. von (1962), *The Ultimate Foundation of Economic Science,* Princeton, NJ: van Nostrand Comp.

Nelson, R.R. and S.G. Winter (1974), 'Neo-classical vs. evolutionary theories of economic growth: critique and prospectus', *Economic Journal,* 84, 886–905.

Nelson, R.R. and S.G. Winter (1977a), 'Simulation of Schumpeterian competition', *American Economic Review,* 67, 271–6.

Nelson, R.R. and S.G. Winter (1980), 'Firm and industry response to changed market conditions: an evolutionary approach', *Economic Enquiry,* 18, 179–202.

Popper, K.R. (1972a), *The Logic of Scientific Discovery,* London: Hutchinson.

Popper, K.R. (1972b), *Conjectures and Refutations,* London: Routledge and Kegan Paul.

Robbins, L. R. (1932), *An Essay on the Nature and Significance of Economic Science,* London: Macmillan.

Senior, N.W. (1938), *An Outline of the Science of Political Economy,* London: Allen & Unwin.

Witt, U. (1985), 'Economic behavior and biological evolution: some remarks on the sociobiology debate', *Journal of Institutional and Theoretical Economics,* 141, 365–89.

Witt, U. (1986), 'Firms' market behavior under imperfect information and economic natural selection', *Journal of Economic Behavior and Organization,* 7, 265–90.

Witteloostuijn, A. van and J.A.H. Maks (1989), 'Walras: a Hicksian *avant la lettre*', *Economie Appliquée,* 41, 595–608.

Witteloostuijn, A. van and J.A.H. Maks (1990), 'Walras on temporary equilibrium and dynamics', *History of Political Economy,* 22, 223–37.

# 9. Gustav Schmoller: an evolutionary economist

## Simon Duindam and Bernard Verstegen

### INTRODUCTION

On 21 January 1995 Professor Fase reviewed a book on John Kenneth Galbraith in a Dutch newspaper, *NRC-Handelsblad*. In this article Fase stated:

> Economists appear in different species. Roughly speaking, there are two, maybe three main groups. On the one side you have those theoretical economists that were inspired by Marshall, Walras and Keynes. They have given the science great abstraction and academic prosperity, and are esteemed highly in their own scientific circles. A narrow, mostly formal manner of discussion is their trademark and academic security without much social anxiety with mutual high esteem a prominent characteristic.
>
> On the other side there is the visionary mainstream, inspired by the German-Austrian organic descriptive, partly sociological-historical tradition. Its trademark is the living economic reality. In leading economic journals, you seldom see this approach, because contemporary academic fashion prefers no-risk puzzling to fantasy-filled reflection about great themes. In between lies the sympathetic island, inhabited by empirical and econometric workers. They are regarded with high esteem, although their work is often not regarded as the real reality. (Our translation)

One of the most important economists in the German-Austrian tradition is Gustav Schmoller. To get a better view on his work and why he is also an important evolutionary economist, it is important to have a closer look at the personality of Schmoller and his way of thinking, a narrative of which can be found extensively in Hansen (1996). Gustav Schmoller (1838–1917) was born in the vicinity of Heilbronn in a family that soon lost its mother. He spent a lot of time in the office of his father, a tax administrator, where he learned the foundations of political economy and economic governance of the state. During his holidays he could often be found in the nurseries of his grandfather Carl-Friedrich Von Gärtner. Gärtner tried to develop plant hybrids using many kinds of experiments. Because of the success of his programme around 1830 there was a departure from the founding axioms of biology, and a new field of research concerning the adaptation and changing of plant species could be opened up. It was for this research that Gärtner was decorated by the Royal Dutch Academy of Sciences.

Following the methods of his grandfather, Gustav Schmoller got his first impressions of a solid research method that could lead to the confirmation or rejection of assumptions, and aims to filter out wrong hypotheses.

Schmoller adopted this approach rather quickly, which initiated the change from a reflective way of thinking to a more active one, combined with a lot of experiments. Important insights that could not be checked in reality by observation or experiment and could fail, did not belong in the house of science according to Schmoller. It is not the deductive derivation from generalizations, which are regarded to be true in advance, that Schmoller saw as the main activity of science. The description of the particular should be used as a starting point, after which generalizations could follow. For Schmoller a prior correct interpretation of a concept, like income, or a scientific description as Adolph Wagner used them, did not exist. In Schmoller's way of thinking the formation of concepts depended on specific situations, so the contents of these concepts could unfold conditional on time and place. Inductive generalization could lead to more general hypothesis and to a more general specification of concepts.

Other than a vision of the cycle of induction and deduction, that comes forward when shaping and testing hypotheses, Schmoller acquired a permanent impression of the possibilities and impossibilities for correcting nature's development, if one has accumulated knowledge of nature by meaningful organization of empirical research activities. The formation of institutions by way of influencing their development, which we will elaborate on in the following paragraphs, can be seen as an extension of this approach.[1]

## METHODENSTREIT

Many scholars accuse Schmoller of lacking the methodological backgrounds, which are so important for science in general. This judgment even remained after Schmoller (1883) wrote down his methodological argument, which we also know as the historical-inductive method, in a long article. In the article he described the vital elements of the methodology used in the natural sciences at the beginning of the 19th century, which discerned it from the methodology of the natural sciences (biology) in the middle of that century, and he showed how this approach could be made feasible for economics. In this last part we also see the influence of Whewell's inductivism. One of the most important clarifications in Schmoller's methodology considered the role of concepts and the classification of their scientific content. The disagreement between Schmoller and many other scientists about the way of reasoning which should be followed in economics is known under the name 'Methodenstreit' [battle of methods]. Actually there have been different battles of method, however with respect to methodology, the 'Methodenstreit' between Schmoller and Carl Menger was the most important one, although Menger was nothing but a substitute for Adolph Wagner, who was Schmoller's real opponent in the social arena.

For a criticism of Schmoller's methods, reference often is made to Menger's classification of economic science. In this important piece, originating from Menger's dissertation, Menger views the insight in the 'generelles Wesen' of our surroundings as the focal point of all theoretical disciplines. A practical elaboration of this approach for economics is found according to Menger in the 'deductive method' developed by John Stuart Mill.[2] Schmoller refers to Menger's dissertation in his *Jahrbuch für Gesetzgebung, Verwaltung und Volkswirtschaft im Deutschen Reich* article in 1883, in which he regards the work of Menger as a part of an obsolete, old-fashioned way of science; a way of thinking that is based on the classical philosophical notion of science of Aristotle, in which definitions are seen as a priori insights into empirical reality.

Menger answered the same year with a furious response, in which he regarded Schmoller's notion of history as ridiculous and rejected his methodological conceptions. Formulated simply, he regarded Schmoller's work as a collection of historical facts without theoretical background.

Menger's ideas correspond with the notion of science generally held in that period, which would entail that economic policy should weed like a gardener the law-like generalizations which come forward from empirical reality, and use them as a priori principles. In his theory, the definition of an ideal situation in the national economy by using the maximization of individual levels of utility plays a very important role.

The fact that his definitions were based on the comparability of different sorts of utility, that could never be filled empirically, already shows that Menger's method would meet criticism. This criticism grew stronger the more abstract his thinking became and the link with reality was neglected. While Adam Smith always used very realistic and extensive descriptions of historical backgrounds, his followers only touched upon those issues which they considered as 'essential causes'.

In Schmoller's theory the deductive approach can be useful, if it is not part of some kind of a priori line of reasoning. The results of deduction should be tested, concepts should be provided with empirical content, hypotheses be liable to change, and so forth. In his opinion, every situation is unique. Sometimes a hypothesis is corroborated and sometimes it is rejected. If a hypothesis is corroborated we can state that the results of the deductive approach contain truth for the given situation.[3] Little by little researchers are generating transcendent knowledge, always after inductive processes. In this approach concepts are not defined axiomatically beforehand, but a gradual development of the content of concepts takes place based on empirical research.

## FINAL REMARKS

Schmoller put the state at the centre of economic analysis. In his view it is the state that can bring societies to a higher economic level, because it can provide for a framework within which complex market processes can take place, by arranging different institutions. So by designing institutions and by influencing their evolutionary path of development, the state can lead a market economy into the right direction and stimulate its economic development. The scientific influence on the design of public governance, as an integral part of economic theory, is another important aspect of Schmoller's contribution to economic science.

Another aspect of Schmoller's approach to economics is his radical support of interdisciplinarity between all aspects of the social sciences, including economics. Practising economics without considering law, sociology, cultural sciences and so on to him was unthinkable. From the outset of his academic career Schmoller had a profound interest in the use of institutions for solving social problems and for bringing coherence into a market economy.

Today, these developments continue in disciplines like law-and-economics, institutional economics, evolutionary economics and economic history (cliometrics). Disciplines that have earned an impressive number of accolades in the last decade, like the Nobel Prizes for Buchanan, Stigler, North, Fogel and Coase.

But it has not been that easy for economists like Schmoller in the years after he died in 1918. As a backlash to the Second World War, the German historical school and its approach lost its popularity and fell into disuse with a lot of economists, but it did not disappear from the world of economic science. In the United States of America Veblen, Commons and Ayres were very successful under the banner of old-institutional economics in the beginning of the 20th century. They regard economics as the science dealing with the study of the structure and functioning of human relations, focused on the provision of goods and services so as to satisfy human needs. It is the study of changing cultural relations that arise in the creation and the possession of scarce material and immaterial goods and services by individuals and groups, in the light of their private and public needs.

They emphasize that the economy is more than only markets and that economic research should go beyond the pure market mechanism, and should address institutions and market structures that shape a market and that are operated by the market. Research should go further than supply and demand, and attention should be directed to institutional arrangements that influence both supply and demand. It is also clear that institutional economists are not satisfied with the mechanisms and principles stemming from neoclassical economics, like purely mechanical analogies, static equilibrium analysis, the search for determinism, simple methodological individualism and optimum analysis. Institutional economists, as Schmoller did, emphasize an organic or more genetic evolutionary conception of the economy; cumulative and open causality; methodological collectivism enriched by a sophisticated methodological individualism; pragmatism and instrumentalism.

However, their approach and the approach of their followers gave way to the power of the neoclassical approach in (business) economics. In particular the statement that the old-institutionalists collected facts without theory, gave the school a low academic standing, after which it proceeded silently, but not without spirit. A lot of followers remain also in Germany, but the influence Schmoller had in the 19th century disappeared, even in the evolutionary economics mainstream. As we have shown in this chapter, we don't think that development is correct, because Schmoller is in every detail an evolutionary economist.

## NOTES

1. This comment is, among others, based on the article 'Theory for accounting or accounting theory: an essay on the interaction between economics and accounting', by Simon Duindam and Bernard Verstegen (2000), *European Journal of Law and Economics*, September, 2, 125–38.
2. John Stuart Mill's method has not been without controversy in England. For example William Stanley Jevons was firmly opposed to the methodological ideas of Mill in his *Principles of Science*.
3. See also Klant (1978).

## REFERENCES

Fase, M.M.G (1995), 'John Kenneth Galbraith', *NRC-Handelsblad*, 21 januari 1995, boekenbijlage.

Gruchy, A.G. (1969), 'Neoinstitutionalism and the economics of dissent', *Journal of Economic Issues* 3, 53–67.

Hansen, R. (1996), *Die praktischen Konsequenzen des Methodenstreits: eine Aufarbeitung der Einkommensbesteuerung*, Berlin: Duncker & Humblot.

Hansen, R. (1998), 'Assessing and tax accounting principles in the German civil and commercial code and the impact on tax compliance', *European Journal of Law and Economics,* 7, 15–46.

Schmoller, G. (1883), 'Zur Methodologie der Staats- und Sozialwissenschaften', *Jahrbuch für Gesetzgebung, Verwaltung und Volkswirtschaft im Deutschen Reich*, 7ᵉ jaargang, Berlin.

Schmoller, G. (ed.) (1921), *Grundriss der Algemeinen Volkswirtschaftslehre*, Leipzig: Duncker & Humblot.

# 10. Austrian economics and 'the other canon': the Austrians between the activistic-idealistic and the passivistic-materialistic traditions of economics

## Erik S. Reinert

### TYPOLOGIES OF ECONOMIC THEORY AND THE TWO CANONS

We have recently argued that when focusing on very long-term longitudinal trends in economics, two ideal types of economic theory appear to have co-existed in parallel over an extended period of time.[1] These ideal types can be seen as constituting two separate *filiations*[2] – to use Schumpeter's term – and they come into occasional methodological clashes. Werner Sombart fittingly calls the first tradition *activistic-idealistic*, a tradition born with the Renaissance. The second type of economic theory he calls *passivistic-materialistic*,[3] a tradition having its origins with Mandeville and Adam Smith and solidifying as the 'a priori method' with David Ricardo. The purpose of this paper is to outline the characteristics of the two traditions – the tradition behind today's mainstream and 'the other canon' – and to discuss the position of Austrian economics in this context.

In most sciences, periodical and radical gestalt-switches terminate old theoretical trajectories and initiate new ones. In a Kuhnian paradigm shift the scientific world moves from a situation when everybody knows that the world is flat, to a new understanding when everybody knows that the world is round. This happens in a relatively short time. Lakatos' idea of 'degenerating scientific research programmes' that gradually shift to 'progressive' ones conveys a similar conception. In this respect economics is different. In economics the theory that the world is flat has been living together with the theory that the world is round for centuries. We describe this apparent lack of paradigm shifts in economics by the co-existence of these two long-term parallel filiations, where weight and influence periodically tilt back and forth between two alternative Weltanschauungen.

Today evolutionary economics – based on a tradition founded by the Austrian Joseph Alois Schumpeter – represents the most important challenge to the mainstream. However, evolutionary economics has, in our view, so far had an unnecessarily limited scope. This tradition now focuses relatively narrowly on innovations, including neither Schumpeter's own interest in financial matters, nor addressing to any extent the broader issues of uneven economic growth and employment on a world level which are, at their origin, intimately tied to Schumpeterian mechanisms. And, by bringing simple 'Schumpeterian' variables into mainstream equilibrium models, his message is being domesticated and made innocuous. As in the case of Keynes, the mainstream again shows a great ability to usurp, absorb, and subdue threatening alternative theories.

As already indicated, the two different canons are based on fundamentally different Weltanschauungen. The lines of the two canons can be traced back to the period when the term economics was first used, to ancient Greece.[4] While today's standard economics is based on a mechanistic and barter-centred tradition, Renaissance economics – the other canon – is dynamic activistic-idealistic, and production-centred. The first tradition belongs to what Werner Sombart calls *ordnende Nationalökonomie*, which is concerned with organizing the economic sphere. The second tradition is what Sombart calls *verstehende Nationalökonomie*,[5] what Nelson and Winter refer to as *appreciative economics*.[6] The first tradition typically explains man's economic activities in terms of physics (of dead matter), the second in terms of biology (of living matter *and* of man's wit and will). The first tradition is represented by Malthus' *dismal science*, the second by Christopher Freeman's *economics of hope*[7] – by the never-ending frontier of human knowledge.

Present mainstream economic theory places itself solidly in a canonical sequence descending from the physiocrats, via Adam Smith and Ricardo to the neoclassical tradition beginning with Jevons and Marshall. The sequence has been made clear to generations of economists as the 'family tree of economics' featured on the inside back cover of many editions of Paul Samuelson's *Economics*. The alternative canon in economic theory runs parallel in time with the tradition of Samuelson's 'family tree'. We have named this alternative type of theory *the other canon or Renaissance economics*. The latter because never before and never after have the values which this canon represents dominated the world picture as they did during the Renaissance. The mainstream canon is clearly a product of the next philosophical period – the Enlightenment – which was in opposition to Renaissance values and outlook on important matters. Rationality and individuality during the Renaissance were based on an image of man as a spiritual being: creative and productive. The Enlightenment had a more materialistic understanding of human rationality and individuality: mechanical and consuming. Today the Renaissance canon – the other canon – tends to disappear in the history of economic thought, as this branch of economics more and more concentrates on the predecessors of neo-classical economics.

In 19th century United States, the other canon dominated economic policy and the land-grant universities, while the standard canon dominated at the Ivy League universities. Typically Cornell University, as the only university that was both land-grant and Ivy League, was for a while teaching two kinds of economics: the British system and the American system. In all presently wealthy nations, an economic policy based on the other canon has served as a mandatory passage point in the history of economic policy. We would claim that the absence of the history of economic policy as a branch of economics to some extent explains why the other canon has been brought into virtual oblivion.

As already mentioned, Renaissance economics is optimistic: the never-ending frontier of knowledge stands in sharp contrast with Malthus' dismal science and with the production theory of mainstream economics, the foundation of which is still today fundamentally a formalisation of Ricardo's static corn economy. Here the main agents of change, new knowledge and the entrepreneur, are both absent. In the middle of the Cold War, in 1955, Nicholas Kaldor made the extremely important point that 'the Marxian theory is really only a simplified version of Ricardo, clothed in a different garb'.[8] It was not at all obvious to most people at the time that the two political extremes were based on what were really only nuances of the same basic Ricardian economic theory. Only long after the fall of the Berlin Wall, in the late 1990s, arguments stressing the similarities of the two political extremes again surfaced in books by Stiglitz[9] and Hodgson.[10]

The cold war between what were in effect two versions of Ricardian economics led to the present crisis of the other canon. As it now is, the healthy Galbraithian balance of countervailing powers between the standard Anglo-Saxon theory and the other canon no longer exists. A hundred years ago the need for a balance of induction and deduction was generally recognized in all schools.[11] On this matter the neoclassical founder Alfred Marshall approvingly quotes the historicist Gustav Schmoller as saying that 'Induction and deduction are both needed for scientific thought as the right foot and left foot are both needed for walking'.[12] Induction has to a very large extent been lost, making mainstream economics tilt very heavily towards the left side of the brain. The essentially mechanical neoclassical economics now dominates the field, and – as we shall see – the prominent 'other canon' aspects of both of Alfred Marshall's early neoclassical economics and of Carl Menger's early Austrian economics have largely been lost.

Several observers have in fact pointed to the similarities between the economics of Alfred Marshall and of Carl Menger.[13] In this chapter we argue that the theories that these two economists founded – neoclassical and

Austrian – suffered a gradual and parallel loss of their other canon aspects over the course of the 20th century.

The following are main characteristics of other canon economics: the fundamental cause of economic welfare is man's productive creativity and morality; the *immaterial* production factors. In order for these ideas to materialize, capital is needed. Capital per se is in this tradition sterile. The Renaissance tradition can be contrasted with the mainstream using Schumpeter's description of the economics of John Rae – a 19th century US economist of the Renaissance canon: 'The essential thing is the conception of the economic process, which soars above the pedestrian view that it is the accumulation of capital per se that propels the capitalist engine'.[14] Whereas classical economics focused on barter, exchange, and the accumulation of material capital, the Renaissance tradition focuses on production based on human creativity. For this reason Renaissance economics emphasizes education, science, incentives, and entrepreneurship.

Mainstream economics defines its origins in the French school of *physiocracy*[15] (that is, 'the rule of nature'), where value is created by nature, and harvested by man. In Renaissance economics value originates through man's wit and will (that is, 'ideocracy' – 'the rule of ideas'). During the mechanization of the world picture, which took place during the materialistically oriented Enlightenment, the defenders of the Renaissance tradition were the anti-physiocrats.[16] The Renaissance tradition is holistic and idealistic – not atomistic and materialistic. Nevertheless, at the core of the system is the individual, set in a complex web of synergetic interrelations. The beneficial effects of these interrelations first became evident in Renaissance towns giving birth to the Renaissance expression of the *common weal* (il bene comune, das Gemeinwohl) – a synergetic understanding of society as being more than the sum of its parts.[17]

The growth of towns and cities brought these synergies into evidence. Towns permitted communication that unleashed individual freedom, creativity, diversification and synergies that together created unprecedented wealth. This was the fundamental observation of one of the earliest bestselling books in economics, *Delle Cause della Grandezza delle Città*[18] written by Giovanni Botero (1543–1617). The English translation, published in London in 1606, is entitled *The Cause of the Greatnesse of Cities*. This argument was to be discussed at great length by Antonio Serra in 1613.[19]

Later nation-building in this tradition tried consciously to reproduce the synergetic benefits of towns on a larger, national scale.[20] In order to achieve this, the sciences of law and administration had to be consciously cultivated and promoted. Renaissance economics emphasizes the crucial role of nation states and the duties of 'the ruler' – that is, government – not only to regulate in order to provide incentives for the creation of welfare (in the old tradition of law and economics), but also the duty of 'the ruler' to initiate projects creating a demand for knowledge-based production. Thus, Renaissance economics has a strong emphasis on institutions. After all, the key enabling institutions of capitalism – like for example patents, banks and standards – were products of Renaissance Italy.

At the core of the Renaissance other canon is the observation that some economic activities produce higher welfare than others, a static and non-systemic observation of welfare being *activity specific*. (As if today: lawyers make more money than people picking lettuce; therefore a nation of lettuce pickers will be poorer than a nation of lawyers). Very soon – before 1500 – this argument is extended into one of synergies: some economic activities are seen as being at the core of systemic synergies that produce and spread welfare locally or nationwide ('where there are many people working with machines, also the shopkeepers are wealthier than in other places, where machines are not used'). There are degrees of understanding of how these systemic synergies develop into positive feedback systems, but the top performance is that of Antonio Serra in 1613, who has a description of Venice as a true autocatalytic system, where increasing returns and diversity – the latter expressed as the number of different professions in a nation (degree of division of labour) – are identified as being at the core of virtuous circles which generate wealth.[21] Naples is the example of the opposite effect in Serra's system, because the production of raw materials is not subject to increasing returns. We also find Adam Smith in *The Wealth of Nations* asking himself: why is there so little division of labour in agriculture? On the other hand agriculture is to him the only 'natural' activity. Smith fails, however, to make the connection that the 'unnatural' imperfect competition is a product of a sophisticated division of labour. Today these synergy-based arguments are found in the works on increasing return by authors like Paul David, W. Brian Arthur,[22] and James Buchanan.[23]

An integral part of the nation-building strategy was a notion that a national market had to be *created* – that such a market did not appear spontaneously. For this reason, communication and state-initiated investments in large-scale infrastructure projects hold a very strong position in the Renaissance tradition, from the dams and irrigation canals of the Sumerian kingdoms via Colbert's canals to Kennedy's interstate road projects. Using modern terms, we could say that the strategy of Renaissance economics was to create *perfect competition* within the national borders and *dynamic imperfect competition* in the export trade. Contrary to the common preconceptions of economics before Adam Smith, 'Competition was often artificially fostered (nationally) . . . in order to organise markets with automatic regulation of supply and demand'.[24] It was commonly agreed that a national competitive advantage had to be created in knowledge-intensive activities before free trade could be established with the most advanced nations.

This new world view of the Renaissance released enormous creativity in all

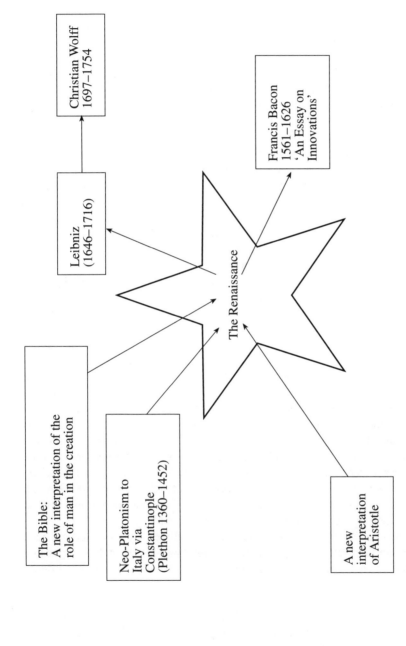

*Figure 10.1   Some factors contributing to the Renaissance*

sciences and arts – the new intellectual freedom gave us Leonardo da Vinci, Michelangelo, Raphael, Kepler and Copernicus. In all arts and sciences the people of the Renaissance still stand out in a heroic light in history, all but the statesmen and economists of the Renaissance. Still today these economists of the Renaissance, who made the modern world possible, come across as the gold-loving caricature that Adam Smith created of his mercantilist predecessors. These economists, however, are the true founders of evolutionary economics. In the spirit of the Renaissance Francis Bacon – Queen Elizabeth's Lord High Chancellor – wrote, around 1605, *An Essay of Innovations.* Bacon became the 'scientific leader of the new industrialist'[25] – urging the use of science to produce manufactured goods and profits. Up until and including James Stuart's 1767 two-volume *Inquiry into the Principles of Political Economy*[26] the term 'innovation' is frequently used, only to disappear with Adam Smith.

Bacon's spirit has often been evoked in order to argue against the mechanical world view of post-Ricardian economics. Richard Jones,[27] the founder of the English historical school, and John Rae[28] were two economists who – as a reaction to the Ricardian system – consciously attempted to 'Baconize' economics again. Also Carl Menger quotes Francis Bacon against what we today would call 'physics envy' when he criticizes 'the attempts to carry over the peculiarities of the natural-scientific method of investigation uncritically into economics'.[29]

Bacon's emphasis of scientific knowledge was very similar to that of Friedrich List more than 200 years later: 'Industry is the mother and father of science, literature, the art, enlightenment, useful institutions and national power . . . The greater the advance in scientific knowledge, the more numerous will be the new inventions which save labour and raw materials and lead to new products and processes.'[30] In this sense, there is a continuity of argument from the Renaissance, through Francis Bacon and Friedrich List to today's evolutionary economics that emphasizes the role of research and development and of innovations for economic welfare. As to natural resources, List says that 'industrialisation will greatly increase the value of a country's natural resources'.[31] This thinking was the basis for economic policy in the resource-rich nations which have achieved general welfare: Canada, Australia, and New Zealand. A manufacturing sector – although one which was not seen as being competitive with that of England – was needed in order to transform the natural resources of a nation into national wealth.

The two types of economics that we have outlined should be seen as 'ideal types' in the Weberian sense. Through time there are several distinguishing features that clearly separate the two canons. A basic one is their different conceptions of the origin of wealth:

1. In the mainstream canon wealth originates from material sources: from nature, that is, land, physical labour and capital. The accumulation of

these assets takes place through trade and war. This accumulation is static, that is, more of the same.

2.   In the Renaissance other canon wealth originates from immaterial sources: from culture, that is, man's creativity and morality. The accumulation of assets takes place through innovations cumulatively changing man's stock of knowledge and his tools (technology). This accumulation is dynamic, that is, more of something new and qualitatively different.[32]

A second major distinguishing feature between the two canons is:

3.   In the mainstream canon the focus of analysis is barter, consumption and accumulation ('man the trader and consumer').

4.   In the other canon the focus of analysis is on production and innovation; productivity being the pineal gland bringing together mind and matter ('man the creative producer').

A third and fundamental difference between the canons is:

5.   The mainstream canon is – since the Aristotelian idea of the complete independence of politics from all other aspects of social life – fundamentally atomistic and mechanical in its analytical approach. The unit of analysis is the atomistic unit (in economics: the individual).

6.   The other canon – since Plato's *Republic* – is fundamentally holistic, organic and synthetical (from synthesis) in its approach (die Ganzheit). The units of analysis include both individuals and their institutions in time and space.

At a very fundamental level, the two canons of economics are founded on two different views of how humans differ from other animals. We shall let Adam Smith represent the material and barter-based canon, and Abraham Lincoln represent Renaissance economics – the immaterial and production-based canon:

Adam Smith:

> The division of labour arises from a propensity in human nature to truck, barter and exchange one thing for another. It is common to all men, and to be found in no other race of animals, which seem to know neither this nor any other species of contracts ... Nobody ever saw a dog make a fair and deliberate exchange of one bone for another with another dog.[33]

Abraham Lincoln:

> ... Beavers build houses; but they build them in nowise differently, or better, now than they did five thousand years ago ... Man is not the only animal who labours; but he is the only one who *improves* his workmanship. These improvements he effects by *Discoveries* and *Inventions* ...'[34]

We also see a consistent pattern of application of the two canons in a *catching-up* framework:

No nation state[35] has ever gone through a transition from poverty to affluence without practising a long period of the immaterial and production-based canon as the fundamental guide for economic *policy*. This is true in France (where a modern starting point for policy could be Louis XI, (1461); and Montchrétien, Jean Bodin, and Sully for theory); England (where a logical starting point for policy is the reign of Henry VII, in 1485); in Germany, the United States (Benjamin Franklin, Alexander Hamilton, Daniel Raymond, Henry Clay, Matthew and Henry Carey, E. Peshine Smith) and Japan (Meiji Restoration). Today we see the production-based economic strategy at work in East Asia. The Third World is essentially an area that has experienced neither a Renaissance-type creative awakening nor any production- and knowledge-based economic canon. Figure 2 shows the family tree of the other canon.

On the practical policy level the two canons produce conflicting recommendations. This is due to the fact that whereas in the Renaissance theory different economic activities offer different potentials for achieving national welfare, in the barter-centred theory all economic activities become qualitatively 'alike'. If anything, in the standard canon superiority is traditionally awarded to agriculture, which is more 'natural' (a) because it delivers nature's produce, and (b) because competition here is more 'natural'; atomistic and 'perfect'.

It is really only after 1960 that the economic policies of Smith and Ricardo have completely won the day in economic policy. The economists of alternative traditions who were crucial to the economic policy are almost completely left out of today's history of economic thought. The last history of economics to give a good coverage of the theories behind 19th century economic policy was Ottmar Spann's *Die Haupttheorien der Volkswirtschaftslehre,* which first appeared in 1911. By 1936 this book had reached 24 editions and a total of 120 000 copies printed in German.[36] There were translations to several languages, and, interestingly, the UK edition was published under the title *Types of Economic Theory,* flagging Spann's awareness of diversity: that there are, indeed, different types of economics, not only one monolithic canon.

Of course, we do not imply that the world is a binary one, where all economists belong either to one tradition or the other. On the contrary, a key characteristic of several important economists is their at times schizophrenic

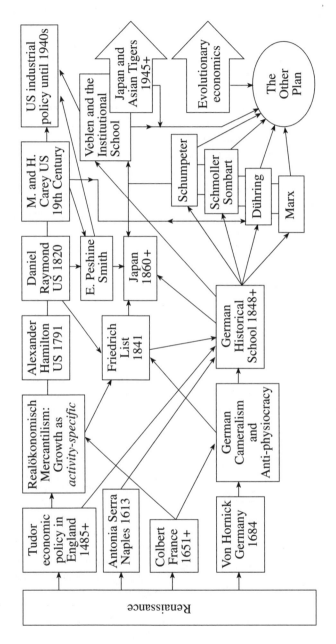

*Figure 10.2  Reality economics: the knowledge- and production-based canon of economic theory*

allegiance to both sets of theory. One example of this is the conflict between the Marshall whose 'Mecca of the economist' lay in economic biology[37] and the Marshall of the appendices to his *Principles* which were deeply steeped in 'physics-envy'. In order to create the equilibrium that characterizes today's physics-based standard economic theory, Marshall paradoxically had to restore to a *biological* metaphor. Increasing returns had been an important argument for industrial policy ever since Antonio Serra in 1613[38] all through the 19th century. In order to reconcile the existence of increasing returns with equilibrium, Marshall uses a lengthy metaphor of firms growing and dying like trees in the forests.[39] This evolutionary growth process supposedly counteracts the tendency towards uneven accumulation caused by increasing returns to scale.[40] The argument that killed all future biological analogies in neoclassical economics was a biological analogy. This biological analogy was important in making economics into what it is today, a profession where a physics-inspired equilibrium is the central gestalt.

Seen from this point of view, Marx also was caught between two paradigms which at one level are mutually exclusive. In terms of his emphasis on technology and economic dynamics, Marx – like Schumpeter – is a clear member of the Renaissance production-based canon. Marx's and Schumpeter's visions have a common basis in the German economic tradition. In Anglo-Saxon economics these two economists come across as extremely original, seen from the German side they are both firmly rooted in that alternative canon. The one aspect of Marx's theory which decidedly belongs to the Anglo-Saxon canon is his use of Ricardo's labour theory of value. The labour theory of value is out of place in the German tradition where entrepreneurship, ideas, knowledge, leadership, and management necessarily contribute importantly to the value added created by physical labour.

*Table 10.1   The two canons contrasted as ideal types*[41]

| Starting point for the standard canon | Starting point for the other canon |
| --- | --- |
| Equilibrium under perfect information and perfect foresight | Learning and decision-making under uncertainty (Schumpeter, Keynes, Shackle) |
| High level of abstraction | Level of abstraction chosen according to problem to be resolved |
| Man's wit and will absent | Moving force: Geist- und Willenskapital<br>Man's wit and will, entrepreneurship |
| Not able to handle novelty as an endogenous phenomenon | Novelty as a central moving force |

| Starting point for the standard canon | Starting point for the other canon |
| --- | --- |
| Moving force: 'capital per se propels the capitalist engine' | Moving force: new knowledge which creates a demand for capital to be provided from the financial sector |
| Metaphors from the realm of physics | Metaphors (carefully) from the realm of biology |
| Mode of understanding: mechanistic ('begreifen') | Mode of understanding: qualitative ('verstehen'), a type of understanding irreducible only to numbers and symbols |
| Matter | *Geist* precedes matter |
| Focused on man the consumer A. Smith: 'Men are animals which have learned to barter' | Focused on man the innovator and producer. A. Lincoln: 'Men are animals which not only work, but innovate' |
| Focused on static/comparative static (a movie of the world) | Focused on change |
| Not cumulative/history absent | Cumulative causations/'history matters'/backwash effects (Myrdal, Kaldor, Schumpeter, German historical school) |
| Increasing returns to scale and its absence a non-essential feature | Increasing returns and its absence essential to explaining differences in income between firms, regions and nations (Kaldor) |
| Very precise ('would rather be accurately wrong than approximately correct') | Aiming at relevance over precision, recognizes the trade-off between relevance and precision as a core issue in the profession |
| 'Perfect competition' (commodity competition/price competition) as an ideal situation = a goal for society | Innovation- and knowledge-driven Schumpeterian competition as both engine of progress and ideal situation. With perfect competition, with equilibrium and no innovation, capital becomes worthless (Schumpeter, Hayek) |
| The market as a mechanism for setting prices | The market also as an arena for rivalry and as a mechanism selecting between different products and different solutions. (Schumpeter, Nelson & Winter) |
| Equality assumption I: No diversity | Diversity as a key factor (Schumpeter, Shackle) |

*Table 1    continued*

| Starting point for the standard canon | Starting point for the other canon |
| --- | --- |
| Equality assumption II: All economic activities are alike and of equal quality as carriers of economic growth and welfare | Growth and welfare are activity-specific – different economic activities present widely different potentials for absorbing new knowledge |
| Both theory and policy recommendations tend to be independent of context ('one medicine cures all') | Both theory and policy recommendations highly context-dependent |
| The economy largely independent from society | The economy as firmly embedded in society |
| Technology as a free good, as 'manna from heaven' | Knowledge and technology are produced, have costs and are protected. This production is based on incentives of the system, including law, institutions and policies |
| Equilibrating forces at the core of the system and of the theory | Cumulative forces are more important than equilibrating ones, and should therefore be at the core of the system |
| Economics as Harmonielehre: the economy as a self-regulating system seeking equilibrium and harmony | Economics as an inherently unstable and conflict-rich discipline. Achieving stability is based on man's policy measures (Carey, Polanyi, Weber, Keynes) |
| Postulates the representative firm | No representative firm. All firms are unique (Penrose) |
| Static optimum | Dynamic optimization under |
| Perfect rationality | uncertainty. Bounded rationality |
| No distinction made between real economy and financial economy | Conflicts between real economy and financial economy are normal and must be regulated (Minsky, Keynes) |
| Saving caused by refraining from consumption and a cause of growth | Saving largely results from profits (Schumpeter) and saving per se is not useful or desirable for growth (Keynes) |

# CANONICAL BATTLES: THE HEAD-ON CONFRONTATIONS

Occasionally the two canons meet head-on in what we have labelled *canonical Methodenstreite*. Below we describe five of these Methodenstreite.

## Canonical Methodenstreit 1: Misselden vs. Malynes (1622–23)

The theoretical conflict between the forefathers of today's mainstream canon and the Renaissance canon has existed at least since the 1622–23 'English' debate between Gerard de Malynes[42] and Edward Misselden,[43] where Malynes represented a static theory rooted in barter and Misselden represented a theory centred around learning and production. Both Misselden and Malynes were Dutchmen from Antwerp working in London. In the history of economic thought, their debate is interpreted as being about exchange controls and the balance of trade.[44] The controversy between the two was an 'acrimonious, even abusive' one, in which 'ink was shed like water'.[45]

However, by going back to the sources, one finds that the main line of attack by Misselden against Malynes is his 'mechanical' view of man – Malynes has left out man's 'art' and 'soul'. Misselden quotes at length a paragraph from Malynes, where Malynes reduces trade to three elements, 'namely, Commodities, Money, and Exchange'.[46] Objecting to this definition, Misselden says: 'It is against Art to dispute with a man that denyeth the *Principles* of Art'. Misselden scorns Malynes for not seeing the difference between a heap of stones and logs and a house – because man's productive powers and his soul, which produce the house, have been left out. A similar criticism can of course be made of neoclassical economics. Typically, after the Renaissance, the wealth of a nation was seen as lying in its capacity to produce, its 'productive powers'.

Misselden represents the acute Renaissance awareness of the enormous territory to be covered between mankind's present poverty and ignorance, and the enormous potentials. This released enthusiasm and energy. The situation recalls Keynes' frustration with the suboptimal situation of the world under the Great Depression. Both the Renaissance philosophers/economists and Keynes were searching for the formula needed to liberate society from its obviously suboptimal position at the time. This is what Keynes called 'salvation through knowledge'.[47] This attitude is very different from man as the passive victim of 'two sovereign masters, pain and pleasure',[48] which is the philosophical foundation of English classical economics.

## Canonical Methodenstreit 2: Anti-physiocracy vs. Physiocracy and Adam Smith (ca. 1770–1830)

The second Methodenstreit between the knowledge-based Renaissance school and the predecessor of today's standard (neoclassical based) economic theory starts in the 1770s with the rise of the physiocratic school in France. It may be said that the physiocratic school in some sense was a reaction to the perversion of Colbertism into a policy of indiscriminate taxation. It was also clearly a reaction of the landowners against Colbert's policy of systematically diverting resources from agriculture to manufacturing.

The physiocrats had an animalistic view of man which was compatible with the philosophical foundations of English classical economics: '. . . sometimes (the physiocrats) regard man as a browsing animal, concerned only with his nourishment, the maximum production of the fruit of the earth as his social ideal'.[49]

The anti-physiocratic movement has received little attention in the history of economic thought. These authors, however, represented the true continuation of Renaissance economics. Interestingly, two of the main opponents of physiocracy in France were clergymen: Abbé Mably and Abbé Galiani, the Neapolitan envoy to the Court of Paris.[50] Galiani was to take a position which in many ways foreshadowed the position of the historical school in late 19th century Methodenstreit: 'Abstract principles are no good for commercial policy. Corn laws which are good in one time or place may be bad in another. . . . The statesman who admired Colbert should not imitate him, but ask himself, "What would Colbert do if he were here now?" '[51] Abbé Galiani's criticism of a very abstract and context-free theory is very similar to the reaction of Reverend Jones against the writings of Ricardo in 1820. Richard Jones was the father of the English historical school of economics, which became very influential during the latter half of the 19th century. The insistence that economic theory and policy must be context-specific is a sure hallmark of other canon economics through the ages.

One of the main opponents of the physiocratic school[52] in France was Forbonnais, who refused to admit that trade and industry are sterile. Also to Forbonnais the main agent creating wealth is man – not nature itself: without human agency *the land itself* is doomed to absolute or relative sterility. Other contemporary French opponents of physiocracy were Accarias de Serrionne, Graslin, Necker, and Linguet.

Perhaps the most ardent anti-physiocrats were found in Germany. Under the heading 'Antiphysiokraten', Humpert's bibliography of the German cameralist school lists 25 works – published between 1771 and 1832.[53] The best known of these works is Johann Friedrich von Pfeiffer's *Der Antiphysiokrat*.[54] Pfeiffer was also the author of the most influential economic work in Germany at the time. Other strong continental opponents of physiocracy were Johann Jakob von Moser, Dohm, and Sonnenfels.

## Canonical Methodenstreit 3: The American System vs. The British System (19th Century United States)

The US opposition to English classical economic theory started with Benjamin Franklin and continued with Alexander Hamilton's 1791 'Report on the Manufactures'. This Methodenstreit on the policy level lasted all through the 1830s, although on the theoretical level English classical economics was to be increasingly taught at the Ivy League universities during the late 19th century. Important economists in this US tradition were Daniel Raymond, Matthew and Henry Carey, John Rae, E. Peshine Smith and many others. The last great economists of this tradition were Richard Ely and Simon Patten, who – like most US economists who studied abroad in the 19th century – studied in Germany. After Thorstein Veblen, this economic tradition continued under the label of institutional economics. Both the general stance against Ricardian economics, and the mental affiliation with German-type economics, continued much as in the 19th century tradition.

On the policy level, the nations industrializing in the 19th century were to take up the example that had been set by England – and later abandoned by her when she had reached world hegemony. Economic thought and policy of all great industrial nations in their pre-take-off period share a core theme of the *activity-specific* nature of growth. Economic growth could only be achieved by including activities with fast technological change and a rapid growth in output in the nation's portfolio of industrial activities. This theme can be followed in economic writings from the early 1500s in Italy and England and France, a little later in the German cameralists. It is introduced to the United States through Alexander Hamilton and his favourite economist, the English mercantilist Malachy Postlethwayt.[55] Two path-breaking volumes in this school were published in 1820 by Daniel Raymond[56] and Matthew Carey.[57] Heavily influenced by Daniel Raymond, Friedrich List's involuntary exile in the US reinforced this already traditional way of thinking in the Germany of the Zollverein. In Meiji Japan the doitsugaku school – favouring the German model – came to be the most influential for the building of society, at least until 1945.[58] In Japan, after 1883, 'a stream of German teachers of political economy and related disciplines continually flowed in'.[59]

A common thread of successful long-distance catching-up through the centuries is a shared distrust of generalized free trade until the nation is firmly established in what was seen to be the *right* economic activities – the *specific activities* which increased the nation's 'productive powers'. Through the dynamic imperfect competition (in other words, Schumpeter's 'historical increasing returns') in these specific activities, real wages could be raised: first in the 'engine' industry and subsequently spreading through the whole national labour market. In the US tradition, by adding skill to the labourer, his price or value (= wage) was increased. This tradition survived in the United States up until and including the economists who were taught by Ely's and Patten's generation. In a letter to the author, dated 16 August 1996, Moses Abramowitz comments: 'I agree in particular that the "residual" and growth in general are industry-specific. That has seemed clear to me since I was a graduate student in the Thirties and read the Kuznets and Burns books . . . '. This certainly points to a 'filiation' between the old American school and present day 'economics of catching up'.

### Canonical Methodenstreit 4: The Historical School vs. Marginalism (1883–1908)

The resounding success of Ricardian economics and its extreme laissez-faire policies during the 1840s provoked a theoretical countermovement following the political events of 1848. The international depression in 1873 further increased the opposition against the classical economic tradition all over Europe. The stronghold of the opposition was in Germany, where the older historical school founded by Bruno Hildebrand – whose book was published in 1848[60] – Karl Knies and Wilhelm Roscher increasingly challenged both the theoretical foundations and practical conclusions of Ricardian economics. Later a new generation of historical economists led by Gustav Schmoller – the younger historical school – for a long time completely dominated German academic and practical economics.

Carl Menger, the founder of the Austrian marginalist school, in 1883 published his book: *Untersuchungen über die Methode der Sozialwissenschaften und der politischen Ökonomie insbesondere*. Menger had dedicated his first book to Wilhelm Roscher – the prominent German economist of the historical school. Menger closed the preface praising recent German economics and hoping that his book 'be regarded . . . as a friendly greeting from a collaborator in Austria'. The reply from Germany to his books was not friendly. Schmoller reviewed the *Untersuchungen* unfavourably in his *Jahrbuch*, and Menger replied in a small book entitled *Errors of Historicism* in 1884.[61] Of all the Methodenstreite, this – the most famous one – is paradoxically the least fundamental of them all. Menger and Schmoller essentially shared the same critical attitude towards the mechanical and barter-based English theory. Their personalities and pride clashed, but compared to Ricardian economics the two are next of kin. This Methodenstreit created a debilitating civil war inside the other canon.

Schmoller wanted theory to be empirically founded, in opposition to the

English classical tradition that founded theory on introspective assumptions, and deducing far-reaching practical conclusions from these abstract structures. This practice was what Schumpeter labelled 'the Ricardian vice'. Today's standard explanation of the Methodenstreit generally fails to point out how similar their criticism of Ricardian economics was. *The New Palgrave* describes the Methodenstreit as follows: '(Schmoller) rejected Menger's deductive method for three chief reasons: its assumptions were unrealistic, its high degree of abstraction made it largely irrelevant to the real-world economy, and it was devoid of empirical content. The theory was therefore useless in studying the chief questions of importance to economists; how have the economic institutions of the modern world developed to their present state, and what are the laws and regularities that govern them? The proper method was induction of general principles from historical-empirical studies.'[62] However, reading through Menger's *Errors of Historicism* with the perspective of what economics has become in the 2000s, it becomes clear how 'other canon' both Schmoller and Menger in fact were.

The historical school was deeply steeped in the German tradition of embracing *die Ganzheit* – the whole. This search for die Ganzheit forced the historical school to cross the boundaries into what in the English tradition were other – and to them unrelated – academic disciplines. In the German historical tradition it would be complete nonsense to exclude any information relevant to the question asked – be it from the realm of climatology, pedagogy or any other branch of human knowledge. In the German tradition economics was a science that integrated all the others. However, it is not at all clear that Menger disagreed with this. Menger drew up a picture – a model – of the economic forces at work, but, like Schumpeter later, he insisted that history was an 'indispensable' tool for the profession.

To Menger, the problem of the historical school was that they suffered from a kind of a 'case-study syndrome': they collected raw materials for a theory, but never got around to establishing a proper theory. This criticism is similar to that of Thorstein Veblen. However, this criticism is more appropriate to some members of the historical school than to others. It is indeed crucial to define what is meant by 'theory'. The marginalist tradition came to seek 'pure theory', a formalist kind of theory that excluded from economics all the forces that in the Renaissance tradition were the driving forces of history. However, of all the marginalists, Menger was clearly the closest to the historical school, as we shall discuss later he both 'invented' marginalism and, at the same time, went far beyond it.

The criticism of the marginalists from the historical school was that the very source of wealth – man's wit and will – had disappeared. This had led to an Entgeistung der Volkswirtschaftslehre, the role of man's wit and will had been left out of the science. The German ethical historical school – with its US followers like Richard Ely and Simon Patten – followed the Renaissance tradition of seeing economics as a normative science, setting out to transform society for the benefit of the common weal. Morality was, to them, rational, and part of the Ganzheit of the economics profession. In contrast, to British empiricist philosophy and classical economics, morality was irrational and based on sympathy (feeling) in the tradition of Hume and Smith. Accordingly, to the English school morality was totally separated from economics.

### Canonical Methodenstreit 5: The US Institutional vs. the Neoclassical School (20th Century)

Institutional economics presents a continuation of the US and German 19th century economics tradition. Institutionalism – a term originally coined only to describe the work of Norwegian-American economist Thorstein Veblen (1857–1929) – continued the radical trend of 'the American system' in opposing the abstract structures of English theory.

The institutionalists were very critical of the established economic doctrine, but most of them did not seek to throw it out completely. Since their theory was *praxisnah* – empirical and close to reality – the institutionalists attracted the attention of policymakers. Academically and in terms of influence US institutionalism peaked in the troubled 1930s, and it may be argued that institutional policymakers in the early 1930s anticipated the Keynesian policy prescription without his elaborate theoretical framework.

Although institutionalism declined rapidly after World War Two – really during the years of McCarthyism – its influence on economic policy-making in Washington still lingers on. Two recent and informative books trace the demise of institutional economics in the United States: Yuval Yonay's *The Struggle Over the Soul of Economics*,[63] and a collection of papers: *From Interwar Pluralism to Postwar Neoclassicism*.[64]

Today Paul Krugman complains that 'It is not just that economists have lost control of the discourse; the kinds of ideas that are offered in a standard economics textbook do not enter into that discourse at all ...'.[65] If we ask ourselves *to whom* the economists have lost control, Krugman lists an alliance of 'policy makers, business leaders and influential intellectuals'.[66] These are the groups which today defend the common sense and pragmatism of institutional economics against the unmitigated rule of standard textbook economics. To the Ricardian vice labelled by Schumpeter we may add the Krugmanian vice: the vice of possessing more relevant economic theories – like for example new trade theory – but refusing to employ these principles in real world economic policy.

Thus, though neoclassicism won the day in academia and in our economic policy towards the Second and Third Worlds, the eclectic pragmatism of the institutional school lives on in policy making both in United States and in Western Europe. In academia, the proponents of this school are today mostly scattered in business schools, departments of government, and of international affairs. As a result of the virtual eradication of other canon economists from departments of economics, the poor countries of the world are still treated to undiluted neoclassical economics as administered by the Washington institutions.

## THE AUSTRIANS AND THE OTHER CANON

Austrian economics in many ways bridges the two canons. If the theory of economics is seen from the angle outlined in the first part of this chapter, the founder of Austrian economics, Carl Menger, his pupil Richard Schüller, and Joseph Alois Schumpeter all stand out as economists whose fundamental attitudes make them other canon economists. At the other end of the historical spectrum – in a process clearly also influenced by the political agenda created by the Cold War – the modern US/Austrian school has, for most practical purposes, strongly approached what we here refer to as the standard canon of economics.

The central idea of Menger's *Grundsätze*[67] is to present a dynamic theory of economic development, which he presents in the fifth paragraph as 'The Causes of Progress in Human Welfare'. In this section we shall attempt to illustrate the similarities between Menger's approach and that of 19th century other canon theorists in the United States, people like John Rae and E. Peshine Smith. Like Menger, these were economists writing in strong opposition to the English classical school.

When reading Menger, it soon becomes clear that this man went far beyond the marginalism he is noted for. As Erich Streissler puts it: 'Menger is unique because he surpassed marginalism at the same time that he created it'. 'To him (Menger), his ideas beyond marginalism were the most precious.'[68] A re-reading of Menger makes it clear that Streissler is right when he explains: 'Menger ... is to a large extent now forgotten precisely because in the reign of his successors in Vienna, the co-reign of Wieser (1903–24) and Böhm-Bawerk (1904–14) – the latter pre-dominating during his life-time – much of what was genuinely Menger's tradition got lost'. We shall argue in this chapter that both neoclassical economics and Austrian economics have followed similar paths away from the visions of their founders, Marshall and Menger, parallel paths away from a focus on production and methodological diversity towards a theory where barter/exchange and lack of diversity dominate. In our terminology, most important 'other canon' elements were lost both in neoclassical and in Austrian economics during the 20th century.

Menger lived long enough to see that his successors were sliding back into 'old errors' of economic science. Menger told Schumpeter that 'The time will come when people will realize that Böhm-Bawerk's theory is one of the gravest errors ever committed'.[69] Menger also charged Böhm-Bawerk directly in his obituary that he had relapsed into old doctrines. Schumpeter identifies these doctrines as the 'Ricardian roots' of Böhm's theories.[70] Already with Menger's first successor in the genealogy of Austrian economics, in 1903, Austrian theory is taking a decisive bend towards the English-based mainstream tradition. One recent book discusses this under the fitting heading of 'The progressive Neglect of Menger's Originality'.[71]

Typically, today's standard economic theory is what Lionel Robbins termed a *Harmonielehre*,[72] a system where the resulting economic harmony is built into the very assumptions of the theoretical structure. There are two types of entrepreneurs in Austrian theory, who have opposite impacts in this respect:

1.  The *Hayekian/Kirznerian entrepreneur* who produces equilibrium and economic harmony, and
2.  The *Schumpeterian entrepreneur*, who produces disequilibrium and disharmony in the form of uneven economic development.

Of these two types of entrepreneurs, the Hayekian version is fundamentally a harmony-producing element of the standard economic canon, whereas the Schumpeterian entrepreneur is the destroyer of equilibrium, the element introducing the novelty and new knowledge that standard theory is essentially unable to handle. As we shall see, the young Schumpeter – as opposed to most other Austrians – also fundamentally disagreed with the notion of equilibrium.

Today the fundamental difference between modern US-Austrian and neoclassical economics seems to be that while neoclassical economics has a mechanical view of equilibrium, the Austrians focus on the process of *reaching* equilibrium, and the need for an entrepreneur to get there.[73] This may indeed have been a crucially important distinction in the debate between central planning and capitalism, but in a post-cold-war world, the differences in policy recommendations that can be derived from the two theories seem less important. Although the intellectual effort underpinning Hayek's laissez-faire towers above the mechanics of basic neoclassicism, the outcome on the policy level does not differ significantly.[74] Nicolai Foss pinpoints the problem: 'It is not only that modern Austrian economics asks different questions and gives different answers, it is perhaps more a fundamentally a matter of modern Austrian economics being unable to ask a number of interesting questions'.[75] Foss then lists the questions about which Austrian economics is silent: 'the process of technological change, its organization and economic consequences, strategic interaction between duopolists, oligopolists, etc., the firm, its organization and activities'. We could also add: diversity of all kinds, including the issue of world poverty, and novelty. The list of questions that are outside the reach of the modern Austrian and of the neoclassical paradigms overlaps to a large degree, although most of these questions were discussed both by Menger and Marshall. This is one reason we here refer to the parallel loss of other canon issues in both sets of theories.

One fundamental element causing this convergence between Austrian and neoclassical economics seems to lie in the loss of the *time* factor in both theories.[76] Focussing on exchange rather than on production, and having accepted Walras' virtually instant equilibrium – the one-minute *tâtonnement* – modern Austrians and modern neoclassicals are both *Harmonielehren*. Here they stand in sharp contrast to Menger and Schumpeter. Menger's tâtonnement takes a century,[77] and in a system with constant innovations equilibrium will hardly ever be reached. Here we find a most important difference between Menger on the one hand and the later Austrians and the neoclassical thinkers on the other: to Menger the theoretical structure was a map of the forces at work, but the final outcome of these forces could neither be fully described, nor quantified. Nor would the final result necessarily be harmonious. Menger thus opens up the way for an economic theory that analyses the world as it is, and where development is potentially an uneven process.

Menger's pupil Richard Schüller writes his two main works while Menger's influence dominates at the University of Vienna, before the 'backsliding'[78] of Wieser and Böhm is much felt. Schüller dedicates both his works to his teacher Menger: *Die klassische Nationalökonomie und Ihre Gegner* (Berlin, 1895) and *Schutzzoll und Freihandel. Die Voraussetzung und Grenzen Ihrer Berechtigung* (Vienna, 1905). There are reasons to believe that Schüller was one of the students who were closest to Menger. This is indicated when – much later, in 1923 – Menger's son, Karl Menger, asks Schüller to write the foreword to the second edition of his father's *Grundsätze*.[79] This edition is published two years after Menger's death at the age of 81, marking the 50th anniversary of the first edition. In his introduction, written just five months after Manger passed away, Karl Menger thanks 'his father's dear friend, Prof. Dr. Richard Schüller', for his 'many valuable suggestions' and for agreeing to write the foreword to the book.

In Schüller, a Mengerian unpolluted by the 'backsliding' Austrians of the next generation, we find a typical other canon economist. When discussing the perennial question of free trade vs. protectionism, Schüller starts with a discussion of how costs develop as a nation specializes in a certain type of activity.[80] This discussion goes right to the core of the trade debate of the other canon from Serra's first description of increasing returns in 1613, limited to manufacturing, and all through the 19th century debates in the US and Germany. Schüller's focus on production rather than on barter, and on increasing returns, makes him a typical other canon economist, whose system is one of uneven benefits from trade caused by the different development in cost structures according to a nation's 'choice' of specialisation. Schüller's increasing returns are found not only in production, but also in finance, advertising and in 'travelling salesmen'.[81] Increasing and diminishing returns are, to Schüller, factors which cause uneven economic growth, and one of many factors which need to be evaluated before deciding whether a nation should protect its manufacturing industry or not.

In Schumpeter's world also, economic development is an uneven process. To Schumpeter 'the upper strata of society are like hotels which are always full of people, but people who are forever changing.'[82] In Chapter 7 of the first edition of his *Theorie der wirtschaftlichen Entwicklung,* Schumpeter makes the following statement on economic equilibrium:

> It lies in the very foundation of our way of thinking that there is no such thing as a dynamic equilibrium. Economic development is in its very nature a disturbance of the existing static equilibrium, without any tendency whatsoever for the system neither to move back to the original point of equilibrium, nor to any other point of equilibrium.[83]

By the time the second edition of this work appears, in 1926, the whole chapter containing this paragraph – *Das Gesamtbild der Volkswirtschaft* – is gone. This 'case of the missing chapter' contains some interesting elements. In his new foreword to the second edition, Schumpeter informs the reader that Chapter 7 has been omitted. Then, later on in the same foreword he comments on the changes that have been made to Chapter 7 – a chapter which is not in the book at all. The same mistake – referring to a chapter which is not there – is repeated in the otherwise carefully edited and commented French translation of 1935. In his foreword Schumpeter comments as follows on Chapter 7, which he must have decided not to publish at the last minute: 'As I reworked it, I agreed with (my) most severe critics, and excused others who did not understand the argument'.[84]

Following the other Austrians coming after Menger, here also Schumpeter moves towards a rapprochement with the standard canon. This rapprochement is also on an issue with almost religious significance: is there such a thing as equilibrium or not, or rather, what kind of questions can be usefully answered by the metaphor 'equilibrium'. In our view the postulate of an equilibrium severely reduces the scope of economic theory, leaving issues of great practical importance outside the paradigm. We can only speculate how much the different factors weighed in Schumpeter's decision to abandon his most fiercely anti-equilibrium stance; the weight of the criticisms, his admiration for Walras' system, or – and this is pure speculation – perhaps that fact that he wanted his work to appeal more to the Anglo-Saxon economic world, where he was to spend the last almost 20 years of his career. We must agree with Streissler that, in general, it is 'because he admired Walras so much that Schumpeter is such a bad guide to the real Austrian achievement, which has always been in complete contrast to Walras'.[85]

With a perspective of more than 100 years, the ties and similarities between the economics of Carl Menger and traditional German economics are many. This is particularly true when the development of mainstream economics since the Methodenstreit is taken into consideration. In commenting on the Methodenstreit, Carl Brinkmann wrote in the *Encyclopaedia of the Social Sciences* that both Schmoller's and Menger's economics were parts of 'the great reaction that had set in against the one-sidedly deductive methods of orthodox utilitarianism . . .'. 'In fact', Brinkmann says, 'there is the same craving for realism, after an age of self-satisfied "pure" reasoning, in the opening pages of Menger's *Principles* as there is in Schmoller's contemporaneous work on the small crafts in Germany.'[86]

The fact that Menger dedicated his first work to Wilhelm Roscher now seems a natural choice, whereas the Methodenstreit appears as a fight between two factions that had more elements in common against the English neoclassical school than what divided them. Based on this, one should have thought that once the personal animosity between Schmoller and Menger disappeared, the two schools should find each other again. If Austrian economics had followed the path embarked upon by Menger, the Methodenstreit would most likely have come down differently in history, less methodologically acute and more of a personal quibble between insiders of the anti-classical movement. The opposite seems to have happened. The more the second and third generation Austrians moved away from Menger, the more relentless became their criticism of the historical school. We suggest that the reason why the Methodenstreit worsened considerably over time – the most vitriolic attack ever on historicism being Mises' in 1959 – is that both Austrian economics and neoclassical economics, in a parallel fashion, moved away from all the other canon aspects which Menger and Schmoller shared. This will be discussed more in detail in the fifth section of this chapter.

The rest of this chapter is dedicated to the discussion of concrete theoretical points where Menger and Schmoller were both on the other canon side, against what developed into the English-Walrasian theoretical mainstream.

In the foreword to the second edition of Carl Menger's *Grundsätze*, his son Karl Menger emphasizes his father's belief that 'the starting point of all inquiry into theoretical economics is the needs of human nature'.[87] This is the classical starting point of German economics since the times of Leibniz and Christian Wolff: the profession is 'anthropocentric', that is, centred on 'man and his needs'. The Germans always saw this as a sharp contrast to the English classical tradition, which is centred on barter, and where – in the end – man is just a 'factor of production'. Menger's roots in German cameralism are discussed by Paul Silverman.[88]

Menger makes the very other canon statement that 'the quantity of consumption goods at human disposal is limited by the extent of human knowledge',[89] evoking the 'never-ending frontier of knowledge' which is so typical of the activistic-idealistic and optimistic alternative canon. Menger here appears to be inspired by the spirit of US economist Erasmus Peshine Smith,[90] whose work was translated to German only in 1878.[91] To Peshine Smith there were two factors of production: (1) nature, and (2) man's wit and will. This is similar to Menger's view that the production in primitive societies depends solely on nature, 'it takes place independent of the wishes and needs of Mankind, and hence, so far as they are concerned, accidental'.[92] When human beings leave primitive society, and 'explore and research the causal mechanisms which produce consumption goods and take control over these processes, the production of consumption goods takes place as before, but their production is no longer coincidental to the wishes and needs of Man. Instead this is a process where Man is in charge and which is organised around Man's needs and purposes within the limits of nature's laws.'[93]

Like John Rae in his 1834 book,[94] Carl Menger sees the division of labour as being a necessary consequence of human innovations and inventiveness,[95] not – like Adam Smith – the other way around. Menger uses a whole section of his *Grundsätze* to refute Adam Smith on this point. This again is the 'anti-English/anti-barter' stance that is typical of the other canon.

Menger also represents the 'economics of time and uncertainty' which in many ways is the antithesis of neoclassical economics. However, as time has evolved, Austrian economics and neoclassical economics – particularly in their policy prescriptions – have converged on something that for all practical purposes is indistinguishable from that of the neoclassical synthesis. Hayek was, of course, sharply critical of any attempt to convert economics into a discipline similar to the natural sciences.[96] Yet, in a post-cold-war world, Austrian economics came to appear as neoclassical economics in words rather than in mathematics. Menger's great map of the forces at work that would hardly ever come even close to their resting position, became a map which was considered accurate enough to reach the same policy conclusions as mainstream neoclassicism.

One important criticism of the other canon tradition against neoclassical economics has traditionally been its emphasis on monetary aspects and the limited role of the real economy of goods and services (what Schumpeter and others called the *Güterwelt*). In 1936, just after Menger's works had been reprinted in German at the London School of Economics, one author saw this as the *key issue* separating neoclassical and Austrian economics. The author, Franz Wien-Claudi of the University of Prague, published a book which was an early attempt to introduce Austrian economics to an English-speaking public. Wien-Claudi claims at that point that 'Hayek's main objection to the modern English School of Economics was that these authors have overestimated the significance of monetary phenomena and undervalued the importance of the events in the world of goods'.[97] However, this point is not listed as one of Fritz Machlup's six ideas that separated Austrian economics from neoclassical economics before World War Two.[98] Again, what was a typical other canon feature of early Austrian economics seems to have been lost.

As the tradition was 'backsliding' into Ricardian and Walrasian economics, Austrian economics became increasingly 'schizophrenic', torn between a *verstehende* and a *mechanistic/ordnende* paradigm. Schumpeter emanated from the Renaissance tradition of the German historical school and spent his life on the hopeless task of formalizing the creative essence of Renaissance economics – of entrepreneurship, novelty, and creative destruction – into the framework of dead equilibrium that is at the core of neoclassical economics. Schumpeter was, indeed, 'a living, breathing contradiction' as Mirowski puts it.[99] We would claim that this contradiction is an inevitable result of attempting to reconcile two paradigms that are irreducible to any common language.

John Bates Clark points to this 'schizophrenia' when he discusses Hayek's *Individualism and Economic Order*. The factors that create disequlibrium and, consequently, those that create the need for economic policy and government intervention are still there in the Hayek of 1949. However, these factors are being pushed more and more into the background as Austrian economics comes of age, 'slides back', and increasingly focuses on addressing the threat from communist central planning:

> Hayek's position on economic policy is baffling: stressing the function of the free market and the dangers of expanding public controls, admitting the necessity of a considerable measure of control, but avoiding adequate definition of the line between the controls he opposes and those he would approve. The present volume contributes little to clarification of this vagueness. This is partly because the volume is a collection of short essays and addresses, in which Hayek repeatedly excuses himself from systematic and specific elaboration on grounds of space; but it seems to be fundamentally a matter of Hayek's method of attacking the analysis of these problems.
>
> He starts with a principle, which he emphasizes as of dominant importance. *He then admits that an opposing principle has validity and some proper scope; but never comes to grips with the question how far the opposing principle may be properly carried, and how it may be kept down to sound methods and limits.* This is a fairly common theoretical method of analysis; and amounts to throwing the pragmatic emphasis, which generally accompanies the inevitable oversimplification of theory, in one direction or the other. If this direction is that in which the next steps need to be taken, this pragmatic effect may be useful, as far as it goes and so long as only those steps are in consideration. If the emphasis is thrown in the opposite direction, as Hayek's is, its usefulness is limited to sounding a very general warning against

possible excesses of wrong methods, but without yielding much useful guidance to those who are earnestly seeking it, aware of dangers but aware also of things that must be done.

In general, Hayek seems to underrate amazingly the seriousness of the problem of assured employment, and the extent of the public intervention it makes inevitable. *He pitches the argument on a mechanistic economic level*, and seems intolerant of attitudes that do not fit that scheme, rather than recognizing their existence and seeking a viable adjustment with them. On this basis, he seems doomed to the role of Cassandra.[100,101]

# THE 20TH CENTURY CLOSING OF THE ECONOMIC MIND

In 1987 Richard Bloom's book *The Closing of the American Mind*[102] became an unlikely bestseller in the US. The aim of the book was to prevent American education – and the United States itself – from degenerating further into what the author perceived as an increasingly low and narrow mental horizon. Bloom describes American society's loss of the foundations in the humanities that were once synonymous with civilization itself. He holds up the Europeans as being better off than the Americans – whom he at one point refers to as 'big babies' – in this respect. However, the 20th century as 'the American century' has insured the diffusion of US values and attitudes also to Europe.

One important aspect of this development was thoroughly analysed already in the early 1960s, in Richard Hofstadter's *Anti-Intellectualism in American Life*.[103] Although the roots of this anti-intellectualism can be traced back to the Pilgrim Fathers, Hofstadter focuses on the 1950s, on McCarthyism, as being the decisive period for the growth of anti-intellectualism. McCarthyism and the Cold War created a demand for a kind of economics that the mechanical versions of neoclassical economics and Austrian economics could both provide. The neoclassical utopia of a market creating harmony and factor price equalization was an important counterweight to the communist utopia and its omnipotent state that promised to wither away.

In this context the 'intellectuals' became a nuisance. The 'intellectuals' had historical and political qualifications and modifications to the clear message of an absolute superiority of the unmollified market economy. American pragmatism under the pressures of the Cold War degenerated into expediency and anti-intellectualism. History – also US history – cluttered the message of the near 'evilness' of state interventions under all circumstances and in all contexts. Removing economics' previously solid foundation in the humanities pried open the way for the rule and dominance of the mechanical models: clear conclusions, but conclusions which in their pure and undiluted form are only valid in a world void of diversity, of friction, of scale affects, and of time and ignorance. The one-handed economist was created, freeing the profession from the nuisance of qualifications – 'on the other hand' – created by the inclusion of historical context and perspective. This new economist was created at the cost of severely limiting the use of experience-based cognition, intuition and *Fingerspitzgefühl* – of qualities that are normally associated with the right half of the brain. The one-armed economist is to some extent also the 'left brain only' economist.

The pure neoclassical techniques in which economic harmony is already solidly built into the basic assumptions – providing results like Samuelson's *factor price equalization* – was the kind of theory that was ideologically and politically in demand. We are not suggesting that this kind of theory was created for political purposes. The theories had been there essentially since Ricardo, but the *demand* for this kind of theorizing rose considerably during the Cold War, sharpening its focus and message, but conveniently leaving aside the mitigating counterarguments of history. John Bates Clark's criticism of Hayek's failure to come to grips with 'the opposing principles' is a case in point. In this way the 'technicians' crowded out the 'intellectuals' of the economics profession. Still today, when Paul Krugman complains that 'economists have lost control of the discourse', his villains are an alliance of 'policy makers, business leaders and influential intellectuals'.[104] Some of Hofstadter's anti-intellectualism is still around when a technical economist like Krugman perceives the 'intellectuals' as being his enemies.

Both neoclassical economics and the Austrian economics of Hayek and Mises provided extremely useful defence mechanisms against what indeed was a communist threat. The question is what to do now, when this battle is won, and the problems of the world are essentially new, while the Cold War versions of neoclassical and Austrian economics are still the only games in town? We suggest that the need to re-establish the countervailing other canon is urgent.

Both neoclassical and Austrian economics came to lose the kind of historical knowledge and experience that is required for the Fingerspitzgefühl necessary for difficult policy decisions. In this respect it is interesting to note that typical also neoclassical economists of the pre-World War Two kind complained about the loss of historical knowledge. In pre-World War Two neoclassicism both theory and history were used as a matter of course. Jacob Viner is one example of this. Viner was largely responsible for eliminating increasing returns from international trade theory on the account that it was not compatible with equilibrium,[105] thus sacrificing the real world in order to keep the 'purity' of the model.

It was indeed a paradox that this happened in the middle of the 'Fordist' paradigm, where increasing returns were at the very core of the wealth-creating economy of the industrialized world. This severed the understanding of the relationship between manufacturing/industry and progress which had been at the core of European and North American economic policy for about 500 years. This is very different from the attitude of the founder of neoclassical economics, Alfred Marshall, who in the early editions of his celebrated *Principles of Economics,* clearly recognized that a nation could improve its position by subsidizing economic activities subject to increasing returns, and tax those subject to diminishing returns (such as agriculture).[106]Just like Austrian economics, neoclassical economics was backsliding away from its founder into Ricardian and Walrasian models already before World War Two.

Yet the very same Jacob Viner wrote a most interesting book on the problem of economic man as a passive being in the hands of 'Providence' – of the invisible hand being a metaphor for Providence, thus bringing laissez-faire and 'passivity as strategy' close to a primitive belief in faith and providence.[107] The same Viner who threw out increasing returns, also years later complains that 'economists have succeeded in being as ahistorical as an educated man can perhaps possibly be'.[108] This shows the dualism so typical of economists both of the Austrian and neoclassical school before World War Two: the real world was kept as a frame of reference that was to be continuously confronted with the theoretical map of 'the forces at work'.

What has been lost is primarily this important skill of going back and forth between the theoretical models and the real world, between theory and experience. The loss of this skill, and a general lack of historical knowledge, contributes to what Veblen calls the *contamination of instincts*: today's standard education economics too often fails to communicate with what to practical people is 'common sense'. In this vein, a distinguished committee of the American Economic Association pointed in 1991 to the danger that 'graduate programs (in economics) may be turning out a generation of too many *idiots savants*, skilled in technique but innocent in real economic issues'.[109]

An Austrian parallel to Jacob Viner – very orthodox but still insisting on the role of history and of the real world – is Fritz Machlup. One of the founders, with Hayek, of the ideologically important Mont Pelerin Society, Machlup received his PhD in Vienna in 1923 and came to the US in 1933. In spite of his orthodoxy, Machlup wrote extensively on 'Schumpeterian' subjects like 'The Supply of Inventors and Invention'[110] and 'The Production and Distribution of Knowledge in the United States'[111]. Machlup was also the supervisor for Edith Penrose's research for her PhD thesis, research that eventually led to the *Theory of the Growth of the Firm*.[112] This book is important as a key foundation for the microeconomics of the other canon. A recent publication on work of Edith Penrose comments that it is 'a fascinating paradox how Machlup, a doyen of neo-classical economics, should have been partially responsible for a work so far removed from the mainstream'.[113] We would suggest that this was much less of a paradox 40–50 years ago that it is now.

This is yet another example of the loss of diversity of scope and tools in the profession.[114]

The economics of Edith Penrose was sharply at odds with textbook theory, but she would not engage in a Methodenstreit: 'Would anyone . . . try to reconcile a football game with a cricket match just because they are both ball games?'[115] Whereas the early Austrians and early neoclassicals were able to play 'both football and cricket', this ability was gradually lost, together with the multitudes of tools and approaches previously used.

In spite of what we today may perceive as a position against the use of history in economics in his *Irrtümer des Historismus,* Carl Menger really goes out of his way to emphasize the important role of history in economics:[116] 'A highly developed theory of economic phenomena is inconceivable without the study of economic history',[117] 'No reasonable person conceals the importance of historical studies for research in the field of political economy',[118] and history is 'indispensable' for theoretical economics.[119] Schmoller and Menger agree that both induction and deduction must be on board, and the Methodenstreit is seemingly about who is to be in the driver's seat. Which of the two is going to be the 'main science' and which should be the 'auxiliary science'? Menger's main objective seems to relegate history to the position as a Hilfswissenschaft (auxiliary science), a term to which he returns again and again. The contestants of the Methodenstreit discuss whether history – which they both see as indispensable to economics – should be an *Überbau* or *superstructure* (Schmoller) or an *Unterbau or foundation* (Menger). From this methodological angle, the Methodenstreit seems to fit the definition of a quibble: an insubstantial argument based on playing with words.

As has been said by many commentators, this particular Methodenstreit seems like a waste of scholarly energy. Seen from today's perspective, Schmoller and Menger were very close in the role they saw for economics, and both were far from today's mainstream. In his first book – of which there is still no English translation – Schumpeter denounced such doctrinal disputes as the Methodenstreit as a waste of time.[120] Each method had its concrete areas of application, and it is useless to struggle for universal validity. To the young Schumpeter, one should enter the theoretical edifice at a level of abstraction where one was likely to find answers to the questions posed. In this spirit we might say that the neoclassical structure is not 'wrong' under its assumptions. It becomes wrong only when – unmitigated by historical observations – it is applied to the real world, where entirely different assumptions are appropriate.

The cases when economists were able to keep both their theoretical models *and* refer back to the many dimensions and complexities of the real world became increasingly rare. Economics came to suffer from what Philip Mirowski calls 'physics-envy'.[121] Also the Austrians 'suffered to some degree from the effects of an intellectual world that expected all science to emulate the rigour of physics', as Allan Oakley puts it in his book on the Austrian school.[122] John B. Clark's 1949 accusation, quoted above, that Hayek 'pitches the argument on a mechanistic economic level, and seems intolerant of attitudes that do not fit that scheme' is indicative of the same development.

We shall let the development of Ludwig von Mises' treatment of *historicism* – comparing his 1933 treatment and his 1957 treatment of the same subject – serve as the last illustration of the development of Austrian economics over time. Mises' treatment of the Methodenstreit went from being a purely academic disagreement in 1933, to being an important ideological and political issue in Austrian economics after World War Two.

In Mises' 1933 *Grundprobleme der Nationalökonomie*,[123] the Methodenstreit is still very much alive, even in the introduction of the book. Mises here presents and caricatures historicism in its 'pure' form. When Sombart is quoted as admitting that 'general economic concepts, which are valid for all economies' do exist, Mises does not take this as an invitation towards a compromise.[124] All through the book, Mises introduces a Methodenstreit type of debate that seems to know few concessions. For example on pages 56 to 59 Mises argues against Gunnar Myrdal that 'Myrdal knows neither the contemporary situation nor the history of our science, and is therefore fighting against windmills'. On pages 129–34 he polemicizes again against Werner Sombart. However, the whole debate is apolitical and – though caustic – purely confined to academic economics.

When Mises again picks up historicism in his *Theory and History*, first published in 1957, the basic criticism is the same, but the treatment very different. (It may be noted that in the 1933 book the author was Ludwig Mises, in the US he is Ludwig von Mises.) Mises comes to the treatment of historicism from a section called 'planning history', which ends as follows: 'It is possible that in a few years all nations will have adopted the system of all-round planning and totalitarian regimentation. The number of opponents is very small, and their direct political influence almost nil. But even a victory of planning will not mean the end of history. Atrocious wars among the candidates for the supreme office will break out. Totalitarianism may wipe out civilization, even the whole of the human race. Then, of course, history will have to come to its end too.'[125]

We shall quote extensively from Chapter 10, 'Historicism', which in a sense represents the last act to be performed in the Methodenstreit (italics are mine):

1.  The Meaning of Historicism
    Historicism developed from the end of the eighteenth century on as a reaction against the social philosophy of rationalism. To the reforms and policies advocated by various authors of the Enlightenment it opposed a programme of preservation of existing institutions and, sometimes, even a return to extinct

institutions. Against the postulates of reason it appealed to the authority of tradition and the wisdom of ages gone by. *The main target of its critique was the ideas that had inspired the American and the French Revolutions and kindred movements in other countries.* Its champions proudly called themselves antirevolutionary and emphasized their rigid conservatism. But in later years the political orientation of historicism changed. *It began to regard capitalism and free trade – both domestic and international – as the foremost evil, and joined hands with the 'radical' and 'leftist' foes of the market economy,* aggressive nationalism on the one hand and revolutionary socialism on the other. As far as historicism still has actual political importance, it is ancillary to socialism and nationalism. Its conservatism has almost withered away . . . '

If the historicists had been consistent, they would have substituted economic history for the – in their opinion counterfeit – science of economics. ( . . . ) But this would not have served their political plans. *What they wanted was to propagandise for their interventionist and socialist programs. The wholesale rejection of economics was only one item in their strategy.* It relieved them from the embarrassment created by their inability to explode the economists' devastating critique of socialism and interventionism. But it did not in itself demonstrate the soundness of prosocialist or interventionist policy. In order to justify their 'unorthodox' leanings, the historicists developed a rather self-contradictory discipline to which various names were given such as realistic or institutional or ethical economics, or the economic aspects of political science (wirtschaftliche Staatswissenschaften). (Mises, 1985, p. 122 italics added)

The line of reasoning against historicism – most of it is not quoted here – is very much like Mises' 1933 treatment of the same subject. But in the 1957 book, the academic antagonism has yielded to what, in the eyes of this writer, comes very close to McCarthyist political propaganda. Historicism is vilified as being the root of most evils of history: not only of socialism. All reactionaries, enemies of 'reason', and also the enemies of the American Revolution, are by definition 'historicists'. Note that the institutional school is, according to Mises, just another name for these 'reactionaries'. Again this contrasts sharply with Menger, who – as Streissler points out – on many points 'was very close to the Institutionalists'.[126]

This piece of Cold War Americana is not complete without a brief account of the alleged 'ideological conflict' between Yale University Press – which originally published the book – and Mises. The disagreement between Mises and his publishers seems to originate in quality problems in the production of Mises' *Human Action*. The press apologizes, and admits that it is not up to standard.[127] This printing problem is by the Mises interpreted an 'ideological conflict between Ludwig von Mises and Yale University Press'. 'Who was it that wanted to harm my husband by producing a bad print, and in that way obstruct the reader?' 'Why did Lu's (Ludwig von Mises') lawyers, who had such a clear case in their hand, decide not to go to court, although Ludwig von Mises so obviously had the right on his side?' Not only does Mises insist that *historicism* is the incarnation of all evil across history from the 'conservative' opponents of the American Revolution to 'revolutionary socialism', but Yale University Press is seen as waging an ideological war against Mises. We have full understanding of an author who sees his press not doing a proper job. However, these kinds of interpretations are only understandable in the context of McCarthyism. Austrian economics had indeed come a long way from Carl Menger.

In many ways the 20th century has witnessed a slow closing of the minds of the economics profession. More than before, economists became the 'eggheads' they were traditionally accused of being in the US: 'people who do not understand everything they know'. Probably the most dramatic event in this development is that the economics profession lost its base and points of reference in the humanities. The early Austrian and neoclassical economists used the theoretical structure as an inaccurate map which was constantly held up and evaluated against real world history, and its philosophy and values were firmly embedded in the humanities. This approach created and allowed methodological diversity and pluralism, a diversity that was lost when the ties between economics and the humanities were slowly severed. We have already mentioned two recent volumes which trace this development in economics, and their titles are descriptive: *The Struggle Over the Soul of Economics*,[128] and *From Interwar Pluralism to Postwar Neoclassicism*.[129]

The founders of both the neoclassical school, Alfred Marshall, and of the Austrian School, Carl Menger, took great care in emphasizing the importance of history in economics. In his preface to the *Principles of Economics*, Marshall spells out the chief influences common to all modern schools of economic thought as biology and history, whereas mathematics is seen as influencing the *form* of the theory.[130] 'It is the business of economics ... to collect facts, to arrange and interpret them, and to draw inferences from them',[131] Marshall says, laying the foundation for economics as an *Erfahrungswissenschaft* (a science of practice), rather than the Ricardian science of a priori assumptions with categories established once and for all.

Both neoclassical economics in general and modern Austrian economics in the United States seem to have taken on many of the characteristics that Bloom ('The Closing of the American Mind') and Hofstadter ('Anti-Intellectualism in American Life') associate with intellectual life in the United States, and spread this attitude to the rest of the world. In terms of economic policy and of belief in 'spontaneous order' Austrian and neoclassical economics seem, for all practical purposes, to be of one mind. The main difference between the two schools seems today to lie in the absence or presence of an equilibrium-making entrepreneur. The foundations of the theory in the humanities are difficult to locate in today's structures, and this economic theory – void of context and of institutions beyond that of the market – indirectly also becomes curiously ethnocentric. If institutions are assumed away in a theory void of time and history, this implicitly assumes that the institutions ruling in one's own country can be taken for granted and can be expected to arise spontaneously and instantly anywhere and in any context. The co-evolution of economic activities and their accompanying institutions is lost.

The collective memory of the tremendous effort it took to build the institutions of civilization was lost from the neoclassical and also to a large extent from the neoAustrian schools. As a German economist put it in 1840: 'As the grown man has long since forgotten the pains it cost him to learn to speak, so have the peoples, in the days of their mature growth of the State, forgotten what was required in order to free them from their primitive brutal savagery.'[132] The policy implications of this proved devastating to economic welfare in the former communist world and in Africa. A re-introduction of brutal savagery has, in some cases, been the result.

US pragmatism in its best sense is related to the *Praxisnähe* in German social sciences: what is wanted is not theory for its own sake, but a practical theory where action is intimately tied to analysis. The same US pragmatism, however, may deteriorate into 'expediency', into going ahead without proper analysis of alternatives and of consequences. After World War Two, Western Europe was given a period of 15 to 20 years to adjust to free convertibility of currency and free trade. Comparing the economic policy applied in Western Europe after World War Two with the 'shock therapy' applied to the former communist world after 1990 provides a good example of how the praxis of economics degenerated from the first definition of pragmatism (operating with a 'practical' theory reflecting the real situation) to the second (going ahead without a proper analysis).

## UNDERSTANDING HUMAN COGNITION: CARL MENGER AND THE KING WHO WANTED TO MAKE THE PERFECT MAP

In the previous section, we looked at Menger's *Irrtümer des Historismus* compared to mainstream economics during the latter half of the 20th century. From this vantage point the Methodenstreit between Menger and Schmoller seems like two other canon economists involved in a relatively minor quarrel. They both agreed on the fundamental importance of history as an indispensable building block for any economic theory. This point was later strongly emphasized also by Schumpeter. From this point of view, Marshall, Menger, Schmoller and Schumpeter all represent a theoretical tradition that is virtually dead in the 2000s.

Only in one aspect does there seem to be a fundamental disagreement between Menger and Schmoller. This disagreement is about the use of past experience in human cognition. In his disagreement with Schmoller, Menger here takes a position that finds its parallel in a short story by Argentine author Jorge Luis Borges about the king who wanted to make the perfect map. The perfect map was seen as one holding all conceivable details, and – obviously – the larger the map, the better it was. Borges tells the story through a fictitious 17th century book, *Viajes de Varones Prudentes:*

> In that Empire, the Art of Cartography achieved such perfection that the Map of one single Province occupied the whole of a City, and the Map of the Empire, the whole of a Province. In time those disproportionate maps failed to satisfy, and the Schools of Cartography sketched a Map of the Empire which was of the size of the Empire and coincided at every point with it.[133]

Norwegian author Tor Åge Bringsværd has a similar story about a man who wants to write world history, and starts with 11 September[134] of one particular year. He found that so many things had happened in the world on that particular date that his history of the world never advanced as far as 12 September of the same year.

Menger criticizes the *Kleinmalerei* or *Mikrographie* of the German historical school, the 'small paintings' they produce of apparently insignificant historical events. Schmoller's publications on cloth production in Strasbourg are attacked by Menger as such a useless micrography. Menger quotes his colleague Emil Sax, and considers him optimistic when he claims that the historical research needed to create a sufficient basis for economics will take 'generations'. Says Menger:

> Should economic history be completed, in the spirit of Schmoller's micrography, before it could go on with theoretical economics, only aeons would suffice. Just think of the meat prices in Elberfeldt! In Pforzheim! In Mühlheim! In Hildesheim! In Germersheim! In Zwickau! And so on. As astronomers had to introduce the concept of light years in their science to measure enormous distances, we economists would at least have to start using the living spans of solar systems as time units, in order only to achieve an approximate idea of the amount of time needed to achieve a complete historical and statistical foundation for scientific research in Schmoller's meaning of the word.'[135]

Hopefully, the parallel between Menger's idea of historicism, Mr. Borges' mapmaking and Mr. Bringsværd's writing of history will now be clear. Menger creates the picture of a map in scale 1 to 1, a complete historical record of every price in every village in Germany (and presumably the rest of the world), which will have to be faithfully drawn in order to create the necessary theoretical foundations for a historical economics. The quote from Menger also gives a flavour of the aggressive and personal, even insulting, style on both sides of the Methodenstreit. In continuation of the meat price argument, Menger accuses Schmoller of being 'naïve' and a 'dilettante', and – closing the book – claims that 'in the future only children and idiots will pay any attention to (Schmoller's) odd theoretical gestures.'[136] This tone was not that unusual among academic economists in Germany at the time. Eugen Dühring's debates with his opponents were possibly even more vitriolic.

The debate over the use of history in economics is fundamentally a debate on human cognition. Schmoller and the German historical school come from a long tradition where history was the raw material for human decision-making. Economics was, like conducting a business, an *Erfahrungswissenschaft* – a science of practice and experience. We shall see below that Schmoller directly inspired the man who created Harvard Business School, a place where management is still today successfully taught as an Erfahrungswissenschaft with the case method of the German historical school.

This view of the role of history contrasts with the philosophical foundations of Adam Smith's economics, which lie in the philosophy of John Locke. In this philosophical tradition the human mind is a passive 'blank slate'. The philosophers behind the other canon – Gottfried Wilhelm von Leibniz and Christian Wolff – were in extreme opposition to John Locke's view of the mind as a 'blank slate' passively receiving impressions. To the other canon philosophers, the mind is fundamentally active, not passive. The mind perceives the world by incessant observations, continuously formulating and reformulating hypotheses based on pre-existing patterns, or schemata, of thought. Feedback mechanisms in this system – important parts of which are clearly subconscious – include intuition, vision and 'gut feelings'. Memorizing series of numbers in large statistical databases, like Menger suggests, is not a part of this system.

In this tradition the mind produces 'clues'. In economics Keynes' biographers call it his 'intuition', while Schumpeter speaks about 'vision'. These theories of the mind are based on a mode of inference called *abduction,* or *phronesis,* Aristotle's third form of knowledge. The tradition was continued by Italian philosopher and historian Giambattista Vico (1668–1744), and continued in the 18th Century in German philosophy, and in the 19th Century both in German and US philosophy. To US philosopher C.S. Peirce '(Induction) can never originate any idea whatever. No more can deduction. All the ideas of science come to it by way of Abduction. Abduction consists of studying facts and devising a theory to explain them. Its only justification is that if we are ever to understand things at all, it must be in this way.' Peirce here continues the role played by the formation of hypothesis in the neoplatonic tradition of Leibniz and Christian Wolff.[137]

English economist Edward Misselden expressed the view that abduction anticipates 'science' in 1623: 'Wee felt it before by sense, but now wee know it by science.' W. Brian Arthur of the Santa Fe Institute is today working on economics and human cognition. Based on work in psychology, a scientific foundation for what was the 'sense' of the historical school is again being established. In an article in *Harvard Business Review*, but without reference to economics, Arthur describes how the study of history builds qualitative *verstehen*:

> What counts to some degree (in hi-tech business) – but only to some degree – is technical expertise, deep pockets, will, and courage. Above all, the rewards go to the players who are first to make sense of the new games looming out of the technological fog, to see their shape, to cognize them. Bill Gates is not so much a wizard of technology as a wizard of precognition, of discerning the shape of the next game.[138]

This is a description of the abductive, qualitative understanding (verstehen) that has been lost in economics. US pragmatism at its best is also 'abductive', and nowhere are the principles of the German historical school being put so consciously to work as at Harvard Business School (HBS). Reading and discussing several cases from real business every day for two years, forcing people to make decisions from real-life cases, produces an 'artificial experience' which develops and fine-tunes the underlying and subconscious system of production and constant and continuous modification of hypotheses. The cases are full of figures, but thinking – like Menger did – that the training for decision making in real life consists of memorizing these numbers is completely missing the point.

There is a consistent discrepancy between how Harvard Business School is rated by the deans of other business schools ('not that brilliant') vs. what HBS graduates are paid (considerably above the graduates of all other business schools). The market is willing to pay a large premium for the systematic and focused artificial honing of abductive reasoning which is unique to this school. HBS students know that they are trained in 'management by gut feeling', there are T-shirts sporting a mock Latin translation of this slogan and the school's coat-of-arms.

The link from Schmoller's historicism to Harvard Business School is direct. The man who created the case method was a student of Schmoller, Edwin F. Gay (1867–1946). Gay is representative of a whole generation of US students who came back imbibed with the attitudes and values of the German historical school, and whose careers formed the economic policy of the United States up until World War Two. We shall therefore look at Gay's career in some detail, as a typical representative of those great American scholars who brought home both their scientific methods and their social consciousness from Germany.

After an MA in Michigan, Gay stayed more than 12 years studying in

Europe, mainly in Berlin, Zürich and Leipzig. He studied under Schmoller and Adolf Wagner, receiving his PhD in Economic History in Berlin in 1902. Studying under Wagner, Gay found himself losing the 'kind of fear of the encroaching action of the state' that he had carried with him from America. 'It was Schmoller, however, who really fired Gay's attentive interest and enthusiasm,' says his biographer.[140]

Gay joined the Harvard faculty in 1902. He was a brilliant organizer and motivator of people, so when Harvard decided to set up a Business School in 1908, Gay was called upon to be its first Dean, a job he kept for ten years. All through his life he was frequently handpicked to launch new ventures, and was constantly called upon for his advice. In spite of his vast knowledge of economic history, he therefore published very little. Although he was very proud of the achievements of the Business School, Gay later regretted giving up so much research and writing time to launching the HBS. However, among his students of economic history at Harvard were Julius Klein and Earl Hamilton, who were to become the foremost economic historians of Spain in the United States.

Gay held the job as Dean of HBS until 1918, but spent the war years in Washington organizing US foreign trade, minimizing international trade (maximizing autarchy!) in order to free as much tonnage as possible of ocean freighters for the war effort. It was here Gay met Herbert Hoover. From 1919 to 1923 Gay worked as the editor of the New York *Evening Post*, and started what became the *Saturday Review of Literature*. From 1923 to 1933 Gay shared the direction of the National Bureau of Economic Research with Wesley Claire Mitchell. He was the first secretary-treasurer of the Council of Foreign Relations, and was the 'moving spirit' in launching *Foreign Affairs* in 1922.

Gay was also elected President of The American Economic Association. Today it is of course absolutely unthinkable that a former Dean of Harvard Business School should be elected President of the American Economic Association. This again goes to show how extremely different and more *praxisnah* mainstream US economics was before World War Two, and how much more intimately the leading economists were integrated into the practical life of the nation.

Gay was very active in promoting better labour legislation and a new Factory Act. His colleagues emphasized that he always saw the 'altogetherness of everything' – the Faustian Ganzheit – and one comments that 'He is an exceedingly important part of the bridge between the social sciences and the humanities.' As a keen observer of economic history, Gay also saw successive waves of industrialization: a sequence of techno-economic paradigms. Under the heading 'Swings of the Pendulum', a history of Harvard Business School states the following about its first Dean:

... he developed a dynamic vision of economic history: it was, he concluded, a record of swings of the pendulum between periods when social controls dominated, and periods dominated by the actions of aggressive individuals. The former periods were static, characterized by security and stability. The latter periods, ushered in by the introduction of new tools, weapons, or other forces, were controlled by the powerful individuals who introduced these forces.[140]

These dynamic periods, Gay felt, were crucial to economic development. The Industrial Revolution, for all its unwelcome side effects, had made possible new levels of productivity and prosperity. The role of the economic historian, as Gay perceived, was to study and comprehend these cycles, and to suggest ways of restraining their excesses. In the famous and voluminous *Hoover Report* – so optimistic before the 1929 crash – Gay's is the only paper that senses that something is not right in the economy.

At the root of the present problem of economics is the loss of the educational tradition that produced people like Gay. The practice lives on, like in the case method that Gay introduced at Harvard Business School – which is a tool right out of Schmoller's historical school of economics – and in the 'businessmen, politicians and intellectuals' who, as Krugman complains, do not listen to textbook economic theory. US history holds a treasure of other canon personalities like Gay, they just become fewer and fewer in economics as the mechanical world view increasingly takes over economics after World War Two, contaminating the healthy instincts of adductive reasoning in the profession. All founders of the American Economic Association had studied in Germany, and most of US economics essentially belonged to the other canon until just after World War Two.

## RELEVANCE LOST: THE PARALLEL PATHS OF AUSTRIAN AND NEOCLASSICAL ECONOMICS

Neoclassical economics travelled a long way from Alfred Marshall's *Wanderjahre* in English industry to Paul Samuelson's factor price equalization – from a production-based understanding of what creates differences in income, to a barter-based *Harmonielehre*. Young Marshall took pride in being able to estimate, with remarkable accuracy, any wage in the industries he visited by observing the skill required for the job.[141] The path travelled by Austrian economics from Menger's insistence that 'the quantities of consumption goods at human disposal are limited only by the extent of human knowledge'[142] to the modern Austrian economics of the US South is equally long and changing.

The trajectories of the two schools of economics are in many ways parallel. Both founders – Marshall and Menger – built theoretical structures as maps of the forces at work. Particularly Menger insisted that his map was extremely inaccurate; he consistently refused attempts to derive 'high degrees of exactness' from a structure that was, by its very nature, sketchy.[143] Over time, their respective maps of forces became rigid structures where time, diversity, friction and complexity disappeared in an increasingly mechanical exercise. Both schools – Austrian and neoclassical – came to focus on barter/market rather than on production. In short, they lost the other canon features of economics that make the structure *praxisnah* (close to the real world) and able to explain important features like uneven economic growth.

The rising threat from communism and the planned economy influenced both schools. The political element, we could even call it the propaganda elements, in the writings of Hayek and Mises is unmistakable. In many ways Samuelson's factor price equalization is more insidious as a tool of propaganda, because the political elements are better hidden under a mathematical garb than in prose. Communism promised that every man should receive according to his needs; Samuelson 'proved' that under a market economy all wage earners would be equally rich! Samuelson here 're-invents' and widens the scope of the *Gesetz des Preisausgleiches* (law of the equalisation of prices) from 'second generation' Austrian economist Friedrich von Wieser, who – in sharp contrast to Menger – believed in 'perfect markets'. In both cases it seems to us that the conclusion – factor price equalization – automatically results from the assumptions. Samuelson's journal articles on this matter were published during the height of the Berlin blockade.

Both neoclassical and Austrian economics lost their embeddedness in real economic life and in society in general. Both drifted away from production into barter and, each in their own way, became fascinated with Walrasian instant equilibrium. In the case of neoclassical economics, the system worked without an entrepreneur. In the case of the Austrians the system needs a Hayekian equilibrium-making entrepreneur. But both theories became static and mechanical, as John Bates Clark pointed out about Hayek. Both types of theory came to produce automatic economic harmony, and both became useful propaganda tools in the Cold War. The Cowles Commission, for neoclassical economics, and the Mont Pelerin Society, for Austrian economics, each in their own way contributed to the development of harmonious economic utopias that were effectively pitched against the communist utopia. In this battle of utopias the *praxisnah* other canon became almost extinct.

Both the neoclassical and Austrian theories lost their ties to a different, and lower, level of abstraction. The *praxisnah* other canon traditionally scorns what German economists Karl Bücher called 'die verschimmelte Schulweisheiten' – the mouldy school truths – of theoretical economics.[145] When these mouldy schooltruths are driven through in economic policy unmitigated by any reference to history or to context – like in the case of the

World Bank and the IMF during the 1990s – they may cause considerable harm.

Menger's economics was also disequilibrium economics, one of uncertainty and of increasing complexity over time. Menger introduces monopoly theory as the general theory. However, both neoclassical and Austrian economics became over time more simplistic and focused on frictionless perfect competition. Economics increasingly became *catallectics* – a science of exchange. Both traditions became more static and void of diversity; they became Harmonielehren. During the 20th century theory stopped being only a starting point for analysis both in neoclassical and Austrian economics, a starting point that was continuously to be compared with historical reality. Theory was increasingly treated as if it were a description of reality itself.

Menger's original Austrian vision was a world of dynamic imperfect competition in a world pushing forward with 'the never-ending frontier of knowledge' as the engine of growth. If Menger was the prototype Austrian economist, Schumpeter was surely the most 'Austrian' of both the second and third generation Austrians. In our view the task in economics is now to reconstruct an appreciative economic theory based on the visions of Menger and Schumpeter, to resurrect an economics profession where 'subjective' theory finds an arena where it meets 'objective' facts.

In the other canon we have attempted to outline the characteristics of this type of theory, and how it contrasts with today's mainstream. The Austrian economics of Carl Menger and Joseph Schumpeter are valuable building blocks in this project. Like other Erfahrungswissenschaften, Menger's theory produced neither accuracy nor any positive theorems. Just like in the other canon and in the historical school, 'truth' – and economic policy – will always be highly *context dependent*.

Menger, the original Austrian economist, was clearly an other canon economist. Echoing other canon criticism of mainstream economics since the publication of Ricardo's *Principles* in 1817, Menger chided Böhm-Bawerk – his successor to the Chair of Economics in Vienna – both for 'the obvious artificiality of his theoretical constructions' and for 'the contradictions between Böhm's fundamental ideas and the real world'.[145]

## NOTES

1. Reinert and Arno Daastøl (2000).
2. 'The relation of one thing to another from which it may say to be descended or derived; position in a genealogical classification.' *The Oxford English Dictionary*, Oxford 1933, Vol. 4, p. 212.
3. Sombart (1928), p. 919.
4. See Reinert & Daastøl, op. cit.
5. Sombart (1930).

6.  Nelson and Winter (1982).
7.  Freeman (1992).
8.  In 'Alternative theories of distribution', in *Review of Economic Studies*, XXIII, No. 2, 1955–6. Reprinted in Kaldor's *Essays on Value and Distribution*, Glencoe, ILL: Free Press, 1960, p. 211.
9.  Stiglitz (1994).
10. Hodgson (1999).
11. At the time most economists have stressed the importance of having access to different theories at different levels of abstraction, see for example Aschehoug, T.H., *Socialøkonomik: En Videnskabelig Fremstilling af det Menneskelige Samfunds Økonomiske Virksomhed*, Kristiania (Oslo), H. Aschehoug & Co. (W. Nygaard), 1903–1908, Three volumes. This was also one of Schumpeter's most important comments to the Methodenstreit in his (1908).
12. Marshall (1961), p. 29.
13. Foss (1998). Erich Streissler looks at the common roots of Menger and Marshall in this (1990).
14. Schumpeter (1954), p. 468.
15. Of which Schumpeter says: 'Its analytical merit is negligible, but all the greater was its success,' Schumpeter, op. cit., p. 175.
16. In Germany the main anti-physiocrat was Johann Friedrich von Pfeiffer, in France Abbé Mably, Accarias de Serrionne, Necker, Forbonnais, Jean Graslin, Abbé Galiani – a Neapolitan envoy at the Court of Paris – and, most critical of them all: Simon-Nicolas-Henry Linguet. For a list of works by German anti-physiocrats, see Humpert (1937), pp. 1031–32.
17. The description of these synergetic effects is clear in Giovanni Botero (1589) and even more so in Antonio Serra (1613). To Serra these 'virtuous circles' have their origins in the increasing returns found in the manufacturing sector, which are absent in agriculture. Machiavelli is also clear on this point: 'Il bene comune è quello che fa grandi le città.'
18. Rome, Vicenzio Pellagalo, 1590.
19. Serra, op. cit.
20. For a discussion of this, see Reinert (1994).
21. For a discussion of this, see Reinert (1999).
22. Arthur (1994).
23. Buchanan and Yong (1994).
24. Eli Hecksher quoted in Polanyi (1944/1957), p. 278.
25. Crowther (1960), p. 97.
26. London, Millar and Cadell.
27. See Rashid (1979).
28. Rae (1834).
29. In the foreword to the *Grundsätze*: Menger (1871). In the English edition (1950, p. 47) of the work, Menger's Latin quote from Bacon is translated as: 'similitudes and sympathies of things that have no reality, they describe and sometimes even invent with great vanity and folly'.
30. Lis (1841), pp. 66–7.
31. Ibid., p. 79.
32. For a discussion of this, see Reinert and Daastøl (1997).
33. Smith (1776), p. 17.
34. Abraham Lincoln, Speech of the 1860 Presidential Campaign.
35. With the possible exception of small city-states, like Hong Kong or San Marino.
36. The US edition is *The History of Economics*, New York, Norton, 1930.
37. Marshall (1890), p. iv.
38. Serra, op. cit.
39. Marshall, op.cit., pp. 315–16.
40. This problem is discussed in Hart (1990).
41. I am grateful the co-authors of this set of ideal types: Leonardo Burlamaqui, Ha-Joon Chang, Peter Evans and Jan Kregel.

42. Malynes (1622, 1623).
43. Misselden (1622, 1623).
44. Schumpeter discusses the controversy between the two men in his (1954), pp. 344–45. See also their respective entries in *The New Palgrave*. In all cases these references are purely to the mechanics of money and exchange.
45. Buck (1942), p. 23.
46. Misselden, op. cit., (1623), p. 8.
47. Ibid., p. 102.
48. Jeremy Bentham (1780), Chapter 1, p.11.
49. Higgs (1897).
50. A good description of Galiani and his unique standing in French society at the time is found in Pecchio (1849), pp. 80–6.
51. Higgs, op. cit., p. 117.
52. The anti-physiocrats are discussed in Weulersee (1910), and in Higgs, op. cit., pp. 102–22.
53. Humpert op. cit., pp. 1031–32.
54. Pfeiffer (1780).
55. It has been shown that Hamilton knew his Adam Smith, but rejected particularly the free trade conclusion. Excerpts from Postlethwayt's *Universal Dictionary of Trade and Commerce* were scattered through Hamilton's Army pay book, see Morris (1957), p. 285. Hamilton's view on the English classical economists was similar to that taken 80 years later by the Japanese, see Morris-Suzuki (1989).
56. Raymond (1820).
57. His pamphlet: *An Address to the Farmers of the United States*.
58. Yagi (1989), p. 29.
59. Sugiyama and Mizuta (1988), p. 32.
60. Hildebrand (1848).
61. Menger (1884). See also Ritzel (1950).
62. Fusfeld (1987), p. 454.
63. Yonay (1998).
64. Morgan and Rutherford (1998).
65. Krugman quoted in Reder (1999), p. 6.
66. Ibid., same page.
67. Menger, op. cit., 1871.
68. Streissler (1972), p. 430.
69. Schumpeter (1954), p. 847.
70. Ibid., p. 846.
71. Gloria-Palermo (1999), pp. 37–75.
72. Robbins (1952), pp. 22–9.
73. This is the main argument in a recent book, Machovec (1995).
74. For an evaluation of Hayek and economic policy, see Streit (1997).
75. Foss (1994), p. 194.
76. With some exceptions in the Austrian tradition.
77. See Streissler, op. cit., p. 440.
78. This is the term Streissler uses in describing Menger's successors.
79. Vienna, Hölder-Pichler-Tempsky, 1923.
80. Schüller, op. cit., starting on p. 9.
81. Ibid., p. 15.
82. Schumpeter (1934), p. 156. This part has been added since the first German edition (1912).
83. Schumpeter (1912), p. 489. All translations, except where otherwise indicated, are our own.
84. *Theorie der wirtschaftlichen Entwicklung*, 1926, p. xiii.
85. Streissler, second op. cit., p. 430.
86. Seligman (1953), p. 167.
87. Menger (1923), p. ix.
88. 'The Cameralist roots of Menger's achievement', in Caldwell (1990).
89. Streissler's translation, in Streissler, op. cit., p. 431.
90. The first of many US editions was Smith (1853).

91. Smith (1853), German edition 1878.
92. (1923), p. 28.
93. Ibid., pp. 28–9.
94. Rae, op. cit.
95. See paragraph 5, 'Über die Ursachen der fortschreitenden Wohlfahrt der Menschen' in his (1871).
96. Hayek (1952).
97. Wien-Claudi (1936), p. 7.
98. See Israel Kirzner's entry 'Austrian School of Economics' in *The New Palgrave*, London, Macmillan, 1987, Volume I, p. 148.
99. Mirowski (1994), p. 5.
100. In Greek mythology, the woman whom Apollo granted the gift of prophecy, but – when she refused to return Apollo's love – made the gift useless by decreeing that no one would believe her predictions.
101. Clark quoted in Hickman, C. Addison (1975) *J. M. Clark*, New York: Columbia University Press, pp. 69–70. My italics.
102. New York: Simon & Schuster.
103. New York: Knopf, 1963.
104. Krugman quoted in Reder, op. cit., p. 6.
105. In his *Studies in the Theory of International Trade*, New York: Harper, 1937, pp. 475–82.
106. Marshall (1890), p. 452.
107. Viner (1972).
108. Viner (1991).
109. 'Report of the Commission on Graduate Education in Economics', in *Journal of Economic Literature*, September 1991, pp. 1044–45.
110. In *Weltwirtschaftliches Archiv*, 85, No. 2, 1960, pp. 210–54.
111. Princeton, NJ: Princeton University Press, 1962.
112. Oxford: Blackwell, 1959.
113. Penrose and Pitelis (1999), p. 5.
114. For a discussion of the loss of tools, see again Morgan and Rutherford (1998).
115. Ibid., same page.
116. Menger (1884), see for example pp. 22, 26, 31, 35, etc.
117. Ibid., p. 22.
118. p. 26.
119. p. 36.
120. Schumpeter (1908).
121. *More Heat than Light. Economics as Social Physics, Physics as Nature's Economics*, Cambridge: Cambridge University Press, 1989. See also De Marchi (1993).
122. Oakley (1997), p. 2.
123. Jena: Fischer, 1933.
124. p. 6.
125. Mises (1985), p. 197.
126. Streissler, op. cit., p. 433.
127. This account is found in Mises, Margit von (1981), pp. 155–63.
128. Yonay (1998).
129. Morgan and Rutherford (1998).
130. Marshall (1890), pp. ix–x.
131. This phrase marks the start of Chapter 3, 'Economic Generalizations or Laws', in Marshall (1961), p. 29.
132. Hoffmann, J.G., introduction to *Lehre von den Steuern*, quoted in Cohn (1895), p. 60.
133. Borges and Casares (1970), p. 123.
134. In: Bringsværd (1974).
135. Menger (1884), p. 38–9.
136. p. 87.
137. For a discussion of this, with references to Peirce, Leibniz and Wolff, see Reinert and Daastøl (1997).

138. Arthur (1996).
139. Heaton (1952), p. 38.
140. Cruikshank (1987), p. 29.
141. Pigou (1925), pp. 358–9.
142. Streissler, op. cit., p. 431.
143. For a discussion of this, see Streissler, ibid., p. 439.
144. Bücher (1919), p. 197. (Title reads *Erster Band, 1847–1890*, but this is the only volume which was published.)
145. Streissler, op. cit., p. 433.

# REFERENCES

Arthur, W. Brian (1994), *Increasing Returns and Path Dependency in the Economy*, Ann Arbor: University of Michigan Press.

Arthur, W. Brian (1996), 'Increasing returns and the new world of business', *Harvard Business Review*, July–August, pp. 100–09.

Bentham, Jeremy (1780), *An Introduction to the Principles of Morals and Legislation*, London: University Paperback.

Borges, Jorge Luis and Adolfo Bioy Casares (1970), *Extraordinary Tales*, New York: Herder & Herder.

Bringsværd, Tor Åge (1974), *Den som har begge beina på jorden står stille*, Oslo: Gyldendal.

Buchanan, James and Yong J. Yoon (eds) (1994), *The Return to Increasing Returns*, Ann Arbor: University of Michigan Press.

Buck, Philip (1942), *The Politics of Mercantilism*, New York: Henry Holt.

Bücher, Karl (1919), *Lebenserinnerungen*, Tübingen: Laupp.

Caldwell, Bruce J. (ed.) (1990), *Carl Menger and his Legacy in Economics*, annual supplement to *HOPE*, vol. 22, Durham, NC: Duke University Press.

Cohn, Gustav (1895), *The Science of Finance* (translated by Thorstein Veblen), Chicago: University of Chicago Press.

Crowther, J.G. (1960), *Francis Bacon. The First Statesman of Science*, London: The Cresset Press.

Cruikshank, Jeffrey L. (1987), *A Delicate Experiment: The Harvard Business School 1908–1945*, Boston: Harvard Business School Press.

De Marchi, Neil (ed.) (1993), *Non-natural Social Science: Reflecting on the Enterprise of 'More Heat than Light'*, Durham, NC: Duke University Press.

Foss, Nicolai (1994), *The Austrian School and Modern Economics: Essays in Reassessment*, Copenhagen: Handelsøjskolens Forlag.

Freeman, Christopher (1992), *The Economics of Hope*, London: Pinter.

Fusfeld, Daniel R. (1987), 'Methodenstreit', in *The New Palgrave Dictionary*, London: Macmillan.

Gloria-Palermo, Sandye (1999), *The Evolution of Austrian Economics From Menger to Lachmann*, London: Routledge.

Hart, Neil (1990), 'Increasing returns and economic theory: Marshall's reconciliation problem', University of Western Sydney discussion paper series, No. E9004.

Hayek, Friedrich von (1952), *The Counter-Revolution of Science. Studies in the Abuse of Reason*, Glencoe, IL: Free Press.

Heaton, Herbert (1952), *A Scholar in Action – Edwin F. Gay*, Cambridge, MA: Harvard University Press.

Higgs, Henry (1897), *The Physiocrats*, London: Macmillan.
Hildebrand, Bruno (1848), *Die Nationalökonomie der Gegenwart und Zukunft*, Frankfurt: Literarische Anstalt.
Hodgson, Geoffrey M. (1999) *Economics and Utopia*, London: Routledge.
Humpert, Magdalene (1937), *Bibliographie der Kameralwissenschaften*, Cologne: Kurt Schroeder.
List, Friedrich (1841), *The National System of Political Economy*, London: Longman.
Machovec, Frank M. (1995), *Perfect Competition and the Transformation of Economics*, London: Routledge.
Malynes, Gerhard (1622), *The Maintenance of Free Trade, According to the three essentiall [sic] Parts . . . Commodities, Moneys and Exchange of Moneys*, London: William Sheffard.
Malynes, Gerhard (1623), *The Center of the Circle of Commerce, or, A Refutation of a Treatise, . . . Lately Published by E.M.*, London: Nicholas Bourne.
Marshall, Alfred (1890), *Principles of Economics*, London: Macmillan.
Marshall, Alfred (1961), *Principles of Economics*, 9th (variorum) edn, London: Macmillan.
Menger, Carl (1871), *Grundsätze der Volkswirtschaftslehre*, Vienna: Wilhelm Brauchmüller. (English edition: *Principles of Economics*, Glencoe, ILL: Free Press, 1950).
Menger, Carl (1884), *Die Irrtümer des Historismus in der deutschen Nationalökonomie*, Vienna: Alfred Hölder.
Menger, Carl (1923), *Grundsätze der Volkswirtschaftslehre*, 2nd edn with an introduction by Richard Schüller, Vienna: Hölder-Pichler-Tempsky.
Mirowski, Philip (1994), 'Doing what comes naturally: four metanarratives on what metaphors are for', in Mirowski (ed.), *Natural Images in Economic Thought*, Cambridge: Cambridge University Press, pp. 3–19.
Mises, Ludwig (1933), *Grundprobleme der Nationalökonomie*, Jena: Fischer.
Mises, Ludwig von (1985), *Theory and History: An Interpretation of Social and Economic Evolution*, Auburn, AL: The Ludwig von Mises Institute.
Mises, Margit von (1981), *Ludwig von Mises: Der Mensch und sein Werk*, Munich: Philosophia Verlag.
Misselden, Edward (1622), *Free Trade and the Meanes [sic] to Make Trade Flourish*, London: Simon Waterson.
Misselden, Edward (1623), *The Circle of Commerce or the Ballance [sic] of Trade*, London: Nicholas Bourne.
Morgan, Mary S. and Malcolm Rutherford (eds) (1998), *From Interwar Pluralism to Postwar Neoclassicism*, annual supplement to *History of Political Economy*, vol. 30, Durham, NC: Duke University Press.
Morris, Richard B. (1957), *Alexander Hamilton and the Founding of the Nation*, New York: Dial Press.
Morris-Suzuki, Tessa (1989), *The History of Japanese Economic Thought*, London: Routledge.
Nelson, Richard and Sidney Winter (1982), *An Evolutionary Theory of Economic Change*, Cambridge, MA: Harvard University Press.
Oakley, Allen (1997), *The Foundations of Austrian Economics from Menger to Mises*, Cheltenham: Edward Elgar.
Pecchio, Giuseppe (1849), *Storia della Economia Pubblica in Italia*, Lugano: Tipografia della Svizzera Italiana.
Penrose, Perran and Christos Pitelis (1999), 'Edith Elura Tilton Penrose: life, contribution

and influence', in *Contributions to Political Economy*, vol. 18, 172ff, published for the Cambridge Political Economy Society by Academic Press.

Pfeiffer, Johann Friedrich von (1780), *Der Antiphysiokrat, oder umständliche Untersuchung des sogenannten physiokratischen Systems für eine allgemeine Freyheit und einzige Auflage auf den reinen Ertrag der Grundstücke*, Frankfurt am Main: Schäfer.

Pigou, A.C. (ed.) (1925), *Memorials of Alfred Marshall*, London: Macmillan.

Polanyi, Karl, *The Great Transformation* (1944/1957), Boston, MA: Beacon Press.

Rae, John (1834), *Statement of Some New Principles on the Subject of Political Economy, Exposing the Fallacies of the System of Free Trade, and of Some Other Doctrines Maintained in the 'Wealth of Nations'*, Boston, MA: Hilliard, Gray & Co.

Rashid, Salim (1979), 'Richard Jones and Baconian Historicism at Cambridge', *Journal of Economic Issues*, **12**(1), 159–71.

Raymond, Daniel (1820), *Thoughts on Political Economy*, Baltimore, MD: Fielding Lucas.

Reder, Melvin W. (1999), *Economics: The Culture of a Controversial Science*, Chicago: University of Chicago Press.

Reinert, Erik (1994), 'Catching-up from way behind: a third world perspective on first world history', in Fagerberg, Jan et. al. (eds), *The Dynamics of Technology, Trade and Growth*, Aldershot: Edward Elgar, pp. 168–97.

Reinert, Erik and Arno Daastøl (1997), 'Exploring the genesis of economic innovations: the religious gestalt-switch and the duty to invent as preconditions for economic growth', *European Journal of Law and Economics*, **4**(2/3), 233–83.

Reinert, Erik (1999), 'The role of the state in economic growth', *Journal of Economic Studies*, **26**(4/5), 268–326.

Reinert, Erik and Arno Daastøl (2000), 'The other canon and uneven economic development: renaissance economics as an immaterial and production-based canon in the history of economic thought and in the history of economic policy', in Reinert, Erik (ed.) *The Other Canon: Evolutionary Economics and Income Inequality*, Aldershot: Edward Elgar.

Ritzel, Gerhard (1950), *Schmoller versus Menger*, Frankfurt am Main.

Robbins, Lionel (1952), *The Theory of Economic Policy in English Classical Economics*, London: Macmillan.

Schumpeter, Joseph Alois (1908), *Das Wesen und der Hauptinhalt der theoretischen Nationalökonomie*, Munich and Leipzig: Duncker & Humblot.

Schumpeter, J. (1912), *Theorie der wirtschaftlichen Entwicklung*, Leipzig: Duncker & Humblot, 2nd edn, 1926. English edition: *The Theory of Economic Development*, Cambridge, MA: Harvard University Press, 1934.

Schumpeter, Joseph A. (1954), *History of Economic Analysis*, New York: Oxford University Press.

Schüller, Richard (1895), *Die Klassische Nationalökonomie und ihre Gegner*, Berlin: Heymann.

Schüller, Richard (1905), *Schutzzoll und Freihandel: Die Voraussetzung und Grenzen Ihrer Berechtigung*, Vienna: Tempsky.

Seligman, Edwin (ed.) (1953), *Encyclopaedia of the Social Sciences*, vol. 1. New York: Macmillan.

Serra, Antonio (1613), *Breve trattato delle cause che possono far abbondare li regni d'oro e argento dove non sono miniere*, Naples: Lazzaro Scoriggio.

Smith, Adam (1776), *Wealth of Nations*, Chicago, University of Chicago Press, 1976.

Smith, E. Peshine (1853), *A Manual of Political Economy*, Putnam: New York. German edition: *Handbuch der politischen Ökonomie*, Berlin: Expedition des Merkur, 1878.

Sombart, Werner (1928), *Der Moderne Kapitalismus*, vol. 2, *Das Europäische Wirtschaftsleben im Zeitalter des Frühkapitalismus*, Munich and Leipzig: Duncker & Humblot.

Sombart, Werner (1930), *Die Drei Nationalökonomien*, Munich and Leipzig: Duncker & Humblot.

Stiglitz, Joseph (1994), *Wither Socialism?*, MA: Cambridge, MIT Press.

Streissler, Erich (1972), 'To what extent was the Austrian school marginalist', *History of Political Economy*, **4**(2), 426–41.

Streissler, Erich Streissler (1990), 'The influence of German economics on the work of Menger and Marshall', in Caldwell, Bruce J. (ed.), *Carl Menger and his Legacy in Economics,* Annual Supplement to *HOPE*, vol. 22, Durham, NC: Duke University Press.

Streit, Manfred E. (1997), 'Constitutional ignorance, spontaneous order and rule-orientation: Hayekian paradigms from a policy perspective', in Frowen, Stephen F. (ed.), *Hayek: Economist and Social Philosopher*, Basingstoke: Macmillan, 1997, pp. 37–58.

Sugiyama, Chuhei, and Hiroshi Mizuta (1988), *Enlightenment and Beyond. Political Economy Comes to Japan*, Tokyo: University of Tokyo Press.

Viner, Jacob (1972), *The Role of Providence in the Social Order*, Philadelphia, PA: American Philosophical Society.

Viner, Jacob( 1991), *Essays in the Intellectual History of Economics*, Princeton, NJ: Princeton University Press.

Weulersee, Georges (1910), *Le mouvement physiocratique en France*, Paris: Alcan. vol. 2, pp. 256–682.

Wien-Claudi, Franz (1936), *Austrian Theories of Capital, Interest, and the Trade-Cycle*, London: Stanley Nott/Allen Unwin.

Yagi, Kiichiro (1989), 'German model in the modernisation of Japan', *The Kyoto University Economic Review*, **59**(1–2), 29–33.

Yonay, Yuval (1998), *The Struggle Over the Soul of Economics*, Princeton, NJ: Princeton University Press.

# Index